THE PARADOX OF GISSING

THE
PARADOX
OF
GISSING

DAVID GRYLLS

London
ALLEN & UNWIN
Boston   Sydney

Allen & Unwin (Publishers) Ltd,
40 Museum Street, London WC1A 1LU, UK

Allen & Unwin (Publishers) Ltd,
Park Lane, Hemel Hempstead, Herts HP2 4TE, UK

Allen & Unwin Inc.,
8 Winchester Place, Winchester, Mass. 01890, USA

Allen & Unwin (Australia) Ltd,
8 Napier Street, North Sydney, NSW 2060, Australia

First published in 1986

British Library Cataloguing in Publication Data

Grylls, David
    The paradox of Gissing.
1.   Gissing, George — Criticism and
interpretation
I.   Title
823′. 8   PR4717
ISBN 0−04−800081−7

Library of Congress Cataloging-in-Publication Data

Grylls, David
    The paradox of Gissing
Bibliography: p.
1.   Gissing, George, 1857−1903—Criticism and interpretation.
I. Title.
PR4717.G79   1986   823′.8   85−30718
ISBN 0−04−800081−7 (alk paper)

Set in 10 on 11 point Baskerville and
printed in Great Britain by
Billing and Son Ltd,
London and Worcester

FOR TRICIA, EDWARD AND EMMA

Contents

Acknowledgements

Anyone who writes a book on Gissing must be grateful for the scholarly and critical work of Jacob Korg and Pierre Coustillas, but I must also thank them on a personal level for their friendship and encouragement. In particular I am grateful to Pierre Coustillas for supplying me with much useful information and responding to my persistent queries with unfailing precision and patience. I am also grateful to Rosemary Stinton for her generous loan of materials, and for first arousing my interest in Gissing; to John Henry, Gail Cunningham and my wife Patricia for their comments on individual chapters; and to Peter Kemp for many valuable discussions and his comments on the final typescript.

For permission to publish extracts from documents in the Carl H. Pforzheimer Library (particularly Gissing's letters and his scrapbook), I am indebted to the Carl and Lily Pforzheimer Foundation, Inc. I am also indebted to the Henry W. and Albert A. Berg Collection of the New York Public Library, and the Beinecke Rare Book and Manuscript Library at Yale University, for access to their Gissing manuscripts and consent to publication.

Preface

George Gissing was a highly cultivated man who lived for many years in squalor and poverty, an aesthete who was also a social critic, a classicist obsessed with contemporary life. His attitude towards the proletarian poor was a peculiar compound of contempt and compassion, just as his appraisal of the upper classes wavered between envy and impatient disdain. A lifelong agnostic, he revealingly confessed, 'If I hold any religion at all, it is *Manichaeism*'.[1] Women he both idealized and despised — and his idealizations were themselves divided between the models of a sensually attractive *grisette* and a pure and refined great lady. Gissing was a proud, sometimes arrogant man, whose self-conscious sense of his own superiority was continually threatened by self-disgust; masochistically, he was often tempted to believe that his own finer qualities and cherished ideals, hopelessly at odds with coarse practicality, deserved to be punished by failure. Above all, perhaps, Gissing was a pessimist — but a pessimist who believed in energy and will power, a pessimist who wrote over twenty books. Convinced that all effort was ultimately doomed, he never ceased to expend effort on his fiction, and in this fiction he never ceased to endorse the individual's struggle for self-improvement, nor to expose the pains and pressures created by social evils. Gissing, in short, was pre-eminently a paradox — unresting, tormented, self-divided.

This book is about those self-divisions: it argues that his quintessential feature as a novelist is his paradoxical imagination, and that this, at least in his finest work, is the source of his peculiar strength. Expounding this argument, the book has three intentions. First, it offers a portrait of Gissing's imagination. Secondly, it offers individual analyses of several of Gissing's major novels. Thirdly, it examines Gissing's fictional development (most explicitly in the conclusion). What unites these three intentions is the notion of paradox. Owing to the circumstances of his early life, as well as to his social and literary predicament, Gissing was an author of severely conflicting impulses. Across the range of his work this creates many weaknesses — contradictions, deadlocks, uncertainties of tone — which are, none the less, frequently intriguing. But the case for Gissing's major novels is also bound up with polarities and conflicts. On reformism, women, poverty and art, Gissing had deeply divided emotions: that was why, at his best, he could write so convincingly about them. His characteristic strengths as a novelist grow out of his imaginative divisions. One such strength is psychological acumen, the perceptiveness that springs — as Orwell noted — from getting inside quite opposite minds.[2] 'I am able to look at both sides, and to laugh at the weaknesses of both', Gissing wrote to his sister, defending *The Emancipated*.[3] Though laughter is certainly not his usual reaction, it is true that Gissing is a master of empathy. Always excellent on anxious or vacillating characters — those who inherit his own torn temperament — he can also write shrewdly about human types who share almost none of his personal responses, providing he can probe to a hidden core of suffering or baffled aspiration. This gift for empathy is what often allows him to write so understandingly about women.[4] His related impulse to think in oppositions is what makes him, elsewhere, so unjust to them.

Gissing's divided imagination creates both strengths and weaknesses — and this is true, too, of the structure of his fiction. Almost invariably, his novels are shaped around conflicting ideas and contrasting groups: ironies, antitheses, juxtapositions comprise their essential medium. In his earlier work, especially, these structural features can be forced and mechanical; later, they confer both subtlety and power. One technical dichotomy in particular will receive recurrent examination, since it posed a creative problem for Gissing which he only gradually resolved. A clue to this dichotomy is neatly supplied by the sub-title of *Will Warburton* (1905) — 'A Romance of Real Life'. All Gissing's novels are in differing degrees both 'romances' and works of 'realism': the perennial challenge he faced as a writer was how to combine the two strands. Gissing's most frequent fictional strategy is to take a definable social evil (the deprivations of the proletariat, the plight of the uncommercial artist, the prospects for untrained single women, the corruptions of metropolitan frivolity), and then to explore its ramifications through a detailed study of personal relations — more specifically, through a love story. In his earlier work, this thematic bifurcation often means that the book breaks into two halves: the love affair is not an adequate vehicle for the social analysis. Later — *New Grub Street* is the best example — Gissing achieves integration. In structure, as elsewhere, an attraction to opposites matures into fruitful union.

Gissing's development as an author was also connected with his split imagination, his fondness for contraries. As my conclusion suggests, that tendency to emotional and intellectual division which is the hallmark of his individual works, making them either confused or complex, can also be traced across his career, which exhibits a persistently self-cancelling pattern, or perhaps a self-critical one. Introspective and stubbornly discontented, he felt compelled to reassess past positions and provide a critique of his earlier work. He did this either by repudiating former values, or, more often, by dissociating himself from their modish or specious exploitation. The process was entirely typical of Gissing, who was always inclined to dissect his own responses. Surveying his career, we might find him, at times, inconsistent, reactionary, or downright perverse. Few readers, though, would call him complacent.

1

Pessimism and Will
Power

The characteristic feel of Gissing's fiction is of busy-ness over-shadowed by despair. People talk, plot, struggle and organize, open up affairs and initiate projects, but inexorably sorrow, frustration and failure begin to close around them. This conflict between energetic aspiration and a certainty that all ambitions are vain is possibly the key to Gissing's self-divisions, for what typifies his treatment of his central values — social reform, artistic integrity, intellectual striving, romantic passion — is the way he remains attached at once to their futility and their necessity. Gissing is a pessimist who believes in will power, an author who exposes the falsity of hope while commending strenuous endeavour. This paradox underlies all his work: before we examine his major themes we need to explore and explain it.

That Gissing and his work are pessimistic might seem to require no laborious proof; but unless we take the measure of his pessimism, we cannot appreciate the scope and significance of his contrary impulses. First, then, Gissing was a pessimist by temperament; this was evident to all who knew him well. Ellen Gissing, the younger of his two sisters, recollected 'that haunting depression which so often attacked my brother ... that strange mental suffering so often his'. His friend Morley Roberts insisted that Gissing 'was truly hopeless, most truly pessimistic'. His ex-pupil Austin Harrison reported that he had never seen 'so sad and pathetic a face'.[1] The scars of Gissing's psychological torment are visible all over his journal and letters; expressions of acute misery punctuate their pages. Depression, he confided to his brother Algernon, visited him periodically; he repeated this years later to Gabrielle Fleury, adding anxiously, 'there is not the slightest fear of my gloomy fits disturbing our happiness, for the simple reason that they *only* come in solitude'. But whether the promised remission occurred is certainly open to question. Gissing's pessimistic tendencies declared themselves very early in life — 'I have given up all hope', he announced when he was 20, 'of anything but starvation and wretchedness' — and clung to him right up to the end.[2] His love letters to Gabrielle, weirdly repetitious and wildly exultant, read like elaborate rituals of self-reassurance. 'I find my old pessimism falling away, melting like mist before the sun,' he enthused. 'No more wandering of the desires — no more restless discontent with life — no more brooding on dark philosophies!' And yet on the very same day — 14 August 1898 — he wrote to Morley Roberts: 'As for me, my literary career is at an end, and the workhouse looms larger day by day. I shouldn't care, of course, but for the two boys. A bad job — a bad job.' In fact it was precisely his 'restless discontent' to which Gabrielle eventually objected. 'He can't be unreservedly happy; it is not in his nature', she concluded.[3] Gissing's discontent, a symptom of his misery, tended to focus on location and climate; hypersensitive to weather and place, he scoured different countries and climatic zones in quest of his impossible ideal. 'In returning to Italy, I am going *home* once more', he assured Eduard Bertz in 1897; five months later he informed his old friend, 'I long to be back in England. I shall never travel again.' Likewise in March 1899 he complained to Gabrielle that he was 'suffering from the heat ... Remember that I was born in the north, and I need a bracing climate.' The following December he wrote to Bertz: 'Are you suffering from the cold? ... This interferes so seriously with one's work. The winter is always a time of darkness within as well as without.'[4]

Despite what is implied in *The Private Papers of Henry Ryecroft*, Gissing never achieved content. His final letters to Morley Roberts are a splendid crescendo of gloom and foreboding, anticipating pauperdom for himself, 'moral and material ruin' for England, butchery and war for the rest of the world. Roberts took it all as Gissing's sense of 'fun', waving his dark premonitions aside as 'fantastic and preposterous'.[5] Given the record of the twentieth century, we can scarcely afford to be equally breezy, but if we look only at those statements of Gissing's in which he remarks on himself and his friends, he does seem to be unduly pessimistic in the strict sense of making doleful predictions that prove to be incorrect. Thus he told Frederic Harrison in 1895 that he could 'hardly hope' to go abroad again; as it happened, he went abroad in seven of the eight remaining years of his life. In January 1896 he advised Henry Hick that his work was 'utterly at a standstill, and probably will be so for twelve months to come': that year he wrote *The Whirlpool* and five short stories. Bertz, he feared in 1895, was 'getting very shaky': at that time Bertz was 43; he lived to the age of 78.[6] But Gissing not only dreaded the future, he loathed the present and pined for the past. Most good things, he thought, were on the way out, from roasted meat to *'really great* men'. 'The deterioration of English butter', he wrote, 'is one of the worst signs of the moral state of our people.' The theatre, too, was in decline, as were decent spelling, Greek speech and the English sense of comfort. Writing in what is today regarded as the golden age of children's literature, he declares, in his critical study of Dickens, 'alas for the whole subject of children's reading nowadays!'[7] Confronted with these and other laments, one cannot but feel in the presence of a morbid temperament.

But Gissing was not just a pessimist by temperament; he was also a pessimist by conviction: in his early twenties he was strongly impressed by the doctrines of Schopenhauer. Schopenhauer's influence, ubiquitous in Gissing, is most plainly apparent in an article he wrote in late 1882, 'The hope of pessimism'.[8] Brutally abbreviated, Schopenhauer's argument is that the ultimate reality (Kant's 'thing-in-itself') is the Immanent Will, which in organic beings manifests itself as the will-to-live. Will, for Schopenhauer, is an evil force, responsible for egotism, conflict, cruelty and inevitable frustration. Misery is the result of the will being thwarted. Happiness, a negative quality, is merely the absence of obstacles to the will; as such it is closely akin to boredom, and indeed human life alternates between boredom and distress. The road to redemption is asceticism, renunciation of the will-to-live. In his article Gissing approves such denial; and he emphasizes Schopenhauer's conviction that acknowledgement of 'the pathos of the human lot' is the only dependable basis of compassion, and hence of morality.[9] In 1882, then, Gissing was a Schopenhauerian. How far he continued, while writing his fiction, to subscribe to Schopenhauer's beliefs is, as we shall see, disputable.

When we examine Gissing's fiction, we find it accords with his temperament and convictions in sentiment, tone and structure. 'All my work', he averred in 1887, 'is profoundly pessimistic as far as mood goes.' The truth of this is demonstrable on a number of levels. First, and most obviously, his fiction is strewn with pessimistic generalizations: 'good things always come too late in this world', 'misery is the key-note of modern life', 'all mirth is unnatural to the reflective mind' — a threnody of sentiments such as these resounds throughout his work.[10] Some are distinctly

Schopenhauerian echoes — the notion, for instance, that non-existence is preferable to even the happiest life;[11] or that happiness itself, being merely 'the exemption from painful shock', is only appreciable in retrospect.[12] Secondly, the burden of such sentiments is endorsed by tone and characterization. Writing to Gabrielle, Gissing explained that his books lacked 'that foolish optimism which is indispensable to popularity'.[13] Optimism, in Gissing's work, is almost invariably foolish. Set against the percipient pessimists — Sidney Kirkwood, for instance, with his 'sad clearness of vision' — are short-sighted smilers like Whelpdale in *New Grub Street*, Barmby in *In the Year of Jubilee*, or Gammon in *The Town Traveller*. Gissing was perfectly capable of mocking a pessimistic poseur — he does so in his short story 'The Pessimist of Plato Road' — but in the main his wiser characters are those who expect the worst.[14]

This brings us to the third and most basic point. Gissing's books are pessimistic in *structure*: pain, frustration, and disillusion are part of their architecture. Without doubt, Gissing's imagination was pulled towards the spectacle of decline and failure — in effect, to the medieval formula for tragedy, prosperity-to-wretchedness. A sketch for a story in the Pforzheimer Library displays the bare bones of this imaginative preference. 'Two scenes,' Gissing writes. 'I. A father and mother with their little child. Happy for its future. Could not bear to think that it would suffer hardship for a day, all bright visions. II. Parents dead, and child, grown up, in some bitterly wretched position.' In the novels such calamitous juxtapositions are sometimes unleashed with almost comparable abruptness. *The Odd Women*, for example, open serenely, with Dr Madden's mellowed hopes for his children, but within a few pages he is thrown from a dog-cart and his orphaned daughters are brought to grief; three are killed off in a couple of paragraphs, one, most appropriately, 'by the over-turning of a pleasure boat'.[15] Grotesque misfortunes, in speeded-up sequence, are also on view in some of the short stories.[16] Normally, however, Gissing was patient in depicting the slow erosion of hope — the entanglements of circumstance, the frailties of character, that conspire to ruin his protagonists' plans. For in Gissing virtually all plans fail: the philanthropic projects of Snowdon and Egremont, the self-serving schemes of Lashmar and Mutimer, the artistic aspirations of Arthur Golding, the theatrical ambitions of Clara Hewett, the musical visions of Alma Rolfe, the complex designs of Godwin Peak — all end in unmistakable failure, leaving only a residue of bitterness and despair.[17]

However, there is one pre-eminent area where failure prevails in Gissing. A fact too easily overlooked is that *all* Gissing's novels are basically romances: what they deal with most persistently is unsuccessful love affairs. These doomed relationships come in two kinds: either the lovers fail to unite, the result being loneliness and misery; or the lovers succeed in uniting, the result being company and misery. A Gissing lover is almost certain to be either thwarted or disenchanted. To list all examples would be tedious, but of Gissing's twenty-one completed novels, no fewer than twelve, in their sexual relationships, contain major failures caused by frustration, while at least nine have failures caused by attrition. Some of his best books contain both: the pattern begins with *Workers in the Dawn* and finds its subtlest expression in *New Grub Street*, where Jasper and Marian fail to unite for the very same reasons, material and emotional, as undermine the union of Amy and Reardon. Here Gissing skilfully interweaves his two types of romantic collapse.

The two alternatives are neatly described by what Gissing said he intended to do in his unfinished novel *Will-o'-the-Wisps*: to show 'the failure of a number of people to gain ends they have set up for their lives, or, if they *do* gain them, their failure to find the enjoyment they expected'.[18] Put like that, it seems to be a Catch 22; and indeed the pervasive presence in Gissing of alternatives *all* of which are hopeless confirms the fact that his work is pessimistic in structure as well as in incident. Of many examples, two must suffice. In *New Grub Street* Amy's desertion of Reardon reveals the inability of a middle-class wife to endure the conditions of poverty. But when Reardon suggests that a man in his position ought instead to marry a work-girl, the suggestion is not only refuted by Biffen, but also impugned by the story of Yule, whose marriage to a woman of the lower class is a miserable fiasco. In *The Odd Women* a traditional marriage, patriarchal and plainly benighted, is set against a more enlightened liaison. The retrograde relationship ends in disaster, but so too, and for very similar reasons - jealousy, power and insecurity — does the seemingly progressive one.

The frequent appearance of this two-pronged trap is connected, of course, with Gissing's refusal to write reformist fiction. When Hardy was accused of pessimism, he would quote a line from his poem 'In Tenebris': 'If way to the Better there be, it exacts a full look at the Worst.' But to Gissing, except in his earliest work, no such defence was open. As Morley Roberts observed in his thinly disguised biography of Gissing, *The Private Life of Henry Maitland*, 'Many of the most pessimistic writers are in reality optimists. They show us the grey in order that we may presently make it rose. But Maitland wrote absolutely without hope.'[19] As ought to be apparent by now, a good deal of evidence could be adduced to corroborate this statement.

But — and here we come to the paradox — despite its pessimistic content, the general effect of Gissing's fiction is not tedious or enervating. Though his books are often grim, they are seldom dreary. Extremely various, thoroughly readable, written with a kind of despondent verve, they sweep the reader into a world of minutely realized social detail, deftly handled psychological suspense and unsparing moral analysis. Commenting on *The Nether World* Adrian Poole has noted the 'discrepancy between the excessive passivity of the two central characters and the energy of the narrator'.[20] But across the range of Gissing's work it is not simply that the pessimistic themes are vitalized by a vigorous narration. The themes themselves are not purely pessimistic. Strangely for an author who believes that plans founder, that optimism usually correlates with crassness, that passion is most often a source of pain, Gissing believes in effort and endeavour, in striving, persistence and determination. The commitment to pessimism coexists with belief in will power.

This belief is frequently implied by a scathing depiction of its opposite. Gissing's work is packed, from beginning to end, with warnings against weakness of will. The sketches and stories, in particular, are draped with drifters and spongers and idlers, and in the novels infirmity of will is a chronic moral affliction. One might notice, for instance, the non-volitional way that Gissing's characters tend to fall into guilt. Gissing is brilliant at describing slides, effected without any conscious decision, into compromising positions. One thinks of Waymark, Thyrza and Hood, of Monica, Eve and Nancy Lord, of Marcian in *Veranilda*.[21] Even where the lapse might seem abrupt — as with Peak's false profession in *Born in Exile* or Glazzard's treachery in *Denzil Quarrier* — it turns out on inspection to have been preceded by a hidden or subconscious slide. Discreditable lapses are related in Gissing to a temporary paralysis of will. So too are passionate impulses. His lovers are motivated by will in the sense of a blind and urgent compulsion (which is close to the Schopenhauerian meaning), but not in the sense of a conscious choice. Quite often they act like automata, as when Thyrza finds herself pulled towards Egremont, or Langley rides westward in *Sleeping Fires*, or Warburton crosses the whole of France in a febrile, infatuated dream.[22] It seems at times like somnambulism — and indeed the very term is used of Peak and Glazzard, and of Otway in *The Crown of Life*, when he courts Olga Hannaford.[23] On awaking from their dream, not a few of Gissing's characters discover they are married or engaged.[24]

Weakness of will, then, brings about marriages; but it also brings about their breakdown; in fact, whether the couple are married or not, it constitutes the primary cause of collapse in most of the amorous relationships. On occasions Gissing was inclined to think that women were even weaker than men. He once made notes on an article by Romanes entitled 'Mental characteristics of women', in which the biologist treated the topic under the headings 'Intellect', 'Emotions', and 'Will'. On the latter Gissing simply noted, 'No firmness of purpose against obstacles ... Less able to concentrate attention', but the article itself went into more detail. Women, the biologist explained, 'are usually less able to concentrate their attention; their minds are more prone to what is called "wandering".' Hence their well-known indecisiveness: 'The proverbial fickleness of *la donna mobile* is due quite as much to vacillation of will as to other unstable qualities of mental constitution.'[25] Whether or not Gissing agreed with this, in practice he makes his men weak, too. Both the sexes lack will power, but in different and characteristic ways. The women are frequently unable to commit themselves wholly to their men; they are blown off course by social propriety or a passion for worldly excitement. The men are unable to assert themselves: too timid, too anxious, or too scrupulous, they lack the courage to act. With circumstantial variations, this pattern recurs again and again: with Kingcote and Isabel Clarendon, with Amy and Reardon, Peak and Sidwell, Peachey and Ada, Harvey and Alma, and other more minor characters.[26] In all these ways, then, Gissing's fiction exposes the moral and emotional dangers of impaired will power.

However, it goes further than that: it positively recommends work and effort, application and perseverance. This is hardly surprising, for Gissing himself was fanatically industrious. As a schoolboy, said his friend Arthur Bowes, 'energy of character, self-reliance and an exorbitant passion for study were his chief characteristics'. 'Rushing off to school with a sharp herring bone in his throat, for fear of missing his first lesson', winning so many prizes he had to take them home in a cab, reading through *Nicholas Nickleby* in a single Sunday afternoon, Gissing seems to justify this description. 'I am sweating violently from 4 a.m. to 11 p.m.', he wrote to Bowes in 1873. Later, sweating over his novels, he would work for up to twelve hours a day, in a manner that terrified Morley Roberts.[27] He also dispatched formidable exhortations, often accompanied with reading lists, to his struggling younger sisters. 'I take it for granted', he wrote to Ellen, 'that you know all Milton's shorter poems by heart.'[28] And he took inspiration from other writers – from Zola ('Lord, how the man toils!'), Dickens ('a wonderfully active ... life'), and even the German classicist Heyne, who, so the story went, laboured for sixteen hours a day, except on the day that he was married, when he had to cut down to eight.[29]

In Gissing's fiction, hard work and a resolute will are tokens of moral distinction. As evidence we might examine in detail *The Emancipated*, published in 1890. This novel is constructed around a series of contrasts, the most obvious being that between the north and the south. The Italian south stands for art and sunshine, while the north (mostly England) harbours puritanism and fog. While Italy is the home of Renaissance and classical culture, of leisure and cosmopolitan polish, England is the seat of a mean, Sabbatarian piety, of factories and provincial gaucheness. But in one respect the contrast cuts the other way: the north is more conducive to sedulous endeavour. Speaking in Italy, Mallard explains that he can do better work in the Hebrides or Norway: 'Here I am not disposed to work.'[30] For Mallard, work consists of art: by trade he is a landscape painter. Brought up in an evangelical household, but adopted by a wealthy bohemian, Mallard embodies an ideal blend. Bluff but sensitive, sceptical but creative, he rejects the restrictions of puritanism; but he also distrusts the kind of modish emancipation that sanctions emotional slackness. The novel is in fact a kind of survey of true and false types of emancipation; and in every case there is a crucial emphasis on will power and hard work.

The plot of the novel, like many of Gissing's, is threaded around two couples. In Part 1 Reuben Elgar wins Cecily Doran, and Mallard has to suffer the anguish of jealousy. In Part 2 the marriage between Reuben and Cecily fails, but Mallard unites happily with Miriam Baske. From the outset both the men and the women are contrasted. On his very first appearance Mallard is announcing, 'I have my work to get on with, and it shall not suffer from the intrusion of idlers', whereas Elgar, we hear, is 'going to the devil' although he appears to have ability. Both men become infatuated with Cecily Doran, but while Elgar submits to his frenzied feelings, Mallard tries hard to resist them. He does not find it easy to succeed. For a time he lingers around, lost in thought and oppressed by turbid emotions. Then, exerting his 'stronger will', he virtually compels Elgar to accompany him to Amalfi, to keep him away from Cecily in Naples. But Mallard, heartsick and tormented by jealousy, is quite unable to concentrate: 'Work! The syllable was like lead upon his tongue, and the thought a desolation in his mind'. When Elgar rushes away and returns to Naples, Mallard sinks into inertia: 'he could not employ himself ...; his mind grew sluggish, and threw a lassitude upon his limbs. The greater part of the day he spent in his room at the hotel, merely idle.' That resumption of work is his only salvation is made explicit in a later passage: 'Never before had he utterly lost the power of working. In every struggle he had speedily overcome, and found in work the one unfailing resource. If he were robbed of this, what stay had life for him henceforth?'[31]

In the event, Mallard recovers his solace. He exits from Part 1, after Cecily's elopement, with a 'haggard but composed face', and begins Part 2 by exhibiting a painting, 'a piece of coast-scenery in Norway, very grand, cold, desolate'. After this bracing return to work, he even goes back to Italy to reassert his self-command: not only to 'convince himself that his freedom was proof against memories', but to finish off thwarted artistic projects, 'thus completing his revenge upon the by-gone obstacles, and reinstating himself in his own good opinion'.[32] But Mallard's main triumph is his union with Miriam, and this too is the outcome of conscientious effort, on her part as well as his. Miriam's development is usually seen as an emancipation from puritanism, from the beaten path of duty to the challenge of art, from the Bartles chapel to the Cappella Sistina — and also from the pleasures of religious animosity to the richer satisfactions of human love. All this is true. But what Gissing also emphasizes is the *energy* involved in Miriam's escape. The book opens with Miriam 'crushed with *ennui*': her sectarianism has begun to thaw, but as yet she has nothing to fit in its place. Italy tempts her to idleness, to the lazy delectation of fruit and music, but it also whets her starved artistic palate. She begins to work at Dante 'with feverish energy', and before long, as Edward Spence informs Mallard, 'she has grappled with whole libraries of solid historians. She knows the Italian poets.' It is not, as Gissing is careful to make clear, that Miriam swots her way to liberation. It is rather that, excited by new ideals, she finds herself possessed of 'unforeseen energy' as she begins to 'qualify herself for the assertion of new claims'.[33] She is also, of course, qualifying herself for Ross Mallard; nothing is more familiar in Gissing than the spectacle of lovers stirred to feats of learning (see Chapter 4, below). In the climactic scene between Miriam and Mallard, the painter invites her to his studio and greets her with the words, 'Can you sew, Mrs. Baske?' Setting her to mend a case for his engravings, he busies himself with two portraits of Miriam, representing her earlier and later personas. Commenting on these, he declares his love, but carefully adds the stipulation, 'When I say that I love her, I don't mean that I am ready to lose my wits when she is good enough to smile on me. I shouldn't dream of allowing her to come in the way of my life's work.' After this, Mallard appears to dismiss her, but instead offers her a cup of tea, which she makes to save his time. The scene ends with a proposal and an embrace, and the last chapter spotlights their married bliss. As Gissing explained to H. G. Wells, 'In Mallard and his wife, at the end, I wanted to show two people who had settled down to a wholesome, unpretending life of work and duties; having got rid of superstitions (old and new), but too old and too wise to make any fuss about it.'[34]

Reuben Elgar, on the other hand, is both unwholesome and pretending; but what makes him most inadequate is his failure in work and duties. Elgar is presented as a man of talent who fatally — and fatalistically — lacks will power. The reasons for his failure feed into the theme of genuine and spurious emancipation. Reacting against his censorious training, Elgar has lurched into desperate defiance of the pietistic laws that still obsess him. This is brought out by the way in which, having planned vaguely to 'go in for literature', he decides to labour for two or three years at 'a great militant book on Puritanism'. Though he rapidly produces a perfervid manifesto, Reuben soon relapses into sullen ennui and takes to frequenting music-halls under cover of calling at the British Museum. At the same time he reverts to prudishness, forbidding his wife to associate with a married woman who has left her husband. It is rather like Tom Buchanan with Gatsby: 'the transition from libertine to prig was so complete.'[35] Or, in another respect, Elgar anticipates Angel Clare in Hardy's *Tess of the d'Urbervilles*, likewise only superficially emancipated from his evangelical background. Reuben, then, revolts against his Christian name, but fails to make an anti-Christian name for himself. A chapter entitled 'Elgar at Work' shows him doodling, whining, prowling around and prating of fatalism. More and more luridly degraded, he eventually gets shot by the husband of an actress. 'Inconstant, incapable of self-direction, at the mercy of the moment's will', Elgar is the opposite of Mallard.[36]

The principal victim of his weakness is Cecily, and her fortunes, too, trace out a moral graph of lethargy and endeavour. Although Cecily is genuinely accomplished, Gissing suggests that her ardour for art partakes more of receptive enthusiasm than of accuracy and application. Surrendering to a momentary, passionate impulse, she elopes with Elgar and finds herself stultified. Her husband's indolence proves contagious and she suffers from a 'creeping paralysis of the soul'. She abandons her studies, lacks a sense of direction, and reacts to provocation with listlessness. Only on breaking away from Elgar does Cecily recover her zest for work. She is discovered, in the final scene of the novel, 'seated with several books open before her', which apparently she has been reading since six in the morning. An easel and an 'open piano' stand in the room, which has 'plain furniture' and 'no mere luxuries'. 'It was a work-room, not a boudoir', says Gissing firmly. Plainly, given the values of this novel, hope remains for Cecily, as a concluding quotation from Boccaccio reassuringly implies.[37]

As if the themes of the main narrative were not resonant enough, Gissing takes care to amplify them through sub-plots and minor characters. Reuben and Cecily have coarsened counterparts in Clifford Marsh and Madeline Denyer. Marsh is a soggy aesthetic *flâneur* who sponges off his stepfather, 'a well-to-do manufacturer of shoddy in Leeds', and like Elgar makes hollow artistic resolves. Mrs Lessingham rapidly spots the resemblance, perceiving that there is quite a bit of Marshiness in Reuben. When Madeline is crippled by an accident, the question of Marsh's fidelity is raised — as is that of Elgar's to Cecily shortly afterwards. Madeline herself, with her pert artistic patter, her anxiety to be modern and avant-garde, makes her début in the novel as a vulgar parody of Miss Doran; her subsequent condition of paralysis and hopelessness becomes — as Cecily realizes — a grim symbol of the latter's own fate. Lack of effort and loss of will power are ubiquitous in *The Emancipated*. There is Musselwhite, the anaemic aristocrat whose 'great task of the day' is killing time until dinner. There is Mrs Travis with her lament, 'I have no perseverance'.[38] At times it seems as if the strenuous

Mallard is surrounded by a veritable epidemic of ennui. Indeed this word is used twice of Elgar, twice of Musselwhite, and three times of Miriam Baske.[39]

The Emancipated, then, is a sustained demonstration of Gissing's respect for the power of the will; it pulls together a series of values that are scattered throughout his work. The question that obviously arises is: how can recommendation of these values coexist with the presence of pessimism? The primary fact to insist upon is that it can and does: in Gissing's work the two tendencies are not incompatible. *The Emancipated* is a brighter book, more bathed in art and light and leisure, than the majority of Gissing's; and since energy prospers where weakness fails, it might appear optimistic. But even here pessimism steals in. Leaving aside the misfortune of Cecily and the harrowing story of Madeline Denyer, the presentation of Mallard is not unclouded. Mallard, after all, is prone to depression: Gissing's description of his countenance — 'rugged, saturnine, energetic' — suggests mournfulness as well as vigour. Just before Mallard hears of Cecily's engagement, and while he is still persisting in hope, Gissing explains in a Schopenhauerian paragraph how this illustrates 'the irony inherent in human fate'. Mallard's view of art is also unconsoling — he is conscious only of 'having progressed an inch or two on the way of infinity' — and when he writes his own epitaph, his words epitomize perfectly the paradox of pessimism and will that might stand not only on his headstone but on that of his creator: 'Here lie I, Ross Mallard ... who spent all my strength on a task which I knew to be vain.'[40]

These words perhaps provide a clue to the nature of this paradox in Gissing. If we look at his first book, *Workers in the Dawn* (1880), a decisive pattern emerges. First, the book is a typical mixture of wretchedness and optimism, of lassitude and energy. Its hero and heroine, Arthur and Helen, are ardent idealists who 'throb' with enthusiasm — 'earnest young people', as Gissing put it, 'striving for improvement in, as it were, the dawn of a new phase of our civilisation.'[41] And yet in spite of all their striving, their passionate concern for art and philanthropy, both come to miserable ends. Radical unhappiness infects their rapture, as they lurch between surges of co-operative zeal and pacing their rooms in isolation and despair. A similar duality appears in the book's attitudes to politics and education. Though parts of the novel are frankly polemical, the rallying paragraphs of satire and protest are subverted by scepticism. The muscular Christian

Mr Heatherley pours cold water on 'schemes of future Utopias'.[42] Education is proclaimed as the only salvation, but the book makes clear in particular cases — the Pettindunds, say, or Carrie Mitchell — that tuition is ineffective.

Arthur Golding's rash marriage to Carrie is the crucial factor that keeps him from fulfilment with Helen Norman. As such, it is the principal cause of their misery, and significantly what brings it about is a defect in Arthur's character. Arthur is a weak-willed idealist, the first of many in Gissing. 'The secret of his life', we are told, 'lay in the fact that his was an ill-balanced nature, lacking that element of a firm and independent will.' As a result, Arthur has been vulnerable to the pressure of adverse circumstances. He has therefore turned to others to direct his activities — first to Will Noble, then Helen. 'In both of these friends he felt the presence of that which he himself lacked — a strong will.'[43] This sounds like an unequivocal judgement — and yet, from what we see in the novel, Golding does not seem to lack a strong will in the sense of determination. He applies himself diligently to his art; like Helen he is a tirelessly patient teacher; with Carrie he is even provokingly determined, driving her into a slatternly fury with his pertinacious corrections. What Arthur lacks is not determination, but rather decisiveness. He cannot discover his *métier*: excessively impressionable, he moves passively between artistic and political engagement. His weakness of will reveals itself not so much as a deficiency of application as a fundamental uncertainty about his ultimate goals.

This kind of weakness, though productive of suffering, is not incompatible with strenuous toil. Indeed, as the end of the novel shows, the suffering simply spurs people on to toil even more. When Helen is lonely and dying of consumption, she perseveres grimly at her evening-class to avoid the thought 'of what her life would become if she yielded to her feebleness or relinquished her work'. Arthur Golding goes even further. When Helen has finally renounced his love, enjoining him to 'strain every nerve' at his art, he accepts the role imposed on him with masochistic grit. Effort here, as so often in Gissing, does not consist — to use a phrase from *Henry Ryecroft* — in 'glad and hopeful energy', but rather in a dogged determination to atone for a mistake. The effort is expended in a context of failure; the protagonist is both industrious and doomed. What we should also notice, however — and this completes the pattern in question — is that Golding, despite his stoic resolution, his almost eager acceptance of pain, continues secretly to live on hope. This hope, Gissing adds, was almost unconscious, 'but for all that it was there, no inconsiderable element of his determined courage'.[44]

Workers in the Dawn establishes a paradigm that helps to explain how pessimism and will power exist side by side in Gissing. The salient features of the pattern are these: a weakness of will in one of the protagonists that makes him or her excessively reliant on other people or on circumstances; a compensatory determination to resist the ensuing disadvantages; and a state of mind in which this resistance, taking the form of strenuous activity, is fuelled by both a conscious acceptance of suffering and the persistence of an almost unconscious hope. Will power is exerted, then, to rectify adversity; the adversity has often been brought about by initial lack of will power. This pattern repeats itself in Gissing, as a few examples will show.

In *Demos* the heroine Adela Waltham, although in love with Hubert Eldon, is misled and pressured by her mother into marrying Richard Mutimer. After this initial weakness of will, she finds her marriage unfulfilling, but tries to repress her reservations by serious and systematic study, particularly of subjects that preoccupy her husband. When Mutimer rewards her with humiliation, she turns instead to asceticism, attempting to accept willingly the hurt that he inflicts. Eventually, however, she has to fall back on a kind of bitter fortitude: 'She was deficient', says Gissing, 'in the strength of character which will subdue all circumstances; her strength was of the kind that supports endurance rather than breaks a way to freedom.'[45] Adela, though, never abandons hope: she continues to think wistfully of Eldon, she does what she can to benefit him, and the last chapter shows that in her heart she had chosen him as her partner.

Great effort of will, in a Gissing novel, is virtually always part of a campaign to make up for some initial setback, quite often an earlier weakness. It therefore partakes less of hope, except of a secret, subconscious kind, than of dogged desperation. The protagonists are weak in decisiveness, in the capacity for conflict and confrontation, but not, as a rule, in perseverance. They lack moral courage, but not stamina; they cling on, rather than break away. Reardon, for example, in *New Grub Street*, is repeatedly presented as exceptionally weak. Racked by financial anxiety, emotionally dependent upon his wife, he is quite unable to concentrate: 'the spring of his volition seemed to be broken'. And yet for a man with a broken spring Reardon works astonishingly hard. He writes — or at least tries to write — for nine and a half hours a day; he rises 'almost to heroic pitch' when completing the last volume of his novel.[46] The effect of all this is hardly cheering, for Reardon is fighting against huge disabilities — not just his lumbago and his sore throats, but the market conditions in literature that condemn him to penury. However, even Reardon's burdens are partly the result of earlier mistakes: his choice of London as a place of work, his choice of fiction as a literary medium, his choice of Amy as a wife.

The final appearance in Gissing's work of the pattern established by *Workers in the Dawn* occurs in *The Crown of Life*. From start to finish Piers Otway is torn between pessimism and will power. Cramming frantically for the Civil Service, Piers is distracted by his love for Irene, thus losing his 'firm will and fixed purposes'. Morally enfeebled, he offends his beloved and penitentially removes himself to Odessa, intent on restoring his fibre. Returning after three years, he tones up with cold baths and dumb-bells and adopts a 'brief, decisive turn of speech': Irene is duly impressed. But Piers is soon reimmersed in gloom when, being illegitimate, he loses his inheritance. He responds by returning to the rigours of business. Coming home to the news that Irene is engaged, he is menaced by despondency once again, but fights 'manfully' against it. The fight assumes its usual form: a desperate concentration on work, a self-punishing battle against temptation, and the nursing of a secret hope.[47]

So *The Crown of Life* goes on: its plot continually arranges tests of the will power of its principals (Irene proves her resolute mettle when she breaks with her fiancé). After yet a third period abroad, Piers is braced for a clinching success: 'His habits were vigorous', we are told. 'Rising very early, he walked across the Park and had a swim in the Serpentine. The hours of the solid day he spent, for the most part, in study at the British Museum.' But at the end of *The Crown of Life*, which has oscillated continually between the poles of exertion and despair, Piers's winning of Irene Derwent is described in an almost elegiac mood. The paradox is evident right to the end; and Piers is the final embodiment of it. 'In Piers Otway's case,' as Gissing suggestively remarks, 'the temper which defies discouragement existed together with the intellect which ever tends to discourage.'[48]

We have seen that this paradox exists in Gissing and to some extent we have seen *how* it exists: the last question to ask is *why*. Two answers may be plausibly offered, one relating to Gissing's convictions, the other to his temperament. The first answer takes us back to Schopenhauer, whom we know to have influenced

Gissing's thought. In Schopenhauer's philosophy, pessimism is not always inconsistent with labour and endeavour. What Schopenhauer terms the will-to-live is not to be identified with what common sense calls will power. As it happens, Schopenhauer himself was notorious for his dogged application. There was no self-contradiction here, because what he was doing, in his own estimation, was exercising pure intellect — quite different from the force of will. Intellect was the origin not only of philosophy, but of literature and — in varying degrees — of all forms of art. Hence, from the inherent evil of the world, there is one escape route other than renunciation. As Gissing puts it in 'The hope of pessimism':

> There is, in truth, only one kind of worldly optimism which justifies itself in the light of reason, and that is the optimism of the artist ... In the mood of artistic contemplation the will is destroyed, self is eliminated, the world of phenomena resolves itself into pictures of absolute significance, and the heart rejoices itself before images of pure beauty.[49]

Does this explain the paradox? Certainly Gissing saw his own work as art, and liked to imagine that his attitude to it was 'that of the artist pure and simple'. As Waymark says in *The Unclassed*: 'The artist is the only sane man. Life for its own sake? — no; I would drink a pint of laudanum tonight. But life as the source of splendid pictures, inexhaustible material for effects — *that* can reconcile me to existence, and that only.'[50] The sentiments are similar to those of Flaubert. Regular, exhausting, artistic work is recommended as the only defence against the grimness of life.[51] Perhaps, then, this is how Gissing managed to acclaim endeavour while facing despair. His fiction, after all, is by no means in favour of just any kind of work. Unlike Samuel Barmby, in *In the Year of Jubilee*, Gissing did discriminate between Matthew Arnold and Samuel Smiles. Frequently, he sets his weak-willed idealists against energetic, coarsely practical men: Egremont and Dalmaine; Reardon and Milvain; Otway and Arnold Jacks.[52] Where the stronger, more practical character is morally approved of by the author, he is usually an artist or an intellectual: consider Waymark, Gabriel and Earwaker, contrasted with Casti, Kingcote and Peak.[53] The vigorous Mallard, we remember, was an artist. If Gissing was indebted to Schopenhauer, he could certainly find sanction in his philosophy, within an acceptance of pessimism, for some kinds of strenuous effort.

But this, of course, is a rather large *if*; there is surely a difference between affinity of outlook and positive indebtedness. It seems as unlikely that Gissing needed Schopenhauer to license his belief in artistic work as that his encounter with the German philosopher was what caused his pessimism. In any case, Gissing did not, in his fiction, consistently endorse Schopenhauerian beliefs. He was deeply ambivalent about renunciation — the possibility or the desirability of 'the calm of achieved indifference'. As a great deal of his fiction indicates, particularly *The Crown of Life*, Gissing, unlike Schopenhauer, continued to believe that sexual passion could find an ideal fulfilment.[54]

The alternative explanation of the paradox invokes Gissing's own temperament — or, rather, the effects on his personality of his early experiences. Perhaps the answer, like so much in this author, goes back to the trauma he received at college, to the episode that snuffed out his scholarly career. On 31 May 1876 Gissing was caught stealing money from the cloakroom at Owens College, Manchester. Expelled from college, convicted of theft, sentenced to one month's imprisonment with hard labour, he was violently twisted in a new direction. Up to this point, his whole being was aligned to academic attainment. After it, his imagination was split. Part of his mind was, it seems, crippled with a permanent disenchantment: what could be hoped for a world in which everything, one's entire edifice of aspiration, could be shattered by a single blow? But another part of him — understandably — could not so readily surrender hope. His single ambition had always been to gain distinction by work and study. Now he would have to work even harder; now he would have to make up for his error by superhuman toil. In this respect the pattern of *Workers in the Dawn* was the pattern of Gissing himself. 'If it be true', he wrote in his commonplace book, 'that the English national characteristic is to act without foresight, and then make up for the negligence by vigour and capability — what an Englishman I am!' Whether or not it was true of the English, it was certainly true of Gissing. He saw himself as one who was locked in a fight against almost impossible odds. Reviewing his life for Gabrielle, he addressed himself in just these terms: 'Consider the story of your life. You began with nothing whatever but a good education. You were self-willed, passionate, foolish, and for years it seemed as if there could be no future for you. Nevertheless, by dint of hard work, you slowly, slowly, made your way in literature.' He was justly proud of his resolute strength. 'Heavens, how I laboured in those days!' he recalled wistfully in *Henry Ryecroft*.[55] And surely, he thought, it demonstrated the

power of his will: his sufferings, as he twice said to Gabrielle,
'would have killed a weaker man'. And yet ... the cause of his
first great mistake, and of later mistakes like his devastating
marriages — could that be called will power, or something
else? Gissing was aware of the oddity here. 'Dear,' he wrote
consolingly to Gabrielle, 'whenever you are uneasy about my
health, remember that I have a very strong *will*' — but he added,
in a bracket, 'in one way'. The point was, as everyone who knew
him insisted, and as he himself was ready to admit, that Gissing's
will was only well developed as a faculty of dogged perseverance.
In terms of stability, of 'rational self-guidance', he was, as he
knew, disastrously weak.[56] That is why his books extol application
and dread indecisiveness.

There is no solid evidence that Gissing was a pessimist before
the catastrophe at Owens College. After that explosion, his world
was darkened; and though he looked for light in his powers of
endurance, his gloom was thickened by a fear that his character
was poisoned by some obscure weakness. He toiled on, to
counteract his dark depression, but excessive toil only made
him more depressed. He accepted suffering as inevitable, but
continued silently to subsist on hope.[57] He tried to believe in
the human spirit; but no one ever had a sharper sense of the
forces that conspire against it. Gissing, in short, believed simultaneously in determinism and determination. In *The Unclassed*
Osmond Waymark expounds two allegories which, he says,
define Pessimism and Optimism. The first, that of Adam and
Christ, recommends pious abnegation and a total denial of
life. The second, that of Prometheus, celebrates 'prowess' and
'aspiration', the triumph of man by 'assertion' and 'strength'.
Waymark seems clearly to favour the second, but a few lines later
he becomes fatalistic: 'I know that I could not have acted otherwise than I did in any juncture of my life; I know that the future is
beyond my control'.[58] The same split allegiance afflicted Gissing;
it became a major paradox throughout his work. In the treatment
of all his central themes, belief in the power of redemptive effort
conflicts with acceptance of defeat or loss. Whether dealing with
art or exile, social reform or the love of women, he is at once
aspiring and despairing, idealistic and disillusioned — in fact, as
self-divided as his own protagonists. This marked dichotomy of
mood and judgement — always the distinctive feature of his
fiction — constitutes the paradox of Gissing.

2

Workers and Reform

I

The conflict in Gissing between pessimism and will power was particularly acute in the years that followed his imprisonment and disgrace. Like Sidney Kirkwood in *The Nether World* he was 'only just recovering from a shock which would leave its mark upon his life to the end, his youth wronged by bitter necessities, forced into brooding over problems of ill when nature would have bidden him to enjoy'. Denied enjoyment, he sought escape through resolution — dogged application to indignant novels and commitment to a cause. His cloven emotions are exposed in a story he dashed off in early 1880, regarding it as merely a parody of Poe. A smouldering little squib about fratricide, 'Cain and Abel' has a hero with the name of Cain but a substitute surname, Hope. 'In worldly prospects', he says, 'I never ceased to improve ... In this respect my career has been exemplary, and I may safely point to it to prove how much can be done by resolute hard work.' The twist is that the man who makes this declaration is speaking from the condemned cell.[1]

Seeing himself likewise as fated to failure even though pledged to resolution, Gissing understandably constructed fictions that embodied these fractured feelings. A symptom of this, not immediately obvious, is that in every one of his first seven novels the theme of sacrifice, or renunciation, is painfully prominent. The protagonists invariably reach a point where they consciously give up their lovers. Helen's sacrifice of Arthur Golding, Kingcote's of Isabel, Emily's of Wilfrid, Egremont's of Thyrza and Thyrza's of Egremont — the line stretches out to the crack of doom. Though it is obvious why Gissing should dwell upon loss, it is less obvious why the spectacle of martyrdom should haunt his imagination. The answer seems to lie in the psychology of sacrifice, which after all combines privation with effort: sacrifice is *voluntary* loss. Hopes may be blasted, lovers renounced, but the concept of sacrifice mitigates the misery with the consolations of will. For Gissing it provided an attractive compound, a unique relief for his peculiar malaise. It was also a dangerously delusive drug, for the truth was that none of his personal sufferings could properly be seen as deliberately, chosen — he hadn't high-mindedly resigned from college; he didn't choose to live in hardship and shame. Perhaps this explains why the reasons for sacrifice are often, in these early books, rather fuzzily conceived. Kingcote forgoes the love of Isabel Clarendon largely through tortuous misunderstandings. Helen Norman refuses to become Arthur's mistress — in a scene that looks back to *The Mill on the Floss* and forward to the end of *The Unclassed* — even though she has earlier been applauded as a valiant defier of convention.[2] At times Gissing seems revealingly unclear how far the emotional martyrdom is desirable or necessary. Emily's renunciation of Wilfrid Athel, in *A Life's Morning*, is offered first as proof of her purity and passion, later as a morbid, self-deceptive reaction to her father's suicide.[3] Such uncertainties, the product of personal involvement, began to disappear from Gissing's fiction as he gradually became more sceptical about the possibility of assuaging anguish with a pose of willed resignation. After *The Nether World* (1889), in which voluntary sacrifice is grimly dismissed as 'the kind of strength which idealism is fond of attributing to noble natures', this theme fades out of his work. Though desolating losses still occur, they are either unmistakably unchosen (as with Reardon and Marian in *New Grub Street*) or eventually accepted without regret (Maurice Hilliard in *Eve's Ransom*, Will Warburton) or even eventually reversed (Edmund Langley in *Sleeping Fires*, Piers Otway in *The Crown of Life*). Dispossessed of his deepest hopes, the older Gissing was much less inclined to confuse eviction with voluntary removal. The will power exerted in sacrifice dried up as a source of solace.[4]

This did not mean, of course, that Gissing was left barren of consoling aspirations or sustaining ideals; will power — a strenuous effort to redeem life's pains — diverted into other streams. Pessimism, however, was equally stubborn, and though Gissing hunted tirelessly for positive values, he tended to wear them out fairly quickly — partly by clashing them against one another, for with his divided and despondent mind he was adroit at spotting the discrepancies between separately valuable aims. The positive value he clutched at in his twenties — then brandished, examined and destroyed in his books — was that of social reform.

After the catastrophe at Manchester, Gissing spent a year in

America, where he experienced for the first time both poverty and democracy. His response to the latter was typically mixed. Approving of the apparent classlessness, he resented the presumption of subordinates (it is interesting to note how in one letter home he shifts from '*Our* democratic notions' to '*They* carry democratic notions').[5] Back in England, and reunited with Nell Harrison (first his mistress, later his wife), he remained depressed by poverty and excited by democracy. 'Returning,' he wrote years later, 'I began a life of terrible struggle in London.' Subsisting on fees from private tuition, he wandered the warrens of the East End and like others before him discovered the poor. What he saw there filled his fiction for over ten years. Appraising this period in his commonplace book, he described it as 'a time of extraordinary mental growth, of great spiritual activity'. As a writer, he added, his childhood, being 'passed in mere comfort', was of no practical use to him. 'The vivid points in my past are certain moments during the period when I was first learning London, and that amid circumstances of hunger and humiliation'; it was then that he acquired his 'intense perception' of the life of the working-class poor.[6] Suffering and empathy made him a rebel. Having been imprisoned and publicly shamed, he was always hypersensitive to humiliation (several of his stories deal wringingly with this, especially 'A Daughter of the Lodge'). And having felt the crushing power of authority, he encouraged himself to regard the lower classes, despite his spontaneous revulsion from them, as likewise victims of injustice. As Waymark says in *The Unclassed*, 'That zeal on behalf of the suffering masses was nothing more nor less than disguised zeal on behalf of my own starved passions ... I identified myself with the poor and ignorant; I did not make their cause my own, but my own cause theirs.'[7]

The emotional displacement at the root of Gissing's zeal helps explain the frequently eccentric shapes that this passion assumes in his fiction. In the late 1870s and early 1880s his turbid feelings of distress and resentment found outlet in three polemical movements: positivism, socialism, and militant agnosticism. All three were proclaimed with self-conscious defiance and his family duly responded with shock. But if we examine this campaigning phase, we can see that Gissing had not really changed; although he shot off in unfamiliar directions, he was always steered to some extent by older and deeper loyalties. The most strident expression of his radicalism was his acrid hostility to the established church. Disgusted by the rise of ritualism, dismayed by the controversial 'burial issue' (the refusal of certain clergymen to bury unbaptized infants), he attended anti-religious lectures and soon offered similar ones himself. With characteristic thoroughness, he devoured David Strauss, Lecky and Gibbon, as well as peppery articles on atheism. His letters home vibrate with anti-clerical vehemence. In one explosive missive to his brother Algernon he rattles off a punishingly full paraphrase of pamphlets obtained from the Liberation Society. 'And what do we deduce from all this? That the Church of England is a monstrosity, an anachronism, an insult to national freedom, and should incontinently be *disestablished* and *disendowed*.' He concludes with the counsel that 'Cathedrals etc.' should be 'confiscated to public use, and used as Government shall determine'.[8]

Gissing had an immediate personal incentive for directing his discontent at the church: his moral transgressions in Manchester could only seem abominable to orthodox piety and it wasn't till some months after this letter that he lived in wedlock with Nell. Despite appearances, though, he was also being moved by earlier commitments. As he told Frederic Harrison (and repeated to Bertz) he had never known 'one moment of enthusiasm for, one instant of belief in, the dogmas of religion'; according to Roberts, his 'one interest in religion' was that 'it was a curious form of delusion almost ineradicable from the human mind'.[9] This cast of thought was the result partly of precocious intellectual inquiry, but partly, too, of his father's influence. Though the other Gissings were conventionally religious, his father, he recalled, had spoken plainly to him once of his 'religious scepticism'. In 1880 he mentioned this to Algernon, arguing, in a letter about positivism, that their father might well have become a disciple if only he had 'had time to become acquainted with all the modern scientific theories'. The face of Gissing's father is occasionally discernible through the pages of the early books. In his notebook 'Reminiscences of my father' Gissing recalls that 'He hated the cant which is contained in vulgarly forced pronunciations of words connected with religion'. In *Workers in the Dawn* the fatuous curate Mr Whiffle betrays his 'fundamentally vulgar nature' through his forced pronunciation of the words 'The Church'.[10] Gissing's contempt for ecclesiastical arrogance, which scandalized his family and seemed a fresh departure, was part of his intellectual patrimony.

A similar attempt to accommodate older values can be seen in the manner of Gissing's allegiance to the cause of social reform. Though ignited by personal observations, his concern took doctrinal form in Comtism and (more doubtfully) in socialism. With their common belief that social transformation could accrue from a theory of historical change, these movements supplied him with hope for the future. Yet before the débâcle at Manchester he had cherished quite different aspirations: it was not through emancipating the people, or establishing a rational social order, but rather through self-cultivation and learning that he then found purpose and meaning. When his social conscience began to stir, an internal struggle was inevitable. Wondering how to reconcile his duty to society with what he regarded as his duty to himself, he decided that reform would have to be effected by culturally fulfilling means. This *rapprochement* proved more difficult than he expected and eventually he gave it up in despair; but for many years his radicalism made unerringly for material that could offer imaginative stimulation or intellectual challenge. Positivism, with its 'wonderful *résumé* of all human knowledge' and its 'scheme of *the history of the world*', seemed to him to offer both (he admitted that when recommending it he always referred 'to its *intellectual* side').[11] Socialism, too, appealed to him for its Continental associations. Introduced to it by his German friend Bertz — 'the only man of *European* culture with whom I have been intimate' — he was soon meeting German socialists in London and reading combustible journals. Bertz's reports of oppression under Bismarck aroused his sympathy and indignation; he utilized them, in September 1880, in three articles he published in the *Pall Mall Gazette* — 'the recognized organ', as he once described it, 'of our most cultured Radicalism'. In these articles on socialism (now available as *Notes on Social Democracy*) he observes that the 'ordinary English capitalist' dismisses such movements as essentially 'foreign'. But their foreignness is precisely what interests Gissing — that and the fact, as he tellingly insists, with reference to Marx, Dühring and Schaeffle, that 'the theory of Socialism rests on the purely scientific inquiries of cultured minds'.[12]

Socialism, it transpires, is exotic and intellectual, equipped with rather attractive connotations of refinement and erudition. One thing Gissing liked about foreign dissent was the chances it provided for translation of texts. In a letter to Algernon which begins with the announcement that his packages have arrived from America and that he now feels satisfied 'with all my possessions once more around me', he laments the outrageous prosecution of the *Freiheit*, a German periodical printed in London and advocating violent revolution. At a meeting about this scandal he 'took some part in the discussion, and certainly knew more of the Socialist matters than anyone there'. At one point, he adds proudly, it was necessary 'to have some passages from the "Freiheit" read out, and as I was the only one present who could translate the German fluently, the duty fell to me'.[13] Cultivation of Continental radicalism was partly, it seems, a continuation of Gissing's attempts to escape from his background by cosmopolitan study. He complained that his Wakefield connections lacked culture, were mentally living in the fifteenth century, and were threatened by 'that abominable narrowness of view which stifles provincial minds'. Part of this narrowness was their queasy shrinking from political philosophies developed abroad (his brother Will, he said, was 'quite savage on the subject of socialists and communists').[14] With Gissing it was very much the opposite: anxious to transcend parochialism, he applauded at alien theatres of conflict: his sanguinary enthusiasm intensified with distance. He would be 'heartily glad', he told Algernon, to hear of a 'fearful revolution' in Germany. He could not condemn political assassination in Russia: 'They are grievously to blame who resolutely obstruct political and social development. Their blood be on their heads!'[15] Clearly it was not only the pleasures of scholarship that exotic politics could afford.

Unfortunately, to tackle the evils around him, he had to return to English politics: and here disappointment supervened. The authentic tones of the disillusioned Gissing reverberate through Eldon's outburst in *Demos*:

> Now in the revolutionary societies of the Continent there is some-
> thing that appeals to the imagination. A Nihilist, with Siberia or
> death before him, fighting against a damnable tyranny — the best
> might sacrifice everything for that. But English Socialism! It is
> infused with the spirit of shopkeeping; it appeals to the vulgarest
> minds; it keeps one eye on personal safety, the other on the
> Capitalist's strongbox; it is stamped commonplace, like everything
> originating with the English lower classes.

The chief spokesman for English socialism in *Demos*, the artisan Richard Mutimer, is constructed to confirm these assertions. As he gratingly harangues a respectable assembly, his smugly xenophobic line of thought ('We are Englishmen — and women — not flighty, frothy foreigners') betrays his parochial limitations: as the author scathingly observes, 'this was not exactly the audience for eulogies of Great Britain at the expense of other countries'. By contrast his sensitive wife, Adela, unnaturally

seduced into social inquiries, at least goes about them in a proper
spirit: a German dictionary beside her, she pores over Schaeffle,
and she finds fascination in French histories of revolution — but
'solely by the dramatic quality of the stories they told'.[16] Adela, in
short, tries to transubstantiate the bread-and-cheese substance of
social analysis into the saving graces of culture. Eventually she
sees that this is a miracle impossible to perform.

Demos was published in 1886, but Gissing made a similar
discovery much sooner; despite his attempts at assimilation,
popular politics were too radical a wrench from his rooted
aspirations. Towards the end of his life he doubted whether he
had ever been a genuine democrat. Henry Ryecroft, confessing
that at one time he called himself a socialist or communist, adds:
'Not for long ... and I suspect that there was always something in
me that scoffed when my lips uttered such things'; elsewhere he
avows that he 'never was' capable of democratic fervour.[17] The
causes of Gissing's disillusion were various. One factor was
his failure to 'reform' Nell, who appears to have reverted, as
their marriage dragged on, to alcoholism and prostitution, and
who not surprisingly evinced little interest in learning about
the classics. Another, closely related factor was his cultural
inflexibility. An intellectual élitist minutely attentive to the
prevailing shibboleths of class,[18] Gissing could scarcely ignore the
fact that although (in his twenties) he found it difficult to admire
the existing aristocracy, and impossible to admire the bourgeoisie,
these classes were nevertheless associated with many pursuits
that he prized. Possibly the socialist millennium would establish
a new set of valuable activities: certainly it would abolish many
old ones. An especial fear of Gissing's was that elegant language
might get trampled by a new regime. At the meetings he attended
he could never help noticing the missing aspirates, the mangled
syntax, the halting clichés, the defective logic. He recoiled from
his comrades in social improvement. Of his working-class
relatives in London, who had introduced him to left-wing
meetings, he reported, 'I fear they put me down for a prig, an
upstart, an abominable aristocrat', but insisted, 'The matter is
entirely intellectual'.[19] It was not entirely intellectual, of course,
but largely temperamental. No directly affirmative and collective
movement could count on Gissing's allegiance for long. All of
them, he felt, were too optimistic: in his opinion there was too big
a gap between the state of humanity they planned for the future
and the inhuman state of the people now. As usual, his positive
impulses were eventually corroded by pessimism.

I I

Many of the tensions in Gissing's treatment of reform are detect-
able in his first two published novels, *Workers in the Dawn* and
The Unclassed. *Workers in the Dawn* (1880) is the most optimistic
of all his books about lower-class life: it is just about equally
balanced between hopefulness and despair. In his unofficial
blurbs for the book Gissing expressed himself vigorously enough.
In an often-quoted letter to Algernon he stated: 'First and
foremost, I attack the criminal negligence of governments which
spend their time over matters of relatively no importance, to the
neglect of the terrible social evils which should have been long
since sternly grappled with. Herein I am a mouthpiece of the
advanced Radical party.' In a lesser-known letter to Frederic
Harrison, however, a considerable vacillation surfaces, an
ambivalence about the East End poor. The novel was the
outcome, Gissing explained, of his 'own strongly excitable
temperament, operated upon by hideous experiences of low life'.
After poking around Whitecross Street and Seven Dials, after
sitting in mean theatres and music-hall pits, he had marvelled at
the gulf between rich and poor — mental as well as material —
and had thought: 'What then is the meaning of those strange
words Morality, Decency, Intelligence ... ? Surely I have wandered
out of the world in which these ideas have any significance; here
they mean nothing, nay, their presence would be the intrusion of
an utterly incongruous element'. He goes on to acknowledge that
the very poor have a quite different 'standard of life and conduct'
from those he calls 'the happier rich'. But he adds: 'I wished to
show the necessity for a personal invasion of these realms of
darkness by those who are able to teach their inhabitants not
only to abandon crime, not only to esteem knowledge, — but to
understand what is meant by the word *Ideal*'.[20] Evidently Gissing
is undecided whether the workers have a different morality or
whether they simply have none. More important, though, is his
uncertainty about the relevance of cultural missionary work. On
the one hand, the presence of middle-class values would be an
incongruous intrusion. On the other, a didactic middle-class
'invasion' is an urgent necessity.

In the novel, the second view prevails: the author's attitude
towards the slums is in the tradition of the 'social explorer'
chronicled by P. J. Keating.[21] This is obvious enough from the
guided-tour opening ('Walk with me, reader, into Whitecross
Street'), but in fact this motif is integral to the plot: Mr Heatherley

tests Helen Norman's mettle by escorting her round the haunts of
the poor; Arthur beckons Carrie to the vilest quarters ('Will you
come for a walk with me?') to expose the evils of drink. That the
characters' morally instructive excursions are designed as
extensions of the opening lecture is suggested by the verbal
parallels. All three itineraries include an inspection of filthy items
of ragged clothing; the 'low, yawning archway' pointed out on the
first tour is echoed in the 'low-browed arches' of the second. But
what is most remarkable about all three descriptions is how
helplessly *un*descriptive they are. They communicate revulsion
rather than perception. 'A foul-mouthed virulence surpassing
description', 'courts and alleys of undescribable foulness',
'women in appearance too ghastly for description' – in each case
the fluent and fastidious narrator is reduced to inarticulate
disgust.[22]

Nevertheless he still favours, for much of the novel, an invasion
of this territory by moral idealists. Large sections of *Workers in the
Dawn*, insisting that the horrors have a social cause, imply faith
in a social cure. Both hero and heroine are active in schemes
for social amelioration. Enthused by the writings of Comte
and Shelley, the earnestly trustful Helen Norman engages in
philanthropy with a dissenting clergyman (even though her own
motives are purely secular) and eventually sets up an evening-
school for working-class girls. Despite discouragement, she
succeeds in making headway. It is not true that, as Jacob Korg
suggests, 'her new philosophy proves inadequate' or that 'she dies
in an exile she has sought as an escape from her failures in social
work and in love'. Her social work is not a failure: it benefits not
only her own moral nature, but also the girls at her evening-class,
where 'her efforts received each week their unmistakable reward'.
She only dies abroad because she has consumption: her tragedy
is supposed to lie in the fact that death cuts her off just at the
moment when her power for good is expanding.[23] Arthur Golding's
philanthropic stirrings take a more political form. When he joins
a working-men's Radical Club organized by the worthy and
resolute Will Noble, Gissing patiently explores its functions
with a fullness and sympathy unique in his work (its only real
competitor is Mary Barfoot's academy in *The Odd Women*). Its
members, all single and teetotallers, pay voluntary subscriptions
to a self-help fund and meet on Sunday evenings in a carpenter's
shed to discuss the politics of poverty. Arthur – excited, like
Gissing himself, by Continental uprising – makes a flaming
speech in favour of the Paris Commune, but Noble soberly excels

him 'in solid force of argument'. Starting from premises as sturdy
and basic as those he finds himself speaking in, Noble argues that
all human beings are in need of shelter, clothing and food: nature
is sufficient to meet this demand, so there must be something
wrong with a social system that fails to provide such necessities.
Noble objects to the idle rich, but not to inequalities of wealth; he
believes that everyone has a right to share in the products of
human labour, but only to a sufficient degree 'properly to sustain
life'. His prescriptions are as moderate as his diagnosis. The
workers are handicapped by poverty, but even more by ignorance.
'In my mind there is only one answer: *We must get taught!*'[24]
Noble's ringing peroration chimes in with other parts of the
novel, which elsewhere supports state schools and free libraries
and education generally.

So far, so optimistic: the intentions are modest, the setbacks
many (even Noble is temporarily disenchanted), but it does seem
that conscientious men and women can make some impact on
deprivation: the novel seems cautiously reformist. In fact it is
much more divided than this: from the very beginning the calls
for action are echoed by cries of despair. For example, in the
book's opening chapter the flaring panorama of toil and misery is
first blamed on the comfortable classes ('We suffer them to
become brutes in our midst') and then located in 'Adam and Eve
Court'. Toil and misery were the first results of the Fall. And,
unfortunately, a number of characters appear to be unredeemable.
The savagery and sadism of the Blatherwicks, the coarseness and
cruelty of the Pettindunds, the stubborn stupidity and cunning of
Carrie — all provide gloomily cogent evidence of the forces
massed against pedagogic zeal. The last example is particularly
telling because Arthur's efforts to reclaim Carrie Mitchell (the
fictional *alter ego* of Nell) are at times specifically associated with
his humanitarian ideals.

This double vision of the hopes for reform is correlated,
throughout the novel, with a bifurcated view of the workers. They
are variously seen as both victims and criminals, objects of
compassion, deserving aid, and objects of physical and moral
abhorrence, who spurn all the aid that is offered. Both perspectives are found in the tours of the slums. In the first, the faces of
the denizens exhibit both 'vice and misery'; in the second, Helen
and Heatherley pass 'from one haunt of abominations to another,
from one scene of heart-rending sufferings to another'. Though
each response was Gissing's own, in the novel he tries to seg-
regate them. The compassionate view is taken by Arthur's

mentor, the printer Tollady. Contemplating the degraded poor, he acknowledges their hideousness, but blames it on the negligence of government and the callous indifference of the rich. Like Sidney with Clara in *The Nether World*, he regards the manifest faults of the poor 'not as characteristics to be condemned, but as evidences of suffering, the outcome of cruel conditions'.[25] The contrasting view is taken by Helen's mentor, the painter Gilbert Gresham. Hearing of Helen's charitable projects, he replies that 'persistent self-brutalisation' has reduced the masses to a state much worse than that of dogs or horses: 'It is my firm belief that their degeneration is actually and literally physical ... that you might as well endeavour to teach a pig to understand Euclid as to teach one of these gaol-birds to know and feel what is meant by honesty, virtue, kindness, intellectuality'. Gresham's eloquence is instantly rejected by Helen and condemned by his character in the rest of the book — sly, selfish, unprincipled. Yet surely it answers to something in Gissing. Of course Gissing's official position, as proclaimed in the letter to Algernon quoted above, was that of Helen and Tollady. But Greshamite sentiments would keep creeping back. Faced with his landlady's loathsome family, Arthur Golding glimpses 'the great truth that education, and education only, working perhaps through generations', could redeem 'the well-to-do labouring classes'. However, in their company, he still feels 'unutterable disgust'. Indeed, his conviction that the Pettindunds are 'too completely sunk in their hoggish slough to be capable of rescue by any single hand' sounds oddly close to Gilbert Gresham on teaching Euclid to pigs.[26]

Gissing remained undecided about the people's capacity for reform: spontaneous loathing and considered indignation were his permanently polarized responses. Where he also revealed uncertainty, though, was in his appraisal of their reformers — especially in his later books, but even in *Workers in the Dawn*. Here, after all, the full-time reformers are not Helen and Arthur but Heatherley and Noble — who, despite their sincerity and decency, are prosaically inferior to their protégés. Helen soon learns that Mr Heatherley, attracted to 'hard details of social life', does not share her own 'richly poetical' nature. Much later, the account of Noble's library — no poetry, no works of imagination — reveals a man immersed in the 'savage facts' of political economy. Eventually, breaking from Arthur Golding, Noble condemns his commitment to art as 'devotion to a mere unreasoning passion'. Even the most worthy and blameless reformers betray some lack of fineness.[27]

The conflict between art and reform is a central theme in *Workers in the Dawn* — it emerges in the story of Arthur Golding — as in most of Gissing's early books. Its significance has been well expounded in Jacob Korg's seminal article 'Division of purpose in George Gissing', which argues that Gissing was continually torn between the impulse to reform and the impulse to create: he wrote fiction with a social and moral mission while believing himself to be purely an artist, and pure art to be non-didactic.[28] Korg's argument fits into the pattern traced here, for though art and reform become rivals in Gissing, they can both be seen as positive values nurtured to resist the insidious despair brought on by the Manchester crisis (one of them, of course, reached back before this; the other was stimulated by it). Pessimism, however, proved its strength by setting these values at variance. Gissing became doubtful about social reform not only because of his negative convictions (the obstinate animality of the masses) but also because of his positive ones (his exalted conception of culture). In *Workers in the Dawn* Helen Norman's father insists that the only worthwhile education is to cultivate emotions through the careful study of English and European poets.[29] It's not clear where this leaves people like the Pettindunds; presumably some of their remote descendants might profit from the *Golden Treasury*. The problem was a very real one for Gissing, whose limited support for social reform, arising from highly personal motives, was apt to confuse what the workers needed with what he felt he needed himself. When this false conflation was brought to light, the result was inevitably disappointment. Altruistic policy, he then concluded, was incompatible with self-cultivation.

Many of the peculiarities, indeed, in Gissing's fictional treatment of reform spring from the fact that his social curiosity was always rooted firmly in his personal pain. Exposing the miseries of the working-class poor, he was also confessing his spiritual anguish; recommending, depicting or rejecting social action, he was signing a personal statement. Several of the fractures we have touched on so far — between pessimism and will power, art and reform, and above all the analysis of public evils and the cathartic release of private obsessions — come out very clearly in *The Unclassed* (1884), where they merit examination. The novel is quintessential early Gissing, packed with his customary ingredients: intelligent and sensitive young people condemned to degrading and ill-paid jobs; a background of slums and social vices; love affairs vexed with jealousy and introspection; a pervasive note of personal bitterness about poverty, injustice, class displacement and orthodox morality. It is also undoubtedly autobiographical — though here complications arise. At first sight the book's two heroes, Osmond Waymark and Julian Casti, appear to be separate embodiments of twinned but conflicting impulses in Gissing — Waymark, novelist, tutor and cynic, representing his more resolute energies; Casti, marital victim and idealist, acting out his despairing fears. Between them, too, they seem to carry the burden of the author's incongruous literary interests. Waymark writes 'desperately modern' fiction on the sordid miseries of contemporary life; Casti plans an epic poem or drama on a subject from a classical source. Before long, however, this neat contrast breaks down: since both men are moulded on Gissing himself, their identities begin to fuse. Waymark's sexual feelings, like Casti's, are ignited by protectiveness and pity: for Gissing passion and compassion were never far apart.[30] Saddled with this susceptibility, Waymark eventually gets similarly entangled. By the end of the book, worn down by misjudgements, squirming in a self-imposed impasse (he loves Ida but feels committed to Maud), he sounds as depleted as his fagged-out friend: 'Unconsciously he had struggled to the extremity of weariness, and now he cared only to let things take their course'. Though Waymark is certainly stronger-willed than Casti, he is not strong enough to resist the author's pessimism. Casti expires racked with consumption after spending a particularly nasty session in the marital torture-chamber. But Waymark is manacled by dual commitments, only understanding his true preference too late. The liberating ending of the novel, in which Waymark leaps happily to Ida from Maud, was probably not part of the original conception, but prompted by George Meredith, the reader for Chapman & Hall.[31]

Even without this ending, however, the novel is not wholly pessimistic, for once again two positive values are propounded, vigorously if ambiguously: social reform and art. The possibility of rectifying social injustice enters into *The Unclassed* in two main areas, the account of Woodstock's slum properties and the story of the prostitute Ida. In both, reclamation is available — indeed the renovation of the slums is directly due to Ida's return to social respectability. Morally rehabilitated, Ida deploys her grandfather's money in schemes for assisting his degraded tenants, and after Woodstock dies of smallpox contracted in his own fetid properties, she even has the slums rebuilt. The main beneficiaries are the younger generation, for Ida's 'common sense' informs her that, though the 'parents could not be reformed', genuine aid can be offered to their offspring, and the novel concludes with the news that 'Especially in the condition of the children improvement was discernible'. One chapter, entitled 'A Garden Party', shows Ida rounding up a gaggle of urchins and benevolently plying them with cakes and games. It seems a nauseous interlude, and the quasi-biblical exhortations surrounding Ida's actions in the first edition — 'Go, and do thou likewise', etc. — suggest that Gissing was ingenuous enough to regard such juvenile diversions as a serious social proposal.[32] In this, however, he was not alone: in the later years of the nineteenth century there were many lady philanthropists like Ida. For instance, Mrs Henrietta Barnett contributed a chapter on 'Women as Philanthropists' to a book certainly known to Gissing and published in the year of *The Unclassed*: Theodore Stanton's compilation, *The Woman Question in Europe* (1884). Mrs Barnett, the wife of a Whitechapel vicar, did charitable work for young girls in the East End. The example she commends to her respectable readers is a party where the hostess entertains her guests as the friends of, say, the local rent-collector (Woodstock in *The Unclassed* is, of course, a landlord) and 'where she opens her garden, her conservatories, and maybe her house for their reception'. Dwelling fondly on one such occasion, devoted to ten or twelve girls, she recalls 'the well-appointed tea-table, the merry-making games ... the soul-speaking music' (at Ida's party there is a tea-table with 'piled plates of cake', dancing and 'merry laughter', and a hand-organ to lighten the girls' hearts). Mrs Barnett concludes with the revelation that during the past ten years she has given or organized three hundred such parties.[33] Evidently, Ida's fairy-banquet was grounded in historical fact.

The more cogent objection to the garden-party chapter is not that it describes a historical fantasy but that it approves a political one. It offers purely personal acts of charity as the single ray of hope for the poor. However sentimental or misconceived, this was certainly deliberate on Gissing's part. Though he long harboured vaguely reformist yearnings, he soon lost his faith in collective action. 'The progress of the masses', he once opined, 'is by no means due to a general effort among them, but to the hard struggle against universal sluggishness of a very few energetic men, — mostly in the enlightened class.'[34] These 'energetic men' did not include MPs. In *The Unclassed* the vanity of Parliament is shown (especially in the first edition) through the character of Woodstock. A ruthlessly exploitative slum landlord, Woodstock also slakes his lust for power through fierce passion for parliamentary politics. Blue Books, Hansard and the Annual Register stimulate his appetite for reading; he revels in all the 'petty details' of squalid electioneering. By contrast he abandons his wretched daughter − Ida's mother − who falls back on prostitution: a narrowly political mentality, we gather, is the father of social vices. When he finally recovers some humanity, adopting Ida to make amends, Woodstock starts to shed his political obsessions (compare the progress of Adela in *Demos*, who moves from arid political tracts to lush garden parties for the poor).[35] All this might seem an odd line to take for a fiction focused on social abuses and produced in a period of legislative reform. Gissing, however, saw Parliament not as an instrument for removing evils but rather as a system for sanctioning them. Woodstock explains that Parliament could not possibly intervene in the slums, since 'These are affairs of private contract'; 'politics *is* business', he declares.[36] Woodstock's perversity makes Gissing's point. Parliament, being shackled to *laissez-faire*, is presented as a broken-down vehicle for rescuing its victims.

Poverty and hardship are implicitly seen as the outcome of individual greed: they can be ameliorated only by individual initiatives. A similar implication emerges from the treatment of prostitution. Gissing was aware of its economic causes (workroom girls, he remarks at one point, cannot afford the luxury of strict virtue), and he repeatedly draws attention to the social prejudice that prostitutes encounter (their children are expelled from school and they themselves sacked from respectable jobs). But he also insists that personality is decisive in determining this particular choice of career: Waymark deludes himself, we learn, in trying to imagine Ida's 'downfall' as the 'irresistible climax of dolorous circumstances'.[37] Even Ida's wrongful imprisonment for theft − in a chapter sardonically entitled 'Justice', she is sentenced to six months with hard labour − is an instance of social bigotry that seems more like a personal apologia. Gissing's indignant pity for Ida springs unmistakably from his own experience − partly from his knowledge of Nell's adversities, even more from his own imprisonment. This helps to explain the inapposite pleas entered in defence of the heroine's conduct − many of which Gissing carefully excised when he later revised the book. The mental pain of a gaol sentence is evoked with quivering intensity: 'Not with impunity can the human mind surrender itself for half a year to unvaried brooding upon one vast misery ... For months Ida's thoughts had gone round and round about one centre of anguish, like a wailing bird circling over a ravaged nest'. Despite this authorial empathy, however, there is one crucial difference between Ida's case and Gissing's: Ida is not guilty as charged. At times, fertile with extenuations, Gissing appears to forget this fact. The besotted Waymark sometimes contends that Ida is pardonable though technically guilty: 'In his habitual conviction of the relativity of all names and things, he could not possibly bring himself to regard this act as a crime. It was an imprudence, a grievous imprudence'. But sometimes he will not believe her guilty at all — 'Not if every court in England proclaimed her so!' Casti shifts his ground with similar agility. Convinced that Ida is innocent of theft, he bitterly protests against society's right to punish even the guilty:

> What right had society to impose its penalties on a living soul, to condemn to anguish a being it had no power to make happy, to disinherit the birthright of liberty in mere revenge for a petty infringement ... ? Theft, forsooth! Who of all those constituting society should make good to her one moment of these months stolen from her short life?

As reflections on the case of Ida Starr — totally innocent and believed to be so — these sentiments are singularly malapropos. Their true significance is autobiographical — as Gissing, in fact, appears to sense, for he quickly tacks on an authorial disclaimer: 'So thought Julian Casti in his anguish ... love soars so high in its faith in the individual soul'. It was this latter passage he was able to cite when defending the book against his brother's worried strictures: 'There I speak in my own person, and what I say in reality controverts all that Casti has just thought'. In his article 'Gissing's revision of *The Unclassed*', Joseph J. Wolff quotes Gissing's comment and concludes that it 'provides most convincing proof of avowals so frequently stated in his letters that characters are made to express their own and not necessarily his opinions'.[38] In this instance, however, it proves just the opposite. It is precisely because the character's opinions are relevant only to the author's situation that Gissing has to add a formal disclaimer. His repudiation of Casti's outburst is a sign of embarrassment.

There are, in any case, other passages where attacks on the social censure of Ida strike a throbbingly personal note. For example, her motives for adopting prostitution: how can anyone, Gissing demands, presume to condemn her unless they can show they have greater self-knowledge themselves?

Only then are your instincts (which is the same as saying your powers of moral judgment) more valid for me than my own, when you prove that you have learnt me by heart, have got at my mystery, appreciate every step which has brought me to my present position, and miss no item in the circumstances, internal or external, which constitute my being. And Ida Starr was not so easily conned by rote.

It is almost startling, at the end of this passage, to realize we are meant to be thinking of Ida: the author's Hamlet-like reproach is so plainly a personal protest.[39] And the remedies for injustice are personal too. Both Ida and her prostitute friend Sally Fisher are redeemed through love of a particular man. Ida's later rescue from poverty and disgrace is effected through her grandfather's change of heart. And when Ida inherits the slums from Woodstock, her zeal for improvement is in direct proportion to her personal experience of oppression.

The treatment of reform in *The Unclassed* — sentimentally philanthropic and coupled to the concept of personal redemption — reflects its origins in the author's feelings of outrage and humiliation. Characteristically, though, this commitment to reform is checked by attachment to a rival value — the creed of art for art's sake. In the early 1880s Gissing recoiled from his erstwhile dalliance with reformist groups and adopted an aggressively aestheticist stance. Since his hero, Waymark, does the same, critics have naturally assumed that the novel is in this respect, too, directly autobiographical. But how far can this argument be sustained? When Waymark announces his fervent belief that art alone offers full satisfaction, in terms very similar to Gissing's avowals in letters of 1883–4, it is tempting to conclude that Waymark *is* Gissing, and *The Unclassed* an advocacy of pure aesthetic detachment. This is the conclusion that, for example, John Halperin underscores.[40] The objection to it is that the novel's structure is designed to undermine Waymark's credo, and that therefore the book is more reformist than its hero. Admittedly, though, this structure is less evident in the shortened second edition.

Gissing revised and curtailed *The Unclassed* in 1895. Though most of the changes were advantageous, especially the larger-scale excisions (a wooden sub-plot concerning the Enderbys was pared down to a melodramatic splinter), some of them unfortunately obscured his intentions. Chipping away at superfluous phrases, Gissing also loosened some structural joints. A number of these were connected with Waymark's increasing disillusion with art. Waymark is characterized from the beginning as reckless, uncaring, irresponsible, but it soon becomes plain that this willed indifference, this vaunted art-for-art's-sake composure, is largely a cultivated pose. It is a pose directed towards things that disturb him — the horrors of slum life that he has to witness, especially in his role as rent-collector, and the tensions implicit in his dealings with Ida: towards, in fact, the two areas where the novel is concerned with reform. Both bring out aspects of his cynicism. Deadened to the pains of its denizens, he writes cool articles about Elm Court; and though he cannot relish his role in eviction, he tries to turn even this to account — 'it cost him a dark hour now and then. But it was rich material; every item was stored up for future use'. He attempts to be similarly unidealistic about his relations with his prostitute girl-friend: 'Confidence in her he had not ... outcome of the cynicism which was a marked feature in his development'. In the first edition his indifference to the slums is much more pointedly conjoined with his would-be indifference to Ida. For example when, speaking about his own fiction, he declares that only art can satisfy, in the first edition he not only adds, 'I repeat that I have absolutely no social purpose in this novel', but continues with a very 1890s-ish speech to the effect that his interest in prostitution is purely that of an aesthetic connoisseur.[41] Lack of interest in social reform is linked with lack of pity for Ida. Likewise — and this link survived the revision — his announcement of his cynical pieces on the slums is preceded by a self-conscious manifesto on the possibility of passionless relations, in which men and women frankly agree to 'tantalise each other agreeably'. Two pages later a brief note from Ida inflames him with crackling jealousy: perhaps, we wonder, his artistic attitudes are just as self-deceiving as his amorous ones.

The unfolding of the story confirms this conjecture. Though allegedly cured of his radical 'ailment', Waymark increasingly breaks out in scruples — in argument with Woodstock, about Ida's feelings, and especially in his shock at Ida's conviction.[42] Cockily attempting to respond to the latter as merely a dramatic 'situation', he finds that 'for all that, his heart was beating violently'. The whole thrust, in fact, of the love story is Waymark's growing recognition that he does indeed love Ida, and not merely desire her, despite the factors that have held him back — his poverty, his anxiety not to raise false hopes, and later his engagement to Maud. The climax of this recognition, and the moment when his nonchalant posture is dropped, is when Slimy, the most snarlingly brutalized tenant, ties him to a garret floor. Attempting to see this, too, as a 'situation' (in the first edition he has Slimy in his novel), Waymark reflects serenely that 'to an artist it might well be suggestive of useful hints'. Pain and time disabuse him and also 'open his eyes' about Ida. He realizes his 'introspection was at fault'. Later, still morosely engaged to Maud, but despairingly in love with Ida, he casts off his cavalier aesthetic indifference: 'Waymark's mood was bitter, but, in spite of himself, it was no longer cynical ... His enthusiasm for art was falling away; as a faith it had failed him in his hour of need'. With respect to Ida, at any rate, Waymark's cynicism melts away. Given the thematic yoking just noticed, we might expect that by the end of the book he would also repudiate his indifference to the poor. But Waymark embraces only Ida. It is she who devotes herself to reform — though like him she finds no cause satisfying without the fulfilment of love.[43]

The Unclassed is a partially hopeful novel. Although the author's pessimism eats away at the positive values he constructs, a small refuge for reformism is left intact: the slums are rendered tolerable, the prostitute morally reclaimed. Waymark's vaunted aestheticism is shown to fail as a sustaining creed, but more because of his need for love than because of his commitment to reform. In Gissing's subsequent working-class novels a similar opposition of values is set up, but in these it is tethered more determinedly to a negative social thesis. In the late 1880s, almost totally rejecting his former ideas of social reform, he contrived in a series of novels to suggest that this ideal could only be pursued as an alternative — and a dangerously uncertain one — to other, more desirable ends.

I I I

Demos (1886), *Thyrza* (1887) and *The Nether World* (1889) are varied novels in setting and conception, but they all attack the notion of social reform by presenting it as hostile to art and culture, and even more as incompatible with love. As these weird antitheses might suggest, they are all intensely subjective novels, and they highlight the fictional problems implicit in the effort to analyse social evils from a passionately personal standpoint. One sign of their essential subjectivity is their concentration on the lives of reformers rather than the reformed. Though purporting to dismiss the value of schemes to assist the working class, they do so almost exclusively from the viewpoint of the benefactors rather than the beneficiaries. As these terms imply, they see social improvement as something handed down from above. None of these books suggests that workers can or ought to control their own fate. *Demos*, in which the socialist employer, Mutimer, is of working-class origin himself, might appear to be an exception to this rule, but in fact one polemical theme of the novel is that power hoists Mutimer above his comrades. Whisked up from worker to industrialist, he becomes a traitor to his class, pushing for his own aggrandizement rather than contending for the dispossessed. At the same time he is supposed to remain true to his class in that he embodies its typical faults. Prosperity magnifies vices in Mutimer that make him betray the working class, but these vices are themselves exhibited as essentially working-class traits. In an early oration after coming into money, Mutimer promises always to remain 'of the people and with the people'. And in a sense — despite the occasional suggestion that he has dwindled to a 'classless agitator' — he does remain *of* the people although he is no longer *with* them. Mutimer, it seems, is doubly indicted — simultaneously the betrayer and the representative of his class.[44]

In *Demos* social reform is condemned through condemnation of social reformers — of their hypocrisy, envy, lust for power and lack of imagination. To a lesser extent this tactic recurs in *Thyrza* and *The Nether World*, in both of which the failure of a philanthropic project is due partly to disturbing weaknesses in the character of its advocate. However, there is also a contrasting case for rejection of reform in these three novels — that, because of their fineness or nobility, the reformers do not find the work fulfilling. Characters like Adela in *Demos*, or Jane and Sidney in *The Nether World*, would rather devote themselves to higher things: respect for nature, concern for culture, an exalted quest for love. Walter Egremont, the weakly decent hero of *Thyrza*, partly qualifies for this group, too: one oddity of this novel is that its reformer fails on account of his praiseworthy as well as his blameworthy qualities. Normally, however, the two causes of failure are distinct and almost contradictory. It is typical of Gissing that his fictional philanthropists should be either too corrupt or too refined, ruined either by lowly morals or lofty aspirations. Social reform, persistently depicted as unworthy by comparison with other ideals, is, it seems, sufficiently worthy to be stultified by shoddy proponents.

Unillumined by Gissing's own biography (which includes his reading of Ruskin and Morris), these dilemmas and alternatives might strike the reader as eccentrically obscure.[45] There seems to be no inherent reason why a passion for improving the condition of the poor should exclude an appreciation of beauty, whether in nature or in art, or why it should conflict with sexual passion of an idealistic kind. Yet Gissing's anti-reformist fictions continually contrive such oppositions, ingeniously fabricating situations in which a zeal for philanthropy is at odds with Nature, Love or Art. Such zeal is largely confined, we discover, to inferior or inadequate human types: the avaricious, the resentful, the incurably visionary; or else the inartistic, the literal-minded, the incorrigibly prosaic. That reformist activity should chiefly appeal to such unappealing human beings — dullards or dreamers, frauds or dupes — is dispiriting enough in itself. What makes the prospect even bleaker is that the edifice of positive values erected to put reform in the shade is, with one or two slender exceptions, equally ruinous by the end of each book. Artistic buddings are buried in ashes, nature is frequently fouled or ravaged, passion is blocked or crushed. Save for the sunny conclusion of *Demos*, these books are closed landscapes of lowering frustration. Cogently depicting social conditions that cry out for urgent alteration, they nevertheless insist that social reform is unavailing or unfulfilling. Other ideals — potentially more satisfying — do exist, the books suggest; but in practice they remain unsatisfied.

So uncompromisingly negative are the arguments deployed — and often so perversely inconsistent — that for explanation we have to look to Gissing's own predicament. The truth was that by the late 1880s he had over-exercised his social conscience to the point of emotional exhaustion. He was tired of the topic of social reform, overstrained by an uncongenial stance. In the novels this personal disenchantment is projected on to his vain reformers. The streak of insincerity in his own commitment — admitted much later in *Henry Ryecroft* — is blown up into the blatant hypocrisy of Mutimer; his yearning to escape into love or culture is intensified, in Adela or Egremont, into feverish obsession. At the same time Gissing strives hard to attain an objective, even documentary, tone, and each story is invested with a sombre thesis. Essentially, then, these novels are personal confessions in the guise of impersonal investigations. What they seem determined to prove is that social reform is ineffective. What they actually show is that social concern is psychologically unsatisfying.

The limitations of these anti-reformist novels, stemming largely from their personal genesis, show up in a problem of fictional structure that haunted Gissing for years: how to adapt the conventions of romance to the requirements of social analysis. Take *Demos*, according to its sub-title 'A Story of English Socialism': its argument is pegged out almost allegorically on a traditional love-triangle. Richard Mutimer, representing democracy, is contrasted throughout with Hubert Eldon, the liberal aristocrat. Inheriting money that ought to be Eldon's, Mutimer becomes an Owenite employer and sets about promoting the socialist cause. As the narrative unfolds, his personal deficiencies are exposed by comparison with Eldon's strengths. The arbiter of this is a woman, Adela, for whose love and loyalty the two men compete. Inexperienced but sensitively scrupulous, she marries Mutimer but comes to loathe him; eventually, after her husband's death, she turns with relief to Eldon. The woman's choice of a particular man emerges, in the novel's symbolic scheme, as a vote for the aristocratic code: what starts as a moral and aesthetic contrast winds up as a political one. This is true even though at the end of the book Adela interprets the path she has taken as suitable only for herself (humanitarian toil, she muses, is simply 'not for her'). In *Henry Ryecroft*, Gissing says the same of himself, claiming that no condemnation of others is implied by his own undogmatic rejection of democratic fervour.[46] In neither case does the reader believe it. In *Demos*, certainly, Adela's decision cannot be uncontentiously personal, for the book's whole polemical strategy is to show how personal attributes are aligned with ideological positions.

If we ask how in detail this is achieved, the first thing we notice is the heavy reliance on guilt by association. The socialist mentality is carefully loaded with a number of other reactions and leanings, all of them unattractive. Mutimer, the socialist, is unimaginative, pledged to utility rather than beauty, to politics rather than art. Ecologically irresponsible, he devastates a valley with industrial filth, just as he defiles an innocent girl with his clumsy and grasping attentions. He lives superficially, from moment to moment, wholly absorbed in external things; and though occasionally he is allowed some virtues — his energy, his intelligence, his devotion to his family — their narrowness is always apparent. Eldon is everything that Mutimer is not: complex, fastidious, intense, refined, and above all aesthetically sensitive. He has no doubt that Mutimer's ugly factory must be closed, pens sonnets inspired by the *Vita Nuova*, goes to Rome to study art, and gets known as an 'admirable' critic.[47] It is not that Eldon has no faults — he is arrogant, prejudiced, reckless, blunt — but in character-descriptions these are always excused: though lacking humility, he is also noble; though prejudiced, yet liberal-minded; though imperious, capable of delicacy. An opposite technique is at work with Mutimer, whose merits are smudged by qualification — he is earnest but also insincere; egalitarian but condescending; self-taught but only half-taught. Our sympathies are also manipulated by the curious circumstances made to prevail in the story of these contrasting men — curious because flatly at variance with the men's representative function. Mutimer, the test-case proletarian, comes into vast property and wealth and enjoys all the perks of a powerful employer. Eldon, the exemplary aristocrat, is wrongfully disinherited and also, in his affair with Adela, made the victim of parochial scandal. It is remarkable, with Eldon, how Gissing reshapes this haughty sprig of a landed family into someone quite closely resembling himself — passionate, rebellious, isolated, and 'wondering in what class of society he would have to look for his kith and kin'.[48] The privileged man becomes disadvantaged, uncertain of his status although born to rule; and the underdog becomes the overlord.

Having fabricated socially symbolic figures and placed them in tendentious circumstances, Gissing devises a series of tests for the self-styled socialists to fail. Hubristically accepting his specimen status ('He would be the glorified representative of his class'), Mutimer puts his own neck in the noose by publicly disclaiming all selfish motives, then activates the drop by deceiving his fiancée and trying to suppress a will.[49] Lest we should fail to connect these offences with Mutimer's ideology, the other reformers are likewise shown to be inspired by disloyalty, hypocrisy and spite. Much of this exposé-work is lumberingly done — we see Cowes and Cullen, the socialist teetotallers, chuntering maliciously over a drink — but one or two cases are more smoothly sustained. For instance, the marriage between Richard and Adela is paralleled by that between Richard's sister, Alice, and his dubious manager, Rodman. Though Rodman is a cunning criminal and Mutimer merely a self-deceived zealot, the two men are related not only as in-laws, but virtually as outlaws. Shifty, but consistently self-interested, Rodman switches off his socialist ardour as soon as his ends are secured. Like Mutimer, but more crudely, he marries for advantage, but in his case this involves bigamy rather than breach of promise. Like Mutimer, too, he treats his new wife with physical cruelty and callous neglect (at Wimbledon Alice 'perished of *ennui*, for she was as lonely as Adela in Holloway'); and after Mutimer has locked Adela in, Rodman adds a cruel extra twist by locking Alice out.

Finally, following the débâcle with the will, both men indulge in speculative ventures, the reformer's compound-interest scheme being matched by the swindler's Irish Dairy Company: both schemes collapse in financial fraud and bitter recrimination. At the end of the novel, blotting Rodman from her heart, Alice marries Mr Keene. Adela likewise banishes the past by marrying Hubert Eldon.[50]

Morally and politically, the crooked Rodman is cast as a burlesque version of Mutimer: a revealing example of the novel's technique of guilt by association. But Gissing tries to go further than this, for in order to clinch his case against the socialists, he needs not only to associate, but also in some way to identify, their public policies with their private vices. Lightnesses in love have to carry the weight of political deficiencies. A central incident in this respect is Mutimer's betrayal of Emma Vine, his working-class fiancée. Partly symbolic of his treachery to the poor, this also discloses his readiness to substitute theory for personal loyalty (his ostensible motive for marrying Adela is to strike a blow against class distinction) and his fundamental insincerity (his real reason is precisely that Adela is a 'lady'). Although in his early boastful pronouncements Mutimer equates fidelity to Emma with fidelity to his principles, in reality 'A suggestion that domestic perfidy was in the end incompatible with public zeal would have seemed to him ridiculous'. At the same time he is able to profit as a lover from his reputation as a man of high aims — 'such a man', Adela's mother concludes, 'could never be brutal in the privacy of his own home'. When he does betray Emma, the repercussions are seismic. His own mother denounces him as a hypocrite; he loses his influence over his sister; his socialist enemies exploit the scandal to discredit him politically. Emma's lonely sufferings are grimly charted and her ailing sister expires of grief. Unwisely attempting to defend himself by conniving at a smear on Emma's character — 'Men with large aims cannot afford to be scrupulous in small details' — Mutimer is forced to discover afresh that ideology can be laid waste by immorality. Not everyone, it is true, accepts this idea. Westlake, hearing of Mutimer and Emma, reflects that 'you cannot expect men to be perfect, and that great causes have often been served by very indifferent characters'. But Westlake, though well-meaning, is merely a theorist. The author's own judgement on the socialists appears rather to be that of Wyvern: 'They are not themselves of pure and exalted character; they cannot ennoble others'.[51]

Given the structure of the novel, no other assumption could

practically be made; in various ways it has to keep reverting to the link between personal motives and political effects. Not infrequently, the results of this are strained. For example, there is considerable confusion about whether or not socialist convictions should be grounded in personal experience. Gissing delights in laying open the rancour that festers at the heart of lofty professions. Sacking a workman, Mutimer attempts to pass off personal resentment as principle. The success of his ideological antagonist, Roodhouse, is dependent on envy, not argument. Adela's brother Alfred is a 'Radical' whose truculent rhetoric is a compensation for his coarseness and 'defective stature'; underlying his tirades against the aristocracy is a personal hatred of Eldon. 'Never trust the thoroughness of the man', mocks Gissing, 'who is a revolutionist on abstract principles; personal feeling alone goes to the root of the matter.' If one set of socialists, however, are excessively and shamefully personal, another set are not personal enough. When Westlake delivers a lyrical address to a middle-class audience at Commonwealth Hall, 'It needed but a glance over this assembly to understand how very theoretical were the convictions that had brought its members together'.[52] The socialists, it seems, cannot win, trapped as they are between the Scylla of Theory and the Charybdis of Envy. Again it is Gissing's biography that explains this gloomy insistence. For him there was no contradiction here, since he knew, from his own experience, that while an ephemeral urge for reform might seek highly theoretical formulas, its sources could be highly personal.

Demos has many strengths as a novel, especially its account of family friction, but as an attack on English socialism it fails to have impact because of its slippage between thesis and narrative. The morbid fervours of political passion are contrasted with the healthy fulfilments of love, but Adela's flight from Mutimer to Eldon has more to do with temperament than with ideology. Throughout the book the purity of nature is praised and the filth of the factories associated with Mutimer. Yet the socialist inspiration of the New Wanley factories is too plainly a fictional convenience: historically, the black marks of industrialism were the result of capitalist enterprise.[53] It is true that Gissing interpolates some more general condemnations of socialism, but these, too, are not adequately substantiated in the personal narrative. The parson Wyvern complacently argues that social reform is not merely unattainable but even undesirable. As a class, the workers are quite satisfied and the wealthy suffer equally with the poor. This is followed by a chapter on Emma Vine, whose 'sorrow' and 'misery' are unambiguously displayed as the consequences of poverty.[54] The book is, however, consistent in its view that class divisions are unalterable — that they necessarily argue, in Eldon's phrase, 'a difference in the grain'. This truth, once acknowledged by Mutimer's granduncle, is corroborated by his mother and his friend Daniel Dabbs; eventually it is recognized by Mutimer himself, who reflects, 'Yes, the old and natural way was better'. The *natural* way: a similar formulation occurs in the course of Adela's anagnorisis, when she contemplates her husband's face on the train: 'He was not of her class, not of her world; only by violent wrenching of the laws of nature had they come together'.[55] As this passage continues, Gissing seems to be groping towards a quasi-evolutionary justification of existing class divisions. His respectful fascination with class will be analysed more fully in Chapter 4, but what might be noted here of his early books is that social reform nearly always involves a painful attempt to bridge class ravines, and that this attempt nearly always collapses because it is 'unnatural'.

It was, ultimately, human nature that Gissing invoked in his vehement rejection of socialist enterprise. Quoting Herbert Spencer in his commonplace book ('There is no political alchemy by which you can get golden conduct out of leaden instincts'), he added: 'Precisely, and the whole answer to Socialism is: that if Society were ready for pure Socialism, *it would not be such as it now is*'. In *Demos* he classifies socialism among 'Movements which appeal to the reason and virtue of humanity, and are consequently doomed to remain long in the speculative stage'.[56] The whole novel insists on the drossy conduct of those in quest of a gleaming Utopia. Human nature is incorrigible, classes are fixed — Gissing scarcely differentiates these views — and though Mutimer may mutate economically, he cannot do so morally: New Wanley is no answer to Old Adam.

It is interesting at this point to turn to *Thyrza*, the successor to *Demos* which was obviously designed as in some ways a contrast to it. Like *Demos*, *Thyrza* is pessimistic about social conditions and their chances of improvement, but unlike *Demos* its case does not rest on a low view of human nature. Though Egremont discourses at the end of the book on 'the contemptibleness of average humanity', this vision is not enjoined by the text.[57] On the contrary, nearly everyone acts admirably. In *Demos* exalted schemes collapse because of the baseness of their perpetrators: in *Thyrza* the same results ensue from the loftiest of motives. The novel is a tragedy of good intentions. Egremont, 'the idealist', is earnestly well-meaning but plucks down calamity on himself and others. Wishing to help Grail, he blights his life; striving to avoid disgracing Thyrza, he embroils her in further scandal. Even at the end, when he breaks Thyrza's heart, he is dutifully willing to marry her: he kills her out of misunderstanding rather than callousness. Gilbert Grail, too, is magnanimous to a fault. He declines the librarianship from a sense of honour when his benefactor falls in love with his fiancée. Almost superhumanly self-controlled, he pardons Egremont for tempting Thyrza away and never reproaches her for leaving; indeed, after years of suffering, he is glad to take her back. As for Thyrza herself, she is repeatedly portrayed in a flattering light whatever her behaviour. Although she runs away from her adoring fiancé, neglects her devoted grandfather, and cuts herself off from her affectionate sister, her compassion and sensitivity are unswervingly kept in view. She remains true to Egremont, forgives Mrs Ormonde, and tries to alleviate Gilbert's sorrow — rather absurdly, at the end of the book, by consenting once again to become his wife when she knows she has not long to live.

The minor characters are similarly altruistic. Though made plausible by everyday human foibles, middle-class persons like Annabel and Mrs Ormonde, or working-class ones like Bunce and Boddy, Luke Ackroyd and Totty Nancarrow, are sympathetic and conscientious. Thyrza's sister Lydia is a masterly vignette of a working girl who, with limited values, has enormous reserves of instinctive kindness and ferocious loyalty. Only the politician Dalmaine and the mean-minded, shopkeeping Bower family might merit the epithet 'contemptible', but even here there are mitigations. Dalmaine, despite his crass commercial ambitions — or rather, it is suggested, because of them — brings about genuine practical reform. Mary Bower, overcoming her spiteful piety, acts humanely in a crisis. And Bower himself, pompous humbug and tattler, 'was not capable of anything above petty mischief'.[38]

Given such a complement of kindly-minded characters, it requires a kind of perverse finesse to engineer a calamity; but this is what Gissing does. The necessary mechanism is sexual attraction. At one point Thyrza explains to her sister that love makes you cruel to other people, and certainly, in this book, it is sexual love that conjures up so much evil, in the sense of misery, from so little evil, in the sense of wrong. The plot is a cat's-cradle of cross-purposes in love.[39] Grail loves Thyrza, but Thyrza loves Egremont. Egremont loves Thyrza, but feels guilty about Grail. Thyrza does not know that Egremont loves her; eventually, when he stops loving her, it is partly because he does not know that she has not stopped loving him. Trammelled up with all this is the network of mistiming between Egremont and Annabel. Initially, he proposes and she refuses; then his feelings for Thyrza tug him away. Apprised of this, Annabel craves for his love, but ultimately overcomes her ardour. At this point Egremont proposes again and Annabel accepts.[60]

Similar impediments and emotional confusions are reduplicated in the secondary plots. Just as Thyrza gets engaged to Grail without love, so Totty gets engaged to Luke Ackroyd. Thyrza loves someone else, of course, and so does Luke — in fact, Thyrza. As Thyrza pines for Egremont, so Lydia pines for Luke. Finally, though, the humbler characters are released from the curse of romantic frustration. The novel's sole satisfactory unions are Totty's unglamorous marriage to Bunce and Lydia's to Ackroyd: the reason why they are satisfactory is that they are rooted in compromise, not passionate idealism. It is not, however, as some critics suggest, that passion and idealism are despised. Thyrza's 'gift of passionate imagination' is not only what 'burned her life away', but also her soul's secret. Egremont's social idealism lifts him above the Tyrrells and Dalmaines, even though it cuts less ice. The book's burden is profoundly pessimistic. Although it is good to be idealistic — passionate, faithful, tender-hearted — it is also painful and self-defeating. In this world only dullards are happy, we learn: finer spirits find it hard to survive.[61]

Precisely this pessimism governs the treatment of social reform in *Thyrza*. As in *Demos*, but for different reasons, an honourable conception bears blighted fruit. Walter Egremont, a young man of working-class background but now of independent means, plans to educate the artisans of Lambeth and fire them with idealism. He offers a series of free lectures, first on English literature, then current affairs, and takes steps to open a free library. Like Mutimer's industrial experiment, this benevolent exercise ends in failure, and its failure is ultimately perceived as having discredited it.

It is here, once again, that problems arise. Though unassumingly titled *Thyrza: A Tale*, the novel, as Jacob Korg has recognized, 'has a clear social thesis; it is a vigorous attack upon mass education'.[62] Even more than in *Demos*, though, the thesis is not properly embodied in the tale. Egremont's programme, supposedly doomed because of its intrinsic limitations, is exploded by sexual responses. It is not the teacher's lectures that injure the pupil (on the contrary, Grail delights in them), but the teacher's intensely requited love for the pupil's wife-to-be. But a mis-handled passion is not the same as a misconceived educational plan. As usual in Gissing, a love affair is superimposed on a social question, but though both are bleakly photographed, they never convincingly coalesce. The result is that, at its very centre, the novel is out of focus.

Against this conclusion, some objections might be urged. The most obvious is that Egremont's scheme does damage Grail, by raising false hopes. Grail only gets engaged to Thyrza because he is supplied with the golden prospect of the new librarianship. Losing Thyrza, he also loses the job; what Egremont offers as a lecturer, he takes away as a lover. But though Egremont's plans increase the hurt to Grail, they cannot be said to cause it. The catastrophe is triggered by sexual passion and not by muddled philanthropy. A more promising line of defence might be that the project launched by Egremont has begun to founder even before he is smitten with Thyrza. He certainly overestimates the number of workmen responsive to lectures on literature — the attendance falls from nine to six — and when, disappointed by this tepid reception, he exchanges his straightforward exposition for a maundering series on 'Thoughts for the present', his unpopularity is confirmed. This is true enough, but not the whole truth. One man does respond perceptively and warmly, and Egremont realizes quite early on that to help Gilbert Grail is the most he can hope for. All sympathetic observers concur, and since Grail's poignant story is retailed in great detail, the reader is left in little doubt that if any initiative could save such a man from a life of permanent mental frustration, it would certainly be worthwhile. We must distinguish, too, between the lectures and the library. Though the lectures trail off into topical vapourings, the library, Walter feels, is 'something solid: it would re-establish him in his self-confidence'.[63] This is the point the reformer has reached immediately before his encounter with Thyrza, which, when all hopes for improvement have been focused on the single issue of Grail and the library, is decisive in destroying them.

We return to the fact that Egremont's project is exploded by something irrelevant to it, his inconvenient desire for a girl. Perhaps, however, it might be argued that to separate the project and the passion in this way is pedantically obtuse. Though undeniably two different things, they issue from a single person-ality, and what they show is that this personality is weak. Certainly Egremont's didactic scheme has a lot in common with his infatuation. Both are the outcome of restlessness, both are attempts to leap over class barriers, and both are inspired by emotional states that turn out to be transitory. Surely, then, it is perfectly plausible that a later expression of idealistic weakness should ruin the effects of an earlier one. The only disadvantage of this interpretation is that, if accepted, it places the book on a gaping thematic fault-line. For Egremont's passion is not presented as infatuation or sentimental weakness, but rather as his single authentic emotion, 'the love which comes to a man but once'.[64] In abandoning Thyrza, as Annabel tells him, he has missed his life's greatest opportunity. Egremont's passion for a working-class girl is not, in terms of the author's approval, on a par with his concern for working-class men. Whereas socially his idealistic bent is increasingly construed as his undoing, sexually and emotionally the reverse is true: here it is rather his betrayal of ideals that makes him an incomplete person.

Though Egremont's passionate love for Thyrza is disastrous for his educational mission, his failure to follow this passion through is presented by Gissing, at the end of the book, as even more disastrous for himself. No doubt the explanation of this curious twist can be found, as Gillian Tindall suggests, in Gissing's wistful memories of Nell — to whom he was, of course, both teacher and lover, thus associating educational zeal with sexual idealization.[65] In the context of his anti-reformist novels the significant point is that, once again, what we have is not a social refutation of a policy for helping the working-class poor, but rather, as in *Demos*, the romantic narrative of how a particular personality finds social work less rewarding than love. The difference from *Demos* is that personal qualities are not correlated here with social results. Not only do the kindly and decent wreak havoc, but the real reformer is the odious Dalmaine, who, like Cornelius Vanderbilt, benefits the people by pursuing his own profit. It is not clear whether Gissing sees the full implications of this stock vindication of *laissez-faire*. Apparently there *is* a political alchemy by which you can get golden conduct out of leaden instincts.

Not even this dismal consolation is available in *The Nether World*, the most pessimistic as well as the most powerful of Gissing's proletarian novels. Similar to its predecessors in some respects, its distinctive feature is its double intensity of eloquent protest and complete despair. In no novel by Gissing is economic affliction depicted with such harrowing exactness. Blackly restricted to the 'nether world' of chronic poverty and crumbling slums — the brief outing to Essex is the only chink of light — it concentrates remorselessly on physical misery and psychological anguish. Appropriately it begins and ends in a graveyard; in between there is sinister and recurrent mention of hospitals, lunatic asylums and gaols.[66] The effigy described in the opening chapter, surmounting the Middlesex House of Detention — 'the sculptured counterfeit of a human face, that of a man distraught with agony' — looms out as a fittingly immovable symbol of the tortured humanity confined in the book. Against a grim background of urban squalor, Gissing elaborates hideous varieties of pain and degradation. Some of these are almost melodramatic: a sickly girl is sadistically tormented in a house containing a decaying corpse; a spirited woman is disfigured by vitriol; a wilting wife is punched senseless by her husband, whose own body is then pierced by the shaft of a cart. But many are convincingly and depressingly inveterate. Destitution, frustration and demoralization are the melancholy norms of the nether world. Unemployment flattens spirits or goads to madness; bestial brawls break out on bank holidays; workers are inflamed or befuddled with alcohol; blackmail and forgery are routinely planned. Starvation and fertility are equally oppressive. One young girl, provoked by hunger, takes to tippling vinegar; others sit on steps 'nursing or neglecting bald, red-eyed, doughy-limbed abortions in every stage of babyhood'.[67] Even more than in Gissing's other work, a lexicon of wretchedness throbs through the prose: 'torture', 'intolerable', 'calamity', 'wound', 'desperation', 'defeated', 'crushed'.[68] A family called Hope is introduced. The father, a rag-picking cripple who drinks, assuages his suffering with blood-curdling threats — of braining, disembowelling, gouging out eyes — directed against his children. Towards the end, in Mad Jack's harangue, the infernal implications of the novel's title are unnervingly confirmed: 'This life you are now leading is that of the damned; this place to which you are confined is Hell!'[69]

Despite such lurid associations, Gissing repeatedly makes it plain that this nether world is economic, a hell constructed by man. His research for the novel was unusually thorough: not only did he scour sociological writings, he put in considerable work on the ground, attending strike meetings and political rallies, touring workshops, exploring locations. Sections of the novel were written, as he said, 'embodying many notes'. The carefully garnered documentary material — evident in the Crystal Palace scenes, the police reports from newspapers, the details about jobs, rooms and rents — does more than make the book socially

credible: it sharpens its political edge.[70] A constant dichotomy
encourages the reader to perceive the book's miseries in political
terms: that between the incarcerating nether world, where each
venial fault putrefies into crime, and a glimpsed but unvisited
upper world, where wealth, leisure and privilege bask.[71] Sidney
Kirkwood, the novel's protagonist, declares: 'We have to fight
against the rich world that's always crushing us down, down —
whether it means to or not'. And Gissing addresses his middle-
class readers without even Kirkwood's qualification. 'Have you
still to learn', he asks sourly, 'what this nether world has been
made by those who belong to the sphere above it?' Denunciations
of 'social tyranny', allusions to the 'slaves of industrialism', are
reinforced by paragraphs that scathingly insist on the economic
relativity of morals ('respect for law is the result of possessing
something which the law exerts itself to guard'), on the bourgeois
confusion of weakness with crime, and, in a passage reminiscent
of Johnson, the presumptuous fatuity of the charitable classes
in expecting gratitude from the poor. As Sidney Kirkwood
concludes, the ubiquitous sufferings are lodged firmly in a social
context: 'With the ripening of his intellect, he saw only more and
more reason to condemn and execrate those social disorders of
which his own wretched experience was but an illustration'.[72]

   In other discourse, the concept of social disorders might
suggest the possibility of social cures; but in Gissing this is not the
case. On the contrary, all prospects for improvement are blocked.
Sidney Kirkwood rejects it and the workers do not want it;
individuals are unable to escape from their fate and collective
remedies are quixotic. Kirkwood resembles Gissing's other
protagonists in that, while embittered by social injustice, he is
practically resigned to it. He has passed through 'the stage of
confident and aspiring Radicalism, believing in the perfectibility
of man, in human brotherhood, in — anything you like that is the
outcome of a noble heart sheltered by ignorance'. He is even
'half-astonished, half-amused' at faith in universal suffrage.
Support for his scepticism seems to be supplied by the nature of
the slum-dwellers all around him, whom Gissing, reverting to his
earliest suspicions, presents as adapted to their degradation. The
inhabitants of Shooter's Gardens, inured to the gruesomeness of
filth and stench, neither know nor desire any other home since
this one provides them with independence — 'that is to say, the
liberty to be as vile as they pleased'. But Gissing then adds
uncomfortably: 'How they came to love vileness, well, that is
quite another matter, and shall not for the present concern us'.[73]

As in *Workers in the Dawn* and subsequent novels, Gissing's reactions to the lowest classes vacillate between indignant pity and censorious repulsion. A similar ambivalence can be discerned in the chapter 'Io Saturnalia', where alertness to environmental pressures alternates oddly with instinctive repugnance ('visages so deformed by ill-health that they excite disgust', etc.). It is curious that a writer who, when discussing Bob Hewett, can assail the readiness of respectable society to appraise working people as criminals can — as in these bank holiday scenes — himself depict them as animals.[74]

If the masses in this book seem hopelessly degraded, individuals seem no less hopelessly trapped. All personal routes to fulfilment are closed. Sidney Kirkwood, with artistic aspirations and talents, is condemned to drudgery as a working jeweller, making luxury goods for the affluent. Clara Hewett, whom he marries, is proud and quick-witted, as well as conceited and selfish. Encouraged by family and school to look forward to something more distinguished than manual toil, she channels her sullenly rebellious spirit into a thrusting theatrical career, capitalizing on her physical attractions and earnestly extending her education in a quest for social acceptance. 'A notable illusion', comments the author; 'pathetic to dwell upon.' For having got the better of a rival actress, Clara has vitriol thrown in her face. Balked in her supreme ambition, lacerated in body and mind, she is forced to fall back on the barren consolation of deploying her histrionic skills to land the role of Kirkwood's wife. It is barren because, despite his love, she is still burnt up by a fiery resentment of everything she has lost. Clara's brother Bob is another example of abilities run to waste. Notwithstanding his energy, intelligence and courage, 'the world to which he belonged', writes Gissing, 'is above all a world of frustration'.[75] The criminal activities to which he resorts as an obscure protest against this frustration are as doomed as his sister's theatrical ambitions. It is indeed a feature of *The Nether World* — discovered not only by Bob Hewett, but by Scawthorne, the Peckovers and Joseph Snowdon — that ultimately crime proves fruitless.

So too, however, does social conscience. In contrast with Gissing's earliest novels, no substantial initiatives for social reform are anywhere visible here. Their spectres are raised only to be dismissed. Revolutionism is represented by the unproductive paroxysms of John Hewett, who, with his bitten lip dripping blood, curses landlords on Clerkenwell Green until 'his face was livid, his eyes bloodshot, a red slaver covered his lips and beard;

you might have taken him for a drunken man, so feebly did his
limbs support him'. (The excesses of drink and of radical oratory
are polemically compounded throughout the book: when John
Hewett finally gets off his soap-box, he also goes on the wagon.)[76]
Contrasting with the hag-ridden frenzies of Hewett is the sober
reformism of a man called Eagles; but this is equally illusory.
Perennially condemning the iniquities of government, Eagles is
bewitched by financial statistics; earning only £2 a week, he
invokes new taxes, juggles with figures, summons up 'Utopian
budgets'. The exertions of middle-class philanthropy are likewise
sardonically waved aside. Miss Lant, a spinster unhappily
numbered among those 'defrauded of their natural satisfactions',
officiously combines with some other ladies to take over a soup-
kitchen formerly run with crude vigour by a working-class
couple. When their meddlesome gentility is coarsely rejected,
they are forced to restore the *status quo*. Gissing offers the episode
as 'significant', but what it signifies most clearly, perhaps, is his
own contradictory reaction to the poor. He mocks the ladies'
indignation about the ingratitude displayed: 'Gratitude, quotha?
— Nay, do *you* be grateful that these hapless, half-starved women
do not turn and rend you.' Within a page, however, he is huffily
expressing his own disapprobation: 'Of all forms of insolence
there is none more flagrant than that of the degraded poor
receiving charity which they have come to regard as a right'.[77]

We might infer from the soup-kitchen fiasco that philanthropy,
to be effective, needs to be administered by working people who,
having grown up among the poor, understand their attitudes and
customs. This, as it happens, is precisely the project of the aged
working man Michael Snowdon, who has suddenly come into
wealth. Theoretically attractive, his scheme expires in the
manner we might expect by now — slowly strangled by the
intricacies of personal relations. At first his idealism appears to
be praised. The man himself is thoughtful and principled,
possessed of 'grave force of character'. He rescues his suffering
granddaughter, Jane, and instructs her in the virtues of compassion. But as he gets older he becomes more careworn. Brooding
on the hardships of his early years, consumed with guilt about his
young bride, Jenny, whom he drove to suicide by the rigour
of his standards, he conceives a grand scheme of benevolent
restitution. Jane — like Ida Starr in *The Unclassed* — shall use her
inheritance to benefit the poor; consecrating her life to a noble
ideal, she shall always remain poor and humble, and only marry
someone who can share such a mission. The man who loves Jane

is Sidney Kirkwood and the chapter in which he is told of the project is 'A Vision of Noble Things'. Even here, though, there are hints that the old man's conception, 'superb' and 'heroic' as it might appear, is in fact an intoxicant delusion. Sidney is first exalted and then dismayed by what it might mean for himself and Jane; she is thrown into painful tumult by the news of her responsibilities. Though both are kind-hearted individuals, neither has a calling for collective philanthropy or sacrificial social concern. Finding yourself committed to such aspirations is a bit like being committed to prison; and in Sidney's reflections they are once again contrasted with other, more desirable values: 'I am no hero ... no enthusiast ... I am a man in love, and in proportion as my love has strengthened, so has my old artist-self revived in me, until now I can imagine no bliss so perfect as to marry Jane Snowdon and go off to live with her amid fields and trees'. As usual, the opposition to social reform is a wistful blend of art, nature and love. From this point on, the convolutions of the plot make the old man's project seem positively twisted. After someone suggests with coarse cheerfulness that he is hoping to profit from marriage to Jane, Sidney breaks out in disgusted scruples and pulls back on a point of honour. But old Snowdon, discounting his granddaughter's feelings, presses forward undeterred: 'Michael had taken the last step in that process of dehumanisation with threatens idealists of his type'. Sidney's morals interweave with others' wiles, and he ends up marrying Clara Hewett. But still the old man talks to Jane about martyr-dom, sacrifice and higher rewards, his grey eyes searching her countenance 'with that horrible intensity of fanaticism which is so like the look of cruelty'. As the noble visionary turns torturer, Gissing reminds us of his dead wife, Jenny, of whom likewise he had 'expected impossible things'.[78] In *The Nether World*, as in *Demos* and *Thyrza*, a desire for reform, at first seemingly untainted, turns rancid after prolonged exposure to the perversities of personal emotion.

What positives remain in this harrowing novel? Only the individual acts of kindness performed in a purely domestic context by Sidney Kirkwood and Jane Snowdon, who meet every year at old Snowdon's grave. Gissing noted that in the last three chapters he wished 'to emphasize that the idealistic social reformer is of far less use than the humble discharger of human duty'. The essence of this ending had been foreseen eight months before he began the book, when Gissing told Hardy he was planning a novel to be set in Clerkenwell. It would be 'dark, but with evening sunlight to close. For there may occasionally be a triumph of individual strength; a different thing from hope for the masses of men'. To measure how far Gissing had come in his disillusion with collective reform we might compare a letter of 1880, the year of *Workers in the Dawn*:

> I mean to bring home to people the ghastly condition (material, mental, and moral) of our poor classes, to show the hideous injustice of our whole system of society, to give light upon the plan of altering it, and, above all, to preach an enthusiasm for just and high *ideals* in this age of unmitigated egotism and "shop".

He added that he would never write a book which did not keep all these ends in view.[79] In fact, however, in the series of novels that followed *Workers in the Dawn* the reformist light was increasingly dimmed until, in the depths of *The Nether World*, it was finally extinguished.

Despite this, the intention to expose injustice was not simultaneously discarded. Even during the writing of *The Nether World*, Gissing declared that his books were, like Daudet's, 'arraignments of society'.[80] In *The Nether World* the arraignment survives, even though all hopes for reform have died. Historically, it is true, such a double reaction to the plight of the proletarian poor was not totally idiosyncratic. A feeling that something ought to be done could coexist, among middle-class observers, with despair or dislike of most concrete proposals. For example, before embarking on *The Nether World*, Gissing read a book by Arnold White, *Problems of a Great City* (1886), from which he 'got some hints'. The 'hints' were in fact substantial and extensive. Many general features of *The Nether World* — pawnshops, overcrowding and unemployment, the distresses of winter and bank holiday excesses — can also be found in Arnold White. So too can many particular details: the retention of a corpse in the living-room until the funeral takes place; the comparison of large 'model dwellings' to barracks; information on Clerkenwell watchmakers and girls in the artificial-flower trade.[81] But perhaps the most notable similarity is the mixture of attitudes that White displays. For although he dilates on the problems of the city, and expresses some anguish for the miseries of the poor, he rejects both charity and political action, 'the baleful introduction of a sickly humanitarianism' and 'the poisonous propaganda of Social Democracy'. His conclusion, with its stress on the moral strength of thoughtful individuals, is remarkably similar to that of Gissing: 'They are most effectually solving the Problems of a Great City who by life and example add wisdom to the sacrifice of self'.[82]

But though Gissing's conclusions were not unique, the route by which he arrived at them was: his social attitudes were intimately indebted to his own traumatic experience. Even his immediate circumstances while working on *The Nether World* are revealing about that novel's tensions. He began it having seen Nell's body in Lambeth, surrounded by sad tokens of her destitution, and having passionately announced in his diary: 'Henceforth I never cease to bear testimony against the accursed social order that brings about things of this kind'. But as he wrote on, he slipped into depression, craving for company and sexual love; privately, he recorded his conviction that he had not long to live. His letters to his family about his own feelings might almost be notes for the novel itself. 'What is the use of complaining when there is no remedy', 'Nothing helps one to endure evils so well as the conviction that they are inevitable'.[83] *The Nether World*, like all his works, was shadowed by his mood during composition. But the spiritual path that led up to this novel's peculiar crossing of arraignment with despair stretched back, of course, further than days or months. It stretched back to Owens College, Manchester, and the paralysing punishment inflicted on him for a moment of philanthropic folly; to his permanently ensuing pessimism and his countervailing search for positive values to give his life meaning again. One of these was reformist concern for the poor, the major subject of his early books. Adopted for intensely personal reasons — as Morley Roberts was the first to point out — it assumed, as we have seen, very personal forms. In the long run it was destroyed by his pessimism and his attachment — deeply personal, too — to alternative ideals. Prominent among these were romantic love, tenaciously prized as 'the crown of life', and aesthetic cultivation, cherished as a refuge from 'unmitigated egotism and "shop"'. After completing *The Nether World*, his last effort on the theme of workers and reform, he went on holiday to Italy and France. In Paris he wrote:

> I experience at present a profound dislike for everything that concerns the life of the people ... All my interest in such things I have left behind in London. On crossing the Channel, I have become a poet pure and simple, or perhaps it would be better to say an idealist student of art.[84]

3

Art and Commercialism

I

Art, for Gissing, was the purest expression of the individual's creative potential; commerce, the dirtiest product of collective greed. The conflict between art and commerce was the subject of his finest book.

The particular merits of *New Grub Street* as a novel — its skilful structure, its psychological subtlety, its successful integration of the social and the personal — will be argued for in detail later, but since the book occupies a central place in the circuits of Gissing's imagination, it might first be useful to trace its connections with other areas of his work and life. The energy that crackles through *New Grub Street* springs partly from its bringing together of polarities — commercial corruption and artistic conscience — which Gissing had pondered for most of his life. Though Gissing's views on art changed over the years, his appraisal of commerce was doggedly consistent. From first to last he loathed and feared it. In his first published story, 'The Sins of the Fathers', devotion to business is associated with coarse materialism and vulgar pride. In his last completed novel, *Will Warburton*, adaptation to a tradesman's life is a social and moral horror. His books abound with dark jibes about business — 'a word', as he says in his study of Dickens, 'which will justify most atrocities'. This revulsion was not based on much personal experience. His own father was a tradesman of a kind — he kept a chemist's shop in Wakefield, which Gissing appears to have regretted. In his travel book, *By the Ionian Sea*, he tells how he met a Calabrian chemist whose shop resembled 'a museum of art': in England, Gissing assured the man, such places were repellently different. Gissing's father himself encouraged such an outlook, for he felt contempt for other Wakefield chemists and kept his children, Gissing remembered, away from those of other shopkeepers. The whole family, it seems, was brought up to view business as a cheap and philistine occupation, based, as his brother William wrote at 16, on 'that mean money-making spirit which is the bane of the world — no music, no poetry, no love in it, only one everlasting stubborn fight'.[1] For twenty-five years much of Gissing's fiction was a vast exegesis of this text.

Towards the end of 1878 Gissing worked as a temporary clerk at St John's Hospital, London. This experience was the only biographical foundation for a lifelong superstructure of lofty disgust. 'A clerk's life ... that is a hideous fate', cries Widdowson in *The Odd Women*; cold water flows down Will Warburton's back as he contemplates applying for such work. To Gissing the prospect was literally hellish. In *A Life's Morning* Hood's 'mercantile clerkships' are described as 'an existence possibly preferable to that of the fourth circle of Inferno'. In Dante the fourth circle harbours Plutus, god of wealth, together with the avaricious and the prodigal, who dance around howling and rolling great weights, which clash together when they meet: an image of endless, fruitless conflict. Gissing's bookish disdain is not, however, reinforced with much practical detail. Hood, he continues with patent impatience, established himself in various businesses, 'vague, indescribable, save by those who are unhappy enough to understand such matters — a commission agency, a life insurance agency and a fire insurance ditto, I know not what'. Commission agents swarm all over Gissing, but their work is invariably dismissed with a snort.[2] Sales jobs, clerkships, shops, counters — all were semi-civilized no-go areas in Gissing's imagination.

However, though the only trade he knew was that of letters, Gissing eventually took some pains to acquire information about finance and commerce. In his scrapbook he pasted clippings from trade and finance journals, compiling a dossier significantly entitled 'Speculation, sport, etc.'. For him the conjunction was natural enough: both activities were idle and vulgar and infected with the evils of gambling. No socialist could have hated the City more. But the nature of his hatred was idiosyncratic. As he noted in his commonplace book — and as Peak repeats in *Born in Exile* — 'The "City" is so oppressive to the spirit because it represents the triumph of the vulgar man'. In *The Crown of Life* there is a similar formulation: 'The brute force of money; the negation of the individual — these, the evils of our time, found their supreme expression in the City of London'. In *Our Friend the Charlatan* Gissing even offers to characterize the faces round the Royal Exchange: marks of weakness, marks of woe — 'self-indulgence' and 'soul-hardening calculation', 'debasing excitement and vulgar routine'.[3] Gissing also studied the Victorian sages, as well as the financial journals, in his search for arguments against *laissez-faire*. Much of his case against the perils of Commerce is similar to that of William Morris in pieces like 'Art and socialism' or 'How we live and how we might live'. In 1883 he commended Ruskin's 'onslaught' on political economy in *Unto this Last*; two years later he made a character in *A Life's Morning* deliver a diatribe on the subject. He also responded keenly to Carlyle, who influenced the longest and most explicit attack on the ethics of free enterprise in his work, the credo of the parson Wyvern in *Demos*. Wyvern declares:

> Thus far I am with the Socialists, in that I denounce the commercial class, the *bourgeois*, the capitalists ... as supremely maleficent ... The very poor and the uncommercial wealthy alike suffer from them; the intellect of the country is poisoned by their influence. They it is indeed who are oppressors ...[4]

The denunciation exists in a vacuum, for capitalist oppression is never dramatized in *Demos*. Even so, it stands out as a startling moment in a book attacking socialism.

Various forms of commercial misery are, however, registered remorselessly in other parts of Gissing's work. First, his main characters are often ruined by business. Innocent investors are plunged into penury as the revelation comes, again and again, that those they trusted have suddenly 'bolted'. Gissing was partly drawing on the plot kitty of earlier Victorian fiction, of course (just as he inherited this tradition in his treatment of wills and bequests). But his actual handling of financial débâcle often goes beyond the merely conventional. In his story 'A Poor Gentleman' the hero becomes bankrupt through a speculation designed to help his country sister and her family. Ignominiously declassed, he lives a double life, but the story concludes with his announcement of the truth. This plot is reworked in *Will Warburton*, in which the hero's feverishly sanguine friend persuades him to go into jam manufacture ('What can be more solid than jam?') with predictably sticky results. Warburton is motivated partly by a wish to assist his provincial mother and sister. He gets out of his jam, and preserves their income, by secretly taking a job as a grocer; eventually, reconciled to his aproned fate, he comes out from behind the counter. The temptation to raise money by dubious means in order to help female relatives in the country is a recurrent predicament in Gissing. Jasper Milvain in *New Grub Street* succumbs to it; Lord Dymchurch in *Our Friend the Charlatan* resists it, though only after a shaming flirtation. Brooding on his mother and sisters in Wakefield, Gissing — who had stolen for Nell Harrison — might also have been tempted to take a gamble for quick money. That he did not was due to his belief that speculation was literally a gamble — and gambling, 'a national curse ... inseparably connected with the triumph of commercialism', is condemned throughout his work.[5]

This leads us to a second effect of business in Gissing — the fact that it is not just financially but also morally damaging. Though poverty demoralizes, so does the attempt to escape from poverty by cultivating commerce. The tragic catastrophe in *A Life's Morning*, James Hood's theft and suicide, is partly provoked by poverty — long years of impecunious anxiety tighten Hood's fingers on the ten-pound note — but partly, too, by his polluting immersion in 'the chicaneries and despicabilities of commerce'. When Dagworthy exploits the theft in order to blackmail Hood's daughter, this is also because 'The trickery and low cunning of the mercantile world was in his blood'. Both improbity and sadistic cruelty are the outcome of a training in trade. Given such effects, Gissing's characters react with understandable horror when they find themselves sucked into the commercial vortex. Will Warburton's suffering as a retail tradesman is not due entirely to social embarrassment. He also has troublesome moral misgivings. He notes his own growing 'acerbity of temper' and reflects that 'a man cannot devote his days to squeezing out pecuniary profits without some moral detriment'. 'A tradesman must harden himself', we learn. Schooled by his cheerfully callous assistant, Warburton learns how to pluck his small profits from the 'toil-worn hand of charwoman and sempstress'. Harvey Rolfe in *The Whirlpool* is slowly pushed down into comparable moral quicksand. Protected at first by his 'profound ignorance' of finance, he is unaffected by the ruinous collapse of Bennet Frothingham's 'pestilent' loan company. Later, impoverished by Frothingham's daughter, he starts dabbling in dark crevices of knowledge. He tries to get hints from City men and pores over financial newspapers, surreptitiously purchased at railway bookstalls, 'taking care that they never fell under his wife's eyes'. The results are morally and physically alarming: 'He felt like one who meddles with something forbidden — who pries, shame-faced, into the secrets of an odious vice. To study the money-market gave him a headache. He had to go for a country walk, to bathe and change his clothes, before he was at ease again.' Spiritually smeared by filthy lucre, Rolfe resembles Dickens's lawyer, Jaggers, who has to wash and gargle after seeing his clients.[6] Frequently in Gissing mercantile activity is redolent of dirt and drains. In *Demos* the unsavoury 'Arry occupies a temporary niche as a 'clerk in a drain-pipe manufactory'. The speculator Enderby in *The Unclassed* raises capital by importing from America 'a scheme for the utilisation of waste product'. The squalid Joseph Snowdon in *The Nether World* works as a salesman for a filter product — 'a business which had the — for him — novel characteristic of serving the purposes of purity'. In this atmosphere it seems a hopeful sign that the well-meaning Peachey, in *In the Year of Jubilee*, toils for a company that makes disinfectants, but in fact these prove to be worse than useless and Peachey is condemned for ignoring this fact because he sees so much of life through 'commercial spectacles'.[7]

Gissing's detestation of tradesmen combined with his dark suspicions of workmen. At the end of *The Whirlpool* defective drains actually cause one character's death: the fitters have 'bungled and scamped their work'. Bungling workmen and bent businessmen, equally in quest of easy cash, malignly collaborate in Gissing's fiction. Speculative builders ravage the countryside with the aid of cack-handed artisans. At the edge of the 'dark patch' of greater London are the Crouch End villas in *The Nether World* — mock-stone bay windows, grinding doors, 'Whatever you touch ... at once found to be sham'. Even more spectacular is the Morgans' house in *In the Year of Jubilee*. Erected on a south London estate, formerly the site of an 'enclosed meadow', now 'fouled with builders' refuse', this brand-new dwelling soon reveals its rotten origins. 'Unlovely vegetation' sprouts from the walls. In winter the pipes burst and flood the building. Plaster falls from the ceilings, stuccoed portions of the front begin to crack and moulder. Everywhere there are piercing draughts which 'often entered by orifices unexplained and unexplainable'. The house is a lath-and-plaster lie: 'From cellar floor to chimney-pot, no square inch of honest or trustworthy workmanship'. The hyperbolic intensity in Gissing's description of this pristine slum seems rather a symptom of his own suspicions than a sober diagnosis of a social malaise. On the subject of commercial exploitation he was often near-hysterical. Just before writing *In the Year of Jubilee* he rejoiced that a sixteen-week coal strike was over: 'We have been paying more than £2 a ton for coals lately, — the result of a swindling confederacy among coal-merchants, who ought to be hanged.'[8]

Another near-capital offence in Gissing's eyes was the block-lettered trade of advertising. In an age of increasing mass production it soon became apparent that profits could be stretched through quantity rather than quality. The main thing required was a transfer of energy from craftsmanship to self-promotion — a tendency denounced by Carlyle in *Past and Present* ('He has not attempted to *make* better hats ... his whole industry is turned to persuade us that he has made such!'). For Gissing, the columns and signboards of advertising were hideous symbols of commercial strife. Advertisements, we learn in *The Unclassed*, summarize 'the principle of universal Competition' with all its 'meanness, ruthlessness, anguish, and degredation'. As Jessica and Barmby wait at King's Cross Station in *In the Year of Jubilee*,

> High and low, on every available yard of wall, advertisements clamoured to the eye: theatres, journals, soaps, medicines, concerts, furniture, wines, prayer-meetings — all the produce and refuse of civilisation announced in staring letters, in daubed effigies, base, paltry, grotesque. A battle-ground of advertisements, fitly chosen amid subterranean din and reek; a symbol to the gaze of that relentless warfare which ceases not, night and day, in the world above.[9]

The vision of unending, infernal conflict recalls the earlier allusion to Dante. *In the Year of Jubilee* (1894) was Gissing's most sustained attack on the ethics and effects of advertising. The 1890s, it has been noted, 'was the period when modern advertising began'. It was also the period when resistance to advertising, usually on aesthetic grounds, began to be voiced systematically. In 1894, the year of Gissing's novel, a periodical was started entitled *A Beautiful World: the Journal of the Society for Checking the Abuses of Public Advertising*. In the novel itself every cranny of the narrative is crammed with spiky observations on the subject. Posing pathetically before her son, Mrs Damerel looks 'rather like a sentimental picture in an advertisement'. Tarrant is left penniless by his grandmother because 'an advertising broker got her in his clutches'. Even the Peacheys' woe-begone nurse-girl is ruined by 'a jewellery tallyman, one of the fellows who sell trinkets to servant-girls on the pay-by-instalment system'. The chief exponent of the new profession is the candidly thrustful Luckworth Crewe, a coarse-grained colour-sergeant of capitalism, who sees himself rather as a champion of modern civilization: 'Till advertising sprang up the world was barbarous. Do you suppose people kept themselves clean before they were reminded at every corner of the benefits of soap?' Gissing's own

response to these pleasant fatuities is given by an art historian in
Our Friend the Charlatan. Recollecting two grotesque posters he has
seen — one of bullocks slaughtered for beef tea, the other for pills
that 'reach their destination' — Sir William Amys says: 'I ask
myself ... what earthly right we have to lay claim to civilization.
How much better it would be always to speak of ourselves as
barbarians. We should then, perhaps, make some endeavour to
improve'. Improvement means something else to Crewe, a
loquacious mouthpiece for both the techniques ('A name is just as
important as the stuff itself that you want to sell') and the values
of contemporary advertising. Enthusiastically, and with no
qualms of conscience, he plans to convert a sleepy seaside village
into a glittering new resort. Eventually he unrolls 'a coloured
picture of Whitsand pier as it already existed in his imagination'.
This picture displays more than the structure: everything in it —
the pier itself, the bathing-machines, the pleasure-boats — is
plastered with placards for purgatives and soap. The advertising
poster depicts advertising posters. Likewise Crewe has promoted
his own agency by writing a guide to advertising. Needless to say,
its printing is paid for by the advertising in its pages.[10]

Not infrequently Gissing differentiates his characters by their
attitudes to advertising. Lionel Tarrant in *In the Year of Jubilee*
is disgusted by advertisements along the pier; in London he
retreats 'from commercial tumult'. The jobless Kingcote in *Isabel
Clarendon* sickens his soul by reading through advertisements.
Will Warburton goes further, and nearly turns his brain:

> In spite of loathing and dread, he began to read the thick-serried
> columns of newspaper advertisement, Wanted! Wanted! Wanted!
> ... To glance over these columns is like listening to the clamour of a
> hunger-driven multitude; the ears sing, the head turns giddy. After
> a quarter of an hour of such search, Will flung the paper aside, and
> stamped like a madman about his room. A horror of life seized
> him; he understood, with fearful sympathy, the impulse of those
> who, rather than be any longer hustled in this howling mob, dash
> themselves to destruction.[11]

Dizziness, madness, contemplated suicide seem extreme
responses to the vacancy columns, even for a Gissing character.
Others express their distaste more quietly. Lord Dymchurch in
Our Friend the Charlatan refuses to lend his name to company
promoters who have 'sought him out with tempting proposals' (in
this period even the crowned heads of Europe gave testimonials
to patent medicines). Eventually he retires into the country, to

devote himself to gardening and silence: 'I don't care to advertise
myself, I don't care to make money.' Being advertised is perhaps
even more atrocious than having to read advertisements. In 'A
Calamity at Tooting' (1895) a teenage girl is devastated by
discovering that when she was two years old, her parents sent her
photograph, complete with testimonial, for use in a baby-food
advertisement: 'There it sat, half-naked in a photographer's
arm-chair, the terrific baby named "Miss Alma Dawson",
sprawling its all too chubby legs, and staring with frightened eyes
out of hollows of fat'. Beneath is reproduced the father's letter:
'Mrs. D. and I are rather proud of our girly-pearly (as we call
her), and we think it only right to let you know that for the
whole of her life she has been fed exclusively upon HOGGAN'S
FOOD', etc. This story is a burlesque variant on Gissing's
favourite theme of the Guilty Secret. Just as Godwin Peak's
college career is stricken by the advent of a shopkeeping uncle, so
too — but here Gissing sees the funny side — it is ruinous for a
respectable Miss to be linked with an advertisement in the
Graphic.[12]

Only insensitive or dubious characters are contentedly sold on
advertising. Joseph Snowdon predictably works for an agency.
Gammon and Polly in *The Town Traveller* are inured to the
advertisements that solicit their attention from every printable
surface in the pub. Mr Florio in *The Crown of Life*, who plans to
stick placards on Hyde Park railings, swinging in the wind with
bells attached, extols the art of advertisement. Significantly,
when Jasper in *New Grub Street* betrays Marian to court a wealthier
woman, she turns out to be the daughter of an advertising
agent.[13]

What were the grounds of Gissing's hatred of commercialism?
Several of them have been hinted at already, but to bring them
into focus we might specify three. Gissing deplored commercialism,
first, because it incited strife; secondly, because it devastated
nature; thirdly, because it appealed to the mob. The first we
might term a moral objection. The conception of life as a violent
competition, in which selfishness and cruelty are required for
survival, runs like a wound through all Gissing's work. The
clichéd concept of 'the battle of life' is luridly revitalized by
frequent metaphors of warfare, bestiality, starvation and overcrowding. 'The world is overfull', says *Isabel Clarendon*, 'and every
day the internecine war grows deadlier.' London, according to
Will Warburton, is a 'vast slaughter-strewn field of battle'; in *The
Crown of Life*, it is 'a huge battlefield calling itself the home of

civilisation'. The traits of animality show through in phrases like 'a brute combat for bread', 'the beastly scrimmage', or 'it is high time that he learnt to fight for his own share of provender'. Living-space is scarce as well as food. Godwin Peak must be taught to 'hit out right and left and make standing-room'. In *New Grub Street* Amy's mother is convinced that 'She must either crush or be crushed' and Reardon knows that if he collapses, 'Those behind will trample over his body ... they themselves are borne onwards by resistless pressure'. Images of choking and strangling abound. Crowded out by five hundred other applicants for a menial job in *The Nether World*, John Hewett hisses, 'I felt like a beast. I wanted to fight, I tell you — to fight till the life was kicked an' throttled out of me!' Warburton, squeezing out the rival grocer, reflects: 'I myself am crushing the man — as surely as if I had my hand on his gullet and my knee on his chest!'[14]

Large parts of this panorama of strife are undoubtedly Darwinian, or, more precisely, Malthusian: a spiralling population, a shortage of food and territory, a struggle for existence, and, of course, the elimination of the weakest. Piers Otway hears in the City of London 'a voice of blustering conquest, bidding the weaker to stand aside or be crushed'. Clara Hewett snarls at a rival actress: 'We have to fight, to fight for everything, and the weak get beaten. That's what life has taught me'. The rival agrees 'with a strangely sudden calmness': that night she throws vitriol in Clara's face. But if strife has biological origins, what becomes of the indictment of commercialism? Clash and conflict in human life are natural, instinctive, unavoidable. At times Gissing does indeed accept this view. 'Man is not made for peaceful intercourse with his fellows', he remarks sadly in *Henry Ryecroft*; 'he is by nature self-assertive, commonly aggressive ... by instinct he is still a quarrelsome creature.' It was of course possible that the commercial ethic was simply an extension of the evolutionary struggle. The link between *laissez-faire* economics and the contemporary prestige of Darwinian doctrine is a commonplace of intellectual history. Yet the evidence that Gissing was a social Darwinist is tenuous and inconclusive. Making notes on Théodule Ribot's *L'Hérédité psychologique*, he was capable of recording, without demur, 'One cause of national degradation, now-a-days, is the success of medicine in keeping alive the unfit'. In *The Whirlpool*, however, his use of Ribot is far from suggesting uncritical approval; and when Rolfe talks fashionable Spencerism ('If a child dies, why, the probabilities are it *ought* to die; if it lives, it lives, and you get survival of the fittest'), the later development of the plot, in which Rolfe's affection for his son is crucial, condemns such bravado as blindly immature. Gissing's usual view, as Jacob Korg has argued, seems to have been that of T. H. Huxley: 'the ethical process is in opposition to the principle of the cosmic process'. Or, as Denzil Quarrier puts it, 'Nature gives no rights ... But civilization is at war with nature, and as civilized beings we *have* rights'.[15]

In this light, the credo of commercial competition seems a brazen spur to barbarism. It has scarred Emily's parents in *A Life's Morning*. It goads on the debt-collector Morgan in *In the Year of Jubilee*. It poisons Warburton's vision of life as he lies awake 'pierced with misery' at the thought of the anguish all around: 'How — he cried within himself — how, in the name of sense and mercy, is mankind content to live on in such a world as this?' Unfettered commercialism, Warburton concludes, is a prompter of 'merciless conflict'.[16]

Gissing's second objection, which we might call ecological, was that commerce devastated nature. We have already witnessed some examples. Both north and south of London, speculative builders were pushing back the frontiers of peace and greenness. Concurrently, rapacious admen like Crewe were discharging modernity along the coasts. In Gissing successful commercialism is frequently associated with pollution — affluence is close to effluence. It was natural to identify commerce with the urban, but Gissing's use of the symbol of the countryside goes obsessively beyond naturalistic explanation. The countryside is a tranquil refuge — ancient, beautiful, relatively empty — from the soiling frenzies of modern trade. Harvey Rolfe has to go for a country walk after poring over financial journals. The country is the opposite of the City and cities, a retreat from both commerce and industrial squalor. This is why Gissing so often concentrates on escapist trips from the outskirts of London. When Waymark in *The Unclassed* walks with two prostitutes to Richmond, joyful simplicity descends on all three 'as the city dropped behind'. Arthur Peachey in *In the Year of Jubilee* carries off his little boy from London's 'gloom and grime ... to the broad sunny meadows and the sweet hop-gardens of Kent'. A chapter entitled 'A Retreat' in *The Nether World* describes, in very similar terms, an escape into Essex from the 'city of the damned': travelling beyond 'the outmost limits of dread', the train eventually enters upon 'a land of level meadows'. Quite often the unspoilt countryside is collated with the innocence of childhood. When one of the prostitutes, entranced by rurality, begins to chatter in the dialect of her girlhood, she anticipates by nearly twenty years the botanizing rambles of Henry Ryecroft, who sings boyhood songs to himself along the lanes. Gissing's accounts of restorative nature are heavily indebted to the Romantic poets. Too often, indeed, his little tapestries of idyll are musty with outmoded poetic locutions ('I hear the birds whose wont it is to sing to me; ever and anon the martins', etc.), but no one could doubt that he responded intensely to nature as a source of sanity and health, in contrast with metropolitan corruption.[17] Prominent among the degradations of the city was commercialism, which Gissing regarded as essentially an anti-natural force. Of course, this contradicted his other belief, that commercialism was all too natural, in that it inflamed man's most predatory instincts. But for Gissing, as for many of his own time and later, there were really two conceptions of nature — one red in tooth and claw, the other green with innocence and peace. Accepting Darwin, he still admired Wordsworth.

Gissing's third objection — a temperamental one — was that commerce depended on appeal to the mob. As the crowd scenes in early books like *Demos* and *The Nether World*, or later ones like *The Town Traveller*, overwhelmingly indicate he despised the mob as a physical entity for its violence, its coarseness, its hysterical emotion. But he also deplored the People as a political entity. Indeed — abetted by the etymology of 'democracy' — he made little distinction between the People and the mob. The People are envious and credulous and narrowly materialistic; the politics of the People, socialism, seems to consist largely, in Gissing's work, of orators haranguing unruly crowds — and crowds, which move easily from clapping to punching, can rapidly mutate into mobs. Commercialism was the third main subject — after hooliganism and socialism — through which Gissing expressed his contempt for the masses. He hated the conditions of mass production — factories, slums, industrial blight — but he loathed mass consumption quite as much. Commercial enterprise, banking on sales, was bound to pander to the *hoi polloi*. It did so first by endorsing their materialism. Will Warburton rejoices that his mother and sister are not like 'the vulgar average of mankind — that rapacious multitude, whom nothing animates but a chance of gain, with whom nothing weighs but a commercial argument'.[18] Gissing's fiction teems with such types. But successful selling also depended on appeal to the judgement of the majority, to the values, tastes and preferences of those without culture, breeding or brains. It followed from this that commercialism — a materialistic movement flattering the masses — was closely akin to socialism.

It was here that Gissing parted company with left-wing critiques of the market. In his condemnation of the City of London, of the jungle ethics of free competition, even in his onslaughts on advertising, 'Thus far', he might have said with Parson Wyvern, 'I am with the Socialists'. He totally diverged from them, of course, in his horror-struck rejection of their remedies ('Why, no man living', says Henry Ryecroft, 'has a more profound sense of property than I'). But Gissing had already begun to branch away by his idiosyncratic formulation of the problem. Like Carlyle's, his arraignments of commerce were also arraignments of democracy. Instead of accepting the incompatibility of economic interest between capitalist and worker, he stressed their supposed compatibility of mental and moral outlook. 'Think how much sheer barbarism there is around us,' says Piers Otway in *The Crown of Life*, 'from the brutal savage of the gutter to the cunning savage of the Stock Exchange!' Compare Maurice Hilliard's sarcastic comment on the centre of Birmingham in *Eve's Ransom*: 'Here are our great buildings, of which we boast to the world. They signify the triumph of Democracy — and of money'. This provocative conflation of forces he dislikes crops up all over Gissing's work. It sometimes necessitates a certain loading of terms. Inveighing against the City in *Born in Exile*, Godwin Peak first declares that 'It represents the ascendancy of the average man', then adds that it stands for 'The power which centres in the world's money-markets — plutocracy'. But the average man is not an international plutocrat. Elsewhere in *Born in Exile* the narrative is contorted to maintain this alignment of the evils of commerce with the threat of the populace. Peak's friend Earwaker is a principled journalist who edits the London *Weekly Post*. The proprietor, Runcorn, 'a wary man of business', cares only for circulation figures and tries to get his editor to lower standards and raise sales. Thus far a cautionary tale about commerce. But Gissing adds the circumstance that the *Post* is an organ of Radicalism. Runcorn prefers the articles of a 'political guttersnipe' called Kenyon; the question of maximizing profits turns into a matter of appeasing the mob. When Earwaker is eventually replaced by Kenyon, he meditates on those who have forced him out: 'Restored to generous calm, he could admit that such men as Runcorn and Kenyon — the one with his polyarchic commercialism, the other with his demagogic violence — had possibly a useful part to play at the present stage of things. He, however, could have no place in that camp.'[19] *That* camp, one notices, rather than those camps. It is hard to imagine any other novelist — unless it be Trollope in *The Warden* — so unqualmishly conflating the newspaper magnate with the Radical agitator.

Gissing's hatred of commercialism was sometimes confounded with his other antipathies; but of that hatred there can be no doubt. Gissing would not be Gissing, though, without some cross-currents of ambivalence. The images he applies to commerce — barbarism, pestilence, pollution, warfare — are apocalyptic with revulsion and fear. Yet commerce was the power that ruled his world. Appalled and overawed by the hordes ranged against him, he tried to solace himself with the thought that the 'business faculty ... is scarcely compatible with a cultured habit of thought'. But compared with the wheelings and dealings of business, cultured habits could not carry you far. Masochistically, he sometimes acknowledged this fact. Though Walter Egremont in *Thyrza* is applauded for his condemnation of commerce, he is rejected with something like contempt for his practical attempts to oppose it. Gissing's own attempts to acquire commercial acumen were invariably short-lived. As a very young man, he toyed with the notion of taking out a mortgage and becoming a *rentier*, but he rapidly abandoned this unlikely 'project of metamorphosing myself into a man of business'. With publishers, at least until the mid-1890s, Gissing was suicidally innocent. Visiting Bentley's in 1889 to discuss publication of *The Emancipated*, he candidly declared that he 'knew nothing' of 'the business side' of authorship. Bentley's were not comparably handicapped. Having offered less for the novel than he wanted, they told him, three years later, that they would gladly be relieved of their more than £50 loss on it: in fact, according to their ledgers, they had lost about £23. Gissing's revenge was oblique and literary. In his Rochester preface to *Barnaby Rudge* he totally supported Dickens's resistance to the trammelling terms he had made with Bentley, vigorously defending the creative author against 'those who deal in men's brains'.[20]

Occasionally, in his fiction as in his life, Gissing would compromise with commerce, but usually it was the kind of compromise that only served to highlight disdain. Bernard Kingcote settles for life in a bookshop, but only when his truest aspirations have been shelved. Will Warburton eventually accepts the grocer's counter, but only a facile reading of the novel could find here an endorsement of trade. The whole treatment of Warburton's reconciliation implies that it needs considerable courage; except on the premise that grocerdom is loathsome, large parts of the book become meaningless. The novel's denouement concerns itself only with the social objections to its hero's role, but as we saw earlier there are moral objections, and these seem to be in no way absolved by Warburton's climactic confession. It is true that Piers Otway in *The Crown of Life* is supposed to be a resolute businessman, but so many special factors are introduced as to turn his work inside out. For him, making money is a means to an end: in the long run, he is bidding for Irene's heart. An idealistic love poet, he cheerfully admits that he is not naturally a merchant. He works in Russia and learns the language; he 'was erudite concerning Russian wool and hemp. He talked about it not like an ordinary businessman, but as a scholar might'. He yearns to explain the Russian soul to the West: at times he sounds more like a cultural attaché than an international tradesman. His charming partner, Moncharmont, is equally extraordinary: born a French Swiss, familiar with Italy, a tolerant cosmopolitan, an occasional composer — 'the world would be a vastly better place', says Piers, 'if its business were often in the hands of such men'. Piers adds that he has never known his partner 'utter an ignoble thought about trade and money-making ... He is a lesson in civilisation. If trade is not to put an end to human progress, it must be pursued in Moncharmont's spirit ... Commerce must be humanised once more'.[21]

In other words, trade must cease to be trade. Given the context for these remarks provided by the rest of Gissing's fiction, one might as well talk about 'humanizing' the techniques of chemical warfare. However much Gissing tried to bend himself to the viewpoint of commercialism, he would always sooner or later spring back to his own, completely contrasting, stance. The more he argues that the perfect businessman is really a scholar, a poet, a musician, the more we suspect that what he is describing is a quite antithetical ideal.

I I

Gissing's first, and almost last, conception of art was of something exalted, rarefied and noble. Art was a potent mode of escape, an asylum from the squalors of everyday life. In this respect it resembled nature — and indeed his passionate feeling for nature had its roots in attention to art. Ryecroft recounts how as a child he slept 'in a room hung round with prints after English landscape painters'; scrutinizing these with juvenile keenness, he developed a love of rural scenery. Later, in the National Gallery, pictures such as Constable's *Valley Farm* offered 'visions of a world of peace and beauty from which I was excluded'. Several of Gissing's characters — Emily Hood, Sidney Kirkwood — inherit a similar love of nature originating in art. Art and nature, throughout his fiction, are constantly coupled as cleansing forces. Perhaps the most ingenuous accounts of art as an antiseptic alternative to life occur in *Workers in the Dawn*, where Golding both practises and appreciates art to escape from harassing circumstance. Deserted by his degraded wife, he solaces himself with a section of the *Odyssey* and a reading from Vasari's *Lives of the Artists*, which seems like experience of a fresh sea breeze after the 'gloom of a manufacturing town'. Eventually, having devoted himself to painting, Golding is encouraged to illustrate a stanza from Tennyson's 'Palace of Art'. Doing so, he spends hours 'in an artist's dreamland, issuing from it purified and exalted'. It might be regarded as singularly ironic that Tennyson's poem should be used in this way, but the irony is not acknowledged by Golding nor, it seems, intended by Gissing.[22]

There are two distinct ways in which art might be seen as an idealistic refuge from everyday life. The first is through restriction of its subject matter, allowing it to treat only of the virtuous, the beautiful, the golden. The second is through the psychology of the artist, who in the act of aesthetic creation is able to transcend mundane concerns. In *Workers in the Dawn* both doors are opened. Golding achieves his greatest liberation through conceiving and executing his work, but he also shrinks from 'hideous' subjects such as those portrayed by Hogarth. After completing *Workers in the Dawn*, Gissing retreated from this latter conception. In a sense, he could hardly do otherwise, given the material in the novel itself — his own art could hardly be more at variance with the art of his artist hero. Nevertheless, he surrendered it reluctantly, and would sometimes revert to the notion that art should confine itself to the intrinsically attractive. Though this notion had a decent pedigree, traceable back at least to Plato, Gissing soon realized that in his own day it was favoured mainly by untutored minds. Instead he turned mainly to the other conception, and here he found contemporary philosophical support. Schopenhauer had argued that aesthetic contemplation was a purely intellectual process which involved a transcendence of conscious desire. The pleasure afforded by art was unique in that it had no connection with the will. It followed from this that artistic sincerity could not strike a bargain with worldly ambition. 'And so do not', Schopenhauer warned, 'degrade your Muse to a whore.' Elsewhere, and even more bluntly, he suggested that essentially there were two kinds of author, those who wrote for the sake of their subject, and those who wrote for money. 'Every author degenerates', he concluded, 'as soon as he writes in any way for the sake of profit.'[23]

New Grub Street might be Gissing's later treatment of this text. But what he first drew from Schopenhauer was belief in the pristine autonomy of art — that through the very nature of aesthetic experience, the realm of art was cordoned off from material concerns. Gissing was always anxious to protect it from practical or utilitarian intrusion. At first, though, he did not perceive the main threat as the poisonous effects of commercialism. The earliest threat came rather from a rival: the seductive appeal of social reform. We have already seen something of Gissing's dilemma, which was not dissimilar to that of Yeats: 'The intellect of man is forced to choose/Perfection of the life or of the work.' The possible compromise — that art should be converted to a didactic vehicle — could not be entertained by Gissing for long. In *Workers in the Dawn* Mr Tollady exhorts Arthur to imitate Hogarth in the cautionary depiction of social and moral deformities. But Arthur, his eyes on ethereal Beauty, can't bear to pile his palette with scrapings from the gutter, however instructive they might be. His personal history blows him between art and reform, but eventually he accepts Helen Norman's ruling that the spirit of art permeates the whole of society and 'ultimately leavens the whole mass'. Arthur, she concludes, should become a 'pure artist'.[24] Her use of the adjective is interestingly ambiguous, for it comprehends both the definitions of purity that competed for Gissing's attention.

In the early 1880s Helen's rarefied convictions were consolidated by reiteration. Again and again in his letters Gissing declares that 'the works of the artist ... remain, sources of health to the world', 'art is the highest product of human life', 'My attitude henceforth is that of the artist pure and simple'. Indeed, he goes even further than Helen, dropping the social-security view of art — with its talk of 'health' and 'benefits' — in favour of an aggressive aestheticism. In the first edition of *The Unclassed*, when Casti asserts that true art works ultimately for human good, Waymark retorts that the artist himself works rather for his own delight. Hogarth, if his pictures had provoked a revolution, would not have rejoiced in the destruction of Gin Lane. By now the purity of art is located entirely in the mind of the artist: to the pure artist all things are pure. Gissing did not always stick firmly to this viewpoint, but he did increasingly believe that art was an alternative to social reform, and for him a preferable one. In *The Unclassed*, as shown earlier, this case is advanced with considerable ambivalence. But in *Demos* Eldon's superfine aesthetics are offered as a delicate but passionate reproach to Mutimer's coarse humanitarianism. Art is identified with the aristocrat. This identification, begun in *The Unclassed*, is frequently brandished in later books. By the time of *Our Friend the Charlatan* (1901) the noble champion of art is literally a baronet. 'Let every one try to civilize himself', says Sir William Amys, who hates commerce and politics; 'depend upon it, it's the best work he can do for the world at large.'[25]

Another threat to art in Gissing's early fiction is that of religious dogma. The ex-Ranter Mike Rumball in *Workers in the Dawn* sneers righteously at little Arthur's 'chalking'. In this case, piety inspires pugnacity. With Maud Enderby in *The Unclassed*, piety makes rather for a swamping sense of guilt. Bobbing pitifully between nature and nurture, she submerges her native aesthetic responses in waves of ascetic neurosis. Like Arnold, Gissing was anxiously aware of the contemporary colonization of art by puritanical criteria (in a small way, his own sisters were missionaries in the cause). Though Christianity purported to be anti-materialistic, its procrustean attempts to convert art to sermon were regarded by Gissing as just one more form of utilitarian distortion. 'The artist should be free', he insists in *The Unclassed*, 'from everything like moral prepossession.' His fullest treatment of this particular tension occurs in *The Emancipated*, which he first thought of calling *The Puritan*. This title referred to Miriam Baske, at first a rigid effigy of provincial religion, later a thoughtful and womanly figure stirred into warm life by Ross Mallard and art. The key moments in her relations with Mallard are all marked by aesthetic experience. At the end, just before his proposal, he presents her with portraits of her two personas — a contrast prepared for many pages before by Miriam's comment on the two bits of stone, one marble, the other travertine, that she has shown to Mallard at Paestum: 'How cold one is, and how warm the other!' In one crucial conversation, situated in the Sistine Chapel, they discuss the power of religious preconception to embarrass aesthetic responses. Gradually but (literally) remorselessly, Miriam discards her religious inhibitions. When

Mallard discovers her in the Sala Rotonda, seated before the Belvedere Apollo, she meets his eyes 'with a look in which self-control was unconsciously like defiance'. Her appreciation of classical nudity betokens her acceptance of both art and sex. In *The Emancipated* art fights free from religion. Gissing's sister Ellen wrote worriedly to him to seek reassurance that Miriam was not modelled upon herself.[26]

In his early work Gissing rejected the principle that art should subordinate itself to a social or religious purpose. Naturally, he was also hostile to art's capitulation to commerce, but only slowly did he come to see this as the greatest danger of all. He hated commercialism *per se*: the encroachment of commercialism on art was for him a horrible blasphemy, an insidious disease. He did not pretend to scientific precision about the true sources of the epidemic. In correspondence with Gabrielle he tended to blame English philistinism. On the Continent he would sometimes sense the presence of a potentially more sensitive audience. A Paris production of *Oedipus Rex* prompted the reflection, 'Great Apollo! What would this become in an English theatre!' The Calabrian people seemed to him to evince 'an innate respect for things of the mind' which was lacking in 'a typical Englishman'. Despite these cosmopolitan leanings, he usually favoured a historical — rather than geographical — explanation of cultural degeneracy. He attributed the commercialization of art to the seedy flowering of mass consumption. This in turn sent out repulsive suckers to the burgeoning of democracy and the growth of elementary education. Since these blights had advanced most rankly in England, his two explanations did not necessarily conflict. Gissing's work bristles with denunciations of the brutal stupidity of the British public. Anything of merit was too difficult for them. In literary matters, Walter Egremont explains, 'the ill word of the mob is equivalent to high praise'. The reason was the feebleness of education conjoined with the power of the market economy. 'When commercial interest is supreme', rages Peak, 'how can the tastes of the majority fail to lead and control?'[27]

In every area, Gissing believed, the sacred enclaves of art and culture were being invaded by unruly hordes. Their most tangible appearance was in tourism. At Shakespeare's house in Stratford in 1888, the 'ghastly thought' struck Gissing of the crowds that piled in at bank-holiday time. The following year he expressed his reservations about the 'gross animals' released into Rome, many of them 'absolute shop-boys and work-girls', proclaiming their 'ignorance and vulgarity' in vile English.

'Every day', he notified Bertz, 'I saw people whom I should like to have assaulted.' The spirit of the masses was made audible, too, in the liltings and jingles of popular music. 'The vulgar song that now-a-days gets popular', Gissing noted icily in his scrapbook, 'generally has a change to the minor, and a waltz refrain.' As early as *Workers in the Dawn* music-hall ditties are mercilessly transcribed, and by *In the Year of Jubilee* half the cast of sham-cultured characters communicates mainly through robust 'sheet-melodies' or mawkishly melting drawing-room songs.[28] The music-halls, of course, blended songs and theatre, and in the demotic theatre of his day Gissing found further deafening proof for his strictures on mass entertainment. He disliked 'the conditions of theatrical exhibition. It is of necessity an appeal to the mob'. He hated 'the contiguity of the vulgar crowd, its base comments, its unintelligent applause'. Explaining in an article 'Why I don't write plays', he expanded his historical diagnosis: 'When the drama flourished in England, it was by virtue of popular interests, for in those days the paying public was the intelligent public.' Now, this Elizabethan ideal has vanished and 'the paying public are the unintelligent multitude' who, seeking amusement after labour, demand the spectacular, the sensational, the obvious. No play without such effects could succeed: 'It would contain no claptrap, no ludicrous outrage of probability, no determined exhilaration at the close'. The most baneful effects, in the theatre, of catering to the multitude could be seen in what happened to classic texts. In his article Gissing cites a mangled adaptation of Daudet's *Fromont jeune*. Elsewhere he mentions cut versions of *Hamlet* — suitably neutered for the 'gross public' by the excision of Ophelia's songs.[29]

Gissing realized that his historical thesis might be challenged. One could argue that the spread of the 'democratic populace' had led to a genuine expansion of culture, not a dilution or a vulgarization. In his fiction he allows this case to be urged by the eponymous charlatan Lashmar: 'England is no longer the stupidly inartistic country of early Victorian times; there's a true delight in music and painting, and a much more general appreciation of the good in literature.' Gissing states the counter-case in *Henry Ryecroft*. True, there are more books of every kind, more cheap editions of classic authors, more works of scholarship and learning. This 'literary traffic' is tiny, however, compared with materialistic activity — as the pages of popular newspapers show. Further (an unusual argument for Gissing), underlying putative intellectuality may well be 'moral barbarism': a trained mind is no guarantee of considerate responses. Finally, as to the greater number of readers, how many read 'with comprehension of their author'? This argument weighed very heavily with Gissing. In *Thyrza* he notes how commonly a book is 'run through without a glance at its title-page'. In his commonplace book he adds that most readers 'are ignorant of the *language* in which good books are written ... when they get thro' a book at all, they follow only the general drift, losing every point of lit. value'. So much for Lashmar's case about reading. No doubt Gissing felt the same would apply to the 'true delight in music and painting'.[30]

Though the quality of reading remained dismally low, the quantity of readers had vastly increased, and so too — equally discouraging for authors — had the quantity of books. 'What hope is there', Gissing asked in 1891, 'for any but either very base or very extraordinary books in such an outpouring of printed matter as now comes forth every week?' His own works could never be popular, he said, for the mob would swarm to others better suited to their taste: 'I fear we are coming to a time when good literature will have a hard struggle to hold its footing at all.' The images of crowding, competition and warfare are applied to books as well as people. The laws of Darwin hold sway in the libraries; the bookshops are fields of elemental strife. 'The struggle for existence among books', says Jasper Milvain, 'is nowadays as severe as among men.' Yet how ironic that these primitive forces should now be unleashed, through commercialism, on the carriers of civilization. As Gissing bitterly exclaims in *Henry Ryecroft*, 'Hateful as is the struggle for life in every form, this rough-and-tumble of the literary arena seems to me sordid and degrading beyond all others'.[31]

Given this new Battle of the Books, what should a hard-pressed author do? Jasper's answer is: adapt to his environment. Amidst the uproar of new publications, only raucous shouting can make itself heard. The accepted techniques of publicity will have to be directed at literature. An author's friends, Jasper believes, can begin by manufacturing rave reviews. This counsel was not so new as it looked. The journalistic promotion of books was not peculiar to Gissing's period. The earliest full-page advertisement in *The Times* was not for a medicine or soap but a book. That was in 1829. The following year Macaulay deplored the malodorous puffing of poets and novelists, complaining that contemporary men of letters were adopting 'devices ... considered as disreputable' even in the lowest trade. By Gissing's day, not only were there more 'devices' — the photograph, the interview, the gossip-column — but, partly owing to the removal of taxes, publicity was spouting from many more outlets. Gissing observed what he once referred to as 'the flood of nauseous & lying eulogy' with a bilious but perceptive eye.[32] A sardonic connoisseur of the literary reviews, he kept a record of their calculated raptures, their errors, imbecilities and contradictions. 'On the whole, is any sort of human work so incompetently performed?' he wondered.[33] He also began to keep a careful chart of the ebbs and flows of literary advertisement. The *Athenaeum* invariably announced a book by Spencer in small type. Writers like Barrie, on the other hand, were swept forward on a tide of acclamation. He himself wished his books to be saved from sinking, but recoiled from the polluting flow of publicity. He was anxious to assure Gabrielle that a paragraph in *Literature*, about the translation of his works into French, had not been communicated by him: 'Never once in my life, directly or indirectly, have I sought this kind of advertisement'.[34] More often, indeed, he had actively repelled it. Like Ross Mallard in *The Emancipated*, he was proudly deficient in the 'properties of the showman'. Unlike Alma Rolfe in *The Whirlpool*, he had no craving to be 'photographed and para-graphed'. He refused his photograph to the London *Figaro*. He declined an interview with the *Pall Mall Gazette*. He even, ironically, achieved some publicity by avoiding it so assiduously. At the same time, and characteristically, he wondered about the wisdom of this resistance. Advising his brother Algernon to collaborate with a write-up in the *Figaro*, he said, 'I am inclined to think that I have behaved rather foolishly in this advertisement business ... we simply cannot afford to be so scrupulous'. Algernon duly materialized as the latest, and perhaps most unlikely, avatar of 'Figaro's Coming Man'. Though Gissing had once grimly reflected that, when he read 'interviews' with authors ('He has built himself a charming little house', etc.), he couldn't help thinking how people would be startled if his own abode and lifestyle were faithfully transcribed, the interviewers eventually tracked him down. One, from America, spelt out his worst suspicions: 'She writes that she is soon going "accross" again. Merciful powers! What a time we live in!' In *Henry Ryecroft* he writes bitterly about the younger generation of 'novelists and journalists awaiting their promotion'.[35]

The rise of journalism, on Gissing's reading, made up one of the murkiest pages in the commercialization of literature. 'Every day', he wrote to Algernon, just after completing *New Grub Street*, 'I learn more decidedly how gross a trade journalism is.' Again the idea was by no means new. Schopenhauer had anticipated Gissing by denouncing the aptly named 'journalists' (the word meant 'day-labourers', he pointed out) who lived solely on the public's folly of wanting to read only what had just been printed. Gissing discriminated carefully between (in ascending order of merit) newspapers, literary periodicals, and books. Newspapers, the meanest organs, he had little wish to scrutinize, and, like his own Lord Dymchurch in retirement, never even saw one for quite long periods.[36] He did, however, subscribe to the view that newspapers spread infection. Schopenhauer's dark contempt for the alarmism of leading articles foreshadowed Gissing's feeling that newspaper hysteria was a principal cause of war.[37] In *Thyrza*, Egremont declares: 'The newspaper is the very voice of all that is worst in our civilisation ... The newspaper has supplanted the book ... These writers are tradesmen, and with all their power they cry up the spirit of trade.' Egremont's eventual report from America that he now reads little but newspapers is not, then, good news about his spiritual condition (shortly after, he abandons Thyrza). In Gissing it is normally the most retarded persons who step forward in defence of the daily press. The half-baked Barmby in *In the Year of Jubilee* is convinced that 'one of our great newspapers' is an apt representative of the Age of Progress (Gissing would undoubtedly have agreed). 'Printed in another way it would make a volume − absolutely; a positive volume; packed with thought and information.' Precious articles of this information − as that the cabs in London, placed end to end, would stretch for no less than forty miles − are continually reissued in Barmby's conversation, attached to the unanswerable *imprimatur*, 'I saw it stated in a paper'.[38]

On the subject of periodicals, Gissing felt more ambivalent. While deploring their effects on cultural health, he remained addicted to them throughout life. In 'An author at grass' (the serial version of *Henry Ryecroft*) he confessed he had a taste for the literary papers largely because he was 'out of it'. Even while writing *New Grub Street*, he went out to purchase the *Review of Reviews* and his final postcard to Morley Roberts concerned a notice in the *Spectator*. In his twenties he had actually thought of running his own weekly. Rather surprisingly, given his contempt for both journalism and advertising, we find him in 1883 proposing to Algernon that they start up a paper, which would have to be forcefully advertised. The paper would be weekly, for the West Riding area, and independent in politics. Algernon could pen a series on ' "Yorkshire Folk-lore," − short, chatty, lively', and

Gissing himself a 'London letter', which he could easily 'concoct ... out of endless publications'. In a later letter Gissing dispatched a prospectus. '*A man must canvass for advertisements*', he insisted. 'The town must be placarded with the announcement.' Needless to say, this project came to nothing, but it was less out of character than it might appear. Its germ was in a letter of two years earlier in which Gissing denounced 'the great bulk' of periodicals as being too blatantly 'written for cash'. Algernon, he continued, ought to 'found some day a good Wakefield paper ... How gladly I would co-operate in such a scheme'. The scheme itself, when it came, was encased in many stipulations. The periodical would accept no 'flatulent correspondence'; it would have 'a strong infusion of fairly good literature'; it would publish the occasional review, but only of 'books worthy of that name'. Manifestly, all the excited talk about receipts, concoctions and placards was meant as a willed concession to business. The project was the brainchild of Edwin Reardon, with management advice from Jasper Milvain. Regional papers were, in any case, less objectionable in Gissing's eyes. In *The Whirlpool*, buying shares in a local paper is equated with rural retirement.[39]

The national periodicals were a different proposition. Of course they varied hugely in quality and audience. At the bottom of the market was the kind of stuff that Ada Peachey reads in *In the Year of Jubilee* — 'illustrated weeklies, journals of society, cheap miscellanies' (the outpourings of Pearson, Newnes and Northcliffe had added to this sediment considerably). At the top were the heavyweight literary monthlies, long established and proud of their titles. What, in Gissing's view, they all had in common was their hypnotizing nature, their spuriousness and their function as substitutes. Penny weeklies, for instance, figure frequently in Gissing, and always as prompters of low-grade illusion. In his Chicago notebook of 1877 he jotted down an idea for a story: 'Woman who has weakened her mind by reading romances, and acts in daily life accordingly.' The story was never written, but the character recurs. Although the idea was not original, Gissing tethered it more closely to cheap periodical literature and pushed it further down the social scale. The Gothic figments of Jane Austen's Catherine Morland seem positively exalted when juxtaposed with the pitiful, degraded, romantic delusions of women like Harriet Smales in *The Unclassed*, Alice Mutimer in *Demos*, or Polly Sparkes in *The Town Traveller*.[40]

The intellectual reviews and magazines were catering for a more ambitious class, but what they were purveying, Gissing thought, was also the prospect of fantasy achievement. In both cases vanity and idleness were the dominant motives of the consumer, but while penny fiction massaged the heart, the literary periodicals flattered the brain: both alike were offering the satisfactions of easy but exciting conquest.As early as 1887 Gissing was planning a satire, *Sandray the Sophist*, on the modern cultivators of periodical literature: although it proved abortive, parts of it were perhaps reused in *New Grub Street*. Reading periodicals, in Gissing, is a compensation for not reading books. Mrs Travis in *The Emancipated* is guilty of this, and so is Mrs Toplady in *Our Friend the Charlatan* who, however, eventually discovers an article exposing the anti-hero, Lashmar, himself an indolent browser through reviews. Lord Dymchurch, by contrast, flings aside a periodical containing a pretentious philosophical article. 'Was it satire or burlesque?' he wonders. Eventually, he connects such trumpery with Lashmar, whom he thinks of, revealingly, as a 'mere sophist ... an unscrupulous journalist'. Pretentious articles are much relied on by the pushy nonentities in Gissing's short stories — the appalling Linda Vassie of 'At High Pressure', the pathetic Philip Dolamore of 'The Pessimist of Plato Road', both of whom spew out half-digested gobbets from the pages of periodicals. Gissing himself well understood the cut-price pleasures of magazines. No one who had not been similarly tempted could have written his short story 'Spellbound', in which the hero sits hunched in a public library, sating himself, month after month, on the illustrated weeklies.[41]

Skimming, we learn in *The Whirlpool*, is 'the intellectual disease of the time'. The periodicals encouraged skimming, and the frothy omniscience they supplied was a threat to more solid reading. It was not only, however, as a reader, but also as a writer that Gissing saw them as tempting alternatives to books. The periodicals offered quick money through short stories. In America Gissing had lived off his stories, but until the early 1890s he was wincingly reluctant to return to this trade. Persuaded to do so by Morley Roberts, he began in 1893 sending stories to the journals edited by Clement Shorter, and even employed an agent, W. M. Colles, to assist him in finding outlets. The results were financially encouraging, but almost at once Gissing scented the tension between commercial and artistic value. 'I am entered upon the commercial path, alas!' he told Bertz. 'But I shall try not to write rubbish.' For the next three years he gave himself over to short stories and short novels (with the exception of *In the Year of Jubilee*). Most of these stories were by no means rubbish, yet Gissing found such cameos uncongenial: 'Only on a large canvas can I do work worth doing.' But though uncongenial, they were also convenient. Not only his chronic shortage of cash, and alterations in the literary market, but also his messy and disrupted home life made Gissing, in the 1890s, favour work in short units. Certainly he compromised during this period, but he never abandoned his artistic conscience. As late as 1898 he was telling the publisher A. H. Bullen that in order to make 'some hundreds a year', he would have to aim firmly at the magazines: 'The problem is, how to do it without degrading myself.'[42]

This was indeed the problem for Gissing; and, as it happened, it confronted him most starkly in the decade after he published *New Grub Street*. In the 1880s, poor but honest, he unhappily did not even have the chance of degrading himself for commercial success. In his earliest work the autonomy of art is threatened by social reform or religion rather than the ruthless intrusions of the market. The commercialization of art, if mentioned, is crudely conceived and briskly dismissed. The cynical Gresham in *Workers in the Dawn* is a painter who courts 'popular favour' and has no 'regard to the dignity of his art'. Clement Gabriel in *Isabel Clarendon* is committed to 'the ideal exactions of art' and refuses to mint money with conventional portraits. The moral antitheses are trite and simple. Gissing always believed that genuine art should be independent of commercial concerns. But at first he also believed that it could be. Writing to the *Pall Mall Gazette* in December 1884, he rejected George Moore's bitter contention that the censorship of literature could be blamed on the circulating libraries. Better to blame it, Gissing argued, on the cowardice of authors. Surrendering themselves to the public's taste, they adopted the 'tradesman's attitude'; anxious not to 'damage their popularity', they shrank from a 'temporary diminution of receipts'. The hopefulness implicit in 'temporary' recurs in Gissing's intransigent conclusion: 'Let novelists be true to their artistic conscience, and the public taste will come round.' (This is what happens with Gabriel: after years of neglect and indigence, he succeeds with both 'the vulgar and the cultured'.) All that the artist need do, it seems, is put up with penury and near-starvation. Sometimes, in fact — as in *Thyrza*, or his early story 'Gretchen' — Gissing would talk as if having money were a positive disadvantage for an artist. By the time he wrote *Henry Ryecroft* he was willing to admit that 'starvation ... does not necessarily produce fine literature'. Even so, he was uneasy about 'carpet authors': better, perhaps, that they should suffer hunger than 'fatty degeneration of the soul'.[43]

Poverty, then, could be a vigorous incentive; it could also —

as Gissing well knew — be a crippling discouragement. This paradox was related to others which Gissing was ultimately unable to resolve. Culture and intellect, he fervently hoped, could serve as a refuge from material care. And yet it was his equally powerful conviction that culture depended on material comfort. In *A Life's Morning* he explores this tension. The heroine, Emily, cultivates art as an ethereal alternative to the sordidness of home. Making beauty her religion, she reads hard at German in her father's 'bare garret' or shelters herself 'beneath the wing of some poet'. The calamity that shatters her father's body also throws down her aesthetic defences. She feels, 'She had presumptuously taken to herself the religion of her superiors, of those to whom fate allowed the assurance of peace, of guarded leisure ... How artificial had been the delights with which she soothed herself !' Aesthetic cultivation, it transpires, can never be exempt from material circumstance. And yet, years later, Emily — impoverished, lonely and pinched in appearance — is still poring over the classics.[44]

New Grub Street deals with Gissing's most pressing dilemma. Convinced that art, by its very nature, should transcend material desires and cares, he could also perceive that in a market economy it was impossible for this to happen. The artist was compelled to make concessions. Yet the market meant the values of the vulgar masses: it meant lethal competition and reckless gambling, superficial reading and venal reviewing, journalism, advertising, interviews, best sellers — it meant the substitution of survival for art. How far, then, should an artist accommodate to the market? At what point might survival as a human being mean the death of creative work? *New Grub Street* is not able to answer these questions, but it does bring them sharply into focus. It is a novel written out of despair and bewilderment, but also out of defiance and integrity. Its epigraph might be what Gissing wrote to Algernon in a letter of 1889: 'the accursed complication of literary endeavour with the struggle for subsistence is, I suppose, one of the most harassing things humanity has ever known'.[45]

I I I

Although *New Grub Street* has some weaknesses, it is one of the great Victorian novels. Its quality arises from a number of factors. First, it embodies its social analysis with complete success in its personal story. As we have seen, Gissing always had difficulty in filtering a social or cultural thesis through the meshes of romantic narrative. In *New Grub Street* he conquers this difficulty. Put simply, he draws an analogy between the literary and the marriage markets, and shows how those who make use of literature will also make use of people. But the analogy is not put simply by Gissing. Rather, it is explored with considerable complexity and — a second distinctive merit — with impressive skills of organization. Though Frank Swinnerton believed that '*New Grub Street* is nearly as arbitrary as *Martin Chuzzlewit*', it is in fact cunningly composed of contrasting and counterpointing themes, with numerous symmetries of incident and motive. Despite this near-schematic structure, it is also — a third strength — psychologically subtle. Though most frequently prized as a 'sociological document', it might equally be valued for its shrewd notation of psychological states.[46] Lastly, *New Grub Street* has vital connections with the rest of Gissing's *oeuvre*. Charged with imaginative energies that crackle only sporadically elsewhere, it transmits his most acrid and powerful statement on the clash between art and commerce.

Like all Gissing's finest novels, *New Grub Street* examines how a social problem bites into individual lives. Actually, the problem is really two problems. The first and deepest is poverty, which Gissing classified as a primary corroder not only of happiness and peace of mind, but of decency and self-respect. The conviction that poverty degrades is voiced by virtually every character — a flaw in the novel, Gissing felt, arising from his own bitterness.[47] Given this corrosive power, however, the immediate problem for the characters is how to stay solvent as practitioners of literature — or, more ambitiously, how to float themselves to wealth. The perennial stresses of poverty are applied to the contemporary crisis of letters. The atmosphere of the novel is unrelievedly literary. All the major characters are attempting to survive on the proceeds of print: they are novelists, journalists, editors, agents, or family dependants of these. (The single exception is Harold Biffen: his problem is how to live not by, but while, producing words.) The particular contemporary challenge they face is the commercialization of literature. With the aristocratic patron replaced by the democratic reading public, literature has become just another commodity, exposed to the forces of the modern market — the imperatives of mass production and consumption, the demand for utility or entertainment, the reliance on recently developed techniques of promotion and publicity. But if poverty corrodes, commercialism pollutes. A writer may leap over the pitfalls of penury, but only, perhaps, to slip into the sewers of mercantile compromise.

The dilemma dealt with is Gissing's own — the conflict between moral integrity and material success. This dilemma is nailed into the narrative on a cross-frame of character juxta-positions. The most obvious contrast is that between Edwin Reardon and Jasper Milvain. Both these men agree that the current standards of the literary world are corrupt; but whereas Reardon rejects them and fails, Milvain exploits them and succeeds. Reardon is a man of the old school (we must specify later what this means) who will not, or cannot, 'make a trade of an art'. Sensitive, conscientious, painfully slow, he strives for work of intrinsic merit rather than ephemeral popular appeal. Jasper is a new man and a tradesman: what he aims at is money and money's benefits — physical comfort, social esteem, travel, luxurious living. Literature for him is a means to this end. Under no illusion about the merit of what he writes, he realizes that success as a writer is not wholly dependent on merit. In the late-Victorian literary market there are other, more serviceable requisites. You must have sufficient capital to finance a flourishing social life: marriage is perhaps the most convenient method of getting your hands on this. You also need influential friends, so that useful reviews can be offered and received, posts can be earmarked, prospects sounded. Recruiting such friends requires diplomatic skills, but also gambler's nerves: patronage from one quarter might well provoke punishment from another. The personal qualities in demand are speed, versatility, cynical detachment and a nose for popular fashion. In short, you must flatter and advertise, cultivate patrons, make connections, and generally pay less attention to your writing than to its successful promotion.

Clearly the difference between Reardon and Milvain is not only moral but temperamental. Reardon is reticent and indepen-dent, Milvain sleekly convivial. Reardon is passionate and pessimistic, Milvain cold and cheerful. This character contrast is obvious, but the juxtaposition of types goes further. At the centre of the novel are two parallel relationships — between the married pair, Amy and Reardon, and the lovers, Marian and Jasper. Like *The Emancipated* before it and *The Odd Women* after, *New Grub Street* is based on the affairs of two couples. Another analogue is *Isabel Clarendon*, in which two couples (Isabel and Bernard, Vincent and Ada) come to grief for related reasons — the excessive attachment to wealth and position of the woman in the first case and the man in the second. The anti-hero, Vincent Lacour, is a prototype Jasper Milvain: a black-haired young egotist, he boasts of his candour but acts with extreme calculation; after flirting with two women at once, he encounters a testamentary setback, and rapidly replaces his un-useful fiancée with a much more promising prospect. The characters in *Isabel Clarendon* are also placed by their attitudes to literature. Bernard and Ada are bookish intellectuals; Isabel is a socialite unacquainted with serious writing.

In *New Grub Street* the crucial pattern in the action is the way that Jasper's relationship with Marian reduplicates Amy's with Reardon. At first, it is true, what we seem to have is a contrast rather than a comparison. Amy and Reardon are breaking apart; Jasper and Marian, it seems, are uniting. But Gissing makes use of his three-volume format both to build up and to undermine this contrast. The first volume concludes with Reardon's despair, and Amy's pursed dissatisfaction, at his failure to prosper through fiction. The second volume, in which the marriage severs, ends with Jasper and Marian's engagement. Both endings, however, are fraught with foreboding. The second, just as much as the first, is overshadowed by financial worry; and the rapturous betrothal is soon betrayed by Jasper's impatience and selfish concern: 'He rose, though she was still seated ... When they had parted, Marian looked back. But Jasper was walking quickly away, his head bent, in profound meditation.' The final curtain goes down, of course, on Jasper and Amy united at last, financially secure and emotionally relaxed, harmonious in repulsive bliss.[48]

This ending is apt, and almost preordained, for Jasper and Amy have much in common. Early in the book Jasper declares that he could never prove attractive to Amy because they are 'too much alike'. His premise is correct though his inference is false. Numerous hints establish the fact that Amy is fascinated by Jasper — by his 'energy and promise of success'. (Jasper, conversely, understanding her well, is rather more sceptical about Amy.) Both are socially ambitious, unromantic, somewhat selfish; at various times they both display a marked disloyalty to Reardon and derive satisfaction from his weakness. They both acknowledge — and more important accept — the moral omnipotence of money, and share the commercial view of literature. They also concur in their conviction that merit must be socially recognized to be of any use. Amy is 'well aware that no degree of distinction in her husband would be of much value to her unless she had the pleasure of witnessing its effect upon others'. When Jasper claims to care only about 'intellectual distinction', his sister Dora sharply objects, 'Combined with financial success'. Jasper's reply is unhesitating: 'Why, that is what distinction means.' Significantly, at the end of the novel, Dora condemns both Jasper and Amy in almost identical terms.[49]

Given these character resemblances, it is scarcely surprising that Jasper and Amy are also alike in their treatment of others. Attracted, perhaps, to their anti-types, they embrace then discard very similar partners. Both Reardon and Marian are introverts whose loneliness has made them sensitive. Warm-hearted but diffident, both hunger for love — hunger being the metaphor used in each case. To Reardon, toiling in poverty, Amy appears like a dazzling light; to Marian, in her bleak life of literary drudgery, Jasper is a 'vision of joy'.[50] Both have moments of murky foreboding, provoked by their partner's responses to money; but in both a craving for sympathy overmasters their suspicion. Marian and Reardon never meet, but Marian closely follows Reardon's path in a downward curve to disaster. Ultimately, the two main relationships are not contrasted but compared. In each a conscientious but nervous *littérateur* seeks escape from isolation through love. Enamoured of ambitious extroverts, both find themselves losing their partners' affection because of a failure to supply them with cash. Just as Amy accepts Reardon's proposal thinking he will one day be wealthy and famous, so Jasper proposes to Marian after news of her inheritance. Reardon's diminishing receipts have their counterpart in Marian's truncated legacy. And as Amy sharply advises her husband to turn out sensational short stories, so Jasper bluntly suggests to his lover that she live by romantic fiction.

The parallels not only run neatly along the narrative, they also plunge down into the characters' emotions. Compare, for instance, the 'fruitless meeting' of the married couple in Chapter 25 with the final meeting, in Chapter 26, of Jasper and Marian in Regent's Park (the latter location chosen by Jasper in order to be 'on neutral ground' — the title of Reardon's book). In the first scene Amy is repelled by Reardon's shabbiness and then begins 'to feel ashamed of her shame'. In the second Jasper notes 'with more disgust than usual, the signs in Marian's attire of encroaching poverty', and yet 'for such feelings he reproached himself, and the reproach made him angry'. The thoughts and feelings of Reardon and Marian, their pride stung by unrequited love, are also directly analogous. Marian refuses to accept an obviously unwilling offer of marriage: 'Do you wish me to be your wife, or are you sacrificing yourself? ... your voice says you promise it out of pity.' This recalls not just Reardon's emotional predicament, but also his actual words to Amy: 'Then you mean that you would sacrifice yourself out of — what? Out of pity for me, let us say.' Other moments, too, are precisely recalled by this final encounter in the park. Much earlier Amy has said to Reardon, of her staunchness under stress of remorseless poverty, 'I can't trust myself if that should come to pass'. In the park Jasper grimly warns Marian that he 'can't trust' himself to remain faithful throughout a protracted engagement.[51] There is even an ironic symmetry in what happens to Marian and Reardon just after they have been abandoned. Marian wrenches herself away to return to work at the British Museum. Reardon resumes his former job as a humble clerk in a hospital. Both return to the very obscurity that preceded their dazzling dreams.

All this might sound rather mechanically schematic, but in fact so gradually are the parallels drawn, and so fully are the individual characters defined, that the dominant pattern of juxtaposition is not obvious until close to the end. The novel is not built simply on the contrast between two men ('Milvain versus Reardon', as one critic has it), but the counterpoint between two relationships, one of which is running ahead of the other, but both of which are eventually played out to a similar plaintive strain.[52] However, Gissing's initial decision to embody his thematic contrast between integrity and worldliness not in two men but in two couples has important effects on the subtlety of the novel's characterization. It means that he cannot make his major characters Morality figures of vice and virtue — else why should the 'virtuous' partner in each couple be attracted at all to the other? If Amy, say, were merely a mercenary succubus, half the book's pathos would be thrown away: Reardon would become just an obtuse dupe, his lasting affection no more than neurosis. As it is, Amy is a character with whom at times we sympathize; Jasper, in the earlier part of the book, we might positively admire. Amy's failings are evident enough. She is cold, self-absorbed and sometimes mean — she never once refers to Marian, for instance, without some suggestion of belittlement. Although, like her predecessor Rosamond Vincy (and her close contemporary Hedda Gabler), magnetized by the theoretical prospect of being wedded to an eminent man, she cannot help, when poverty comes, putting herself first: 'What is to become of me — of us?'

(Contrast Marian to Jasper: 'And why shouldn't I go on writing for myself — for us?' Amy's correction is a tactical cover-up; Marian's a generous afterthought.) Amy, released from her husband's restrictions, mutates into a perfect high-society animal — purring, glossy, beautifully groomed, but always with a latent hint of savagery as soon as she senses a threat. However, her hardness to Reardon is qualified by impulses of guilt and compassion. And, for quite a time, she is dutiful even by Victorian standards — tiptoeing around the tiny flat, scrupulously attentive to her baby, servicing her husband with silence and meals. What most explains her conduct is her social background. Like her mother, she is instinctively committed to the dictates of respectability. Refined, intelligent, educated, she is tarnished and ultimately corroded by the customary responses of her class. Eventually Reardon realizes this, feeling that 'It was entirely natural that she shrank at the test of squalid suffering'.[53] Given the book's emphasis on the debasing power of penury, Amy's flight to security and comfort is at least comprehensible. Her behaviour is not so much morally outrageous as socially commonplace.

Jasper, too, is no prodigy of evil — but Jasper's personality is a tricky subject that might best be looked into later. Switching for a moment to Reardon and Marian, we find that in their moral portraiture, too, the pigmentation is flecked. Marian is intense, fastidious and decent, but she has enough purely human urges to make her entirely credible. Though timid, she is no paragon of trusting innocence. 'Her candour was allied with clear insight', Gissing writes, 'into the possibilities of falsehood; she was not readily the victim of illusion.' This makes her temporary belief in Jasper the more poignant and the less straightforward: it points up the stubbornness of her emotional desires, as well as the tantalizing ambiguity of Jasper's overtures. Her dutifulness as a daughter, too, is carefully distinguished from conventional submission. Though patient to a fault with her fractious father, she resists his sly and presumptuous parleys when he thinks she has become an heiress. Money fortifies her self-respect. And yet, at the same time, her attachment to Jasper makes her 'compromise with her strict sense of honour'. She would even find it acceptable, we are told, if he pleaded with her 'to neglect her parents for the sake of being his wife. Love excuses everything, and his selfishness would have been easily lost sight of in the assurance that he still desired her'. Marian responds intensely to

Jasper's embraces because what he seems to offer is romantic liberation: 'All the pedantry of her daily toil slipped away like a cumbrous garment'.[54]

Similarly wounded, Edwin Reardon reacts with more self-pity than Marian and less resilience. As Gissing told Bertz, 'Reardon ... has the *beau rôle*'; yet few leading men could be less charismatic. Reardon is characterized quite deliberately as 'a weak and sensitive man' or, in another authorial formulation, a man of 'aesthetic sensibility' allied to 'moral weakness'.[55] This weakness is not lack of principle but rather a shortage of executive power. An exhausted, self-torturing perfectionist, he requires long stretches of time and serenity, as well as large doses of connubial affection, to achieve his well-crafted but modest productions. Thrown into the arena of the modern market, he has no chance against the literary lions who entertain the mass audience. Yet Reardon refuses to go down to defeat with the stoic taciturnity of a martyr. Instead he cries out in anxiety and embitterment, vacillates with his wife between bluster and pleading, daydreams, despairs and then frantically resumes his doomed efforts to postpone his demise. The author firmly resists the temptation to idealize his disintegrating hero. Amy's snappish impatience with her husband is rendered quite as understandable as his moral resentment of her.

Nevertheless, we never lose sight of the fact that Reardon is genuinely a victim of an unjust commercial system. In a penetrating passage at the start of Volume 3, Gissing explains how Reardon survives, after the traumatic parting from Amy, 'by force of commiserating his own lot'. According to conventional moral thinking, there are two distinct categories of victim — those who are genuinely deserving of pity and those who indulge in self-pity. Gissing, however, appreciates that these two categories are often one. Reardon dramatizes his own catastrophe — haunting the streets where his wife is staying, wallowing in elegiac poetry, seeking out the poorest eating-houses, even staring at his image in shop mirrors 'with pleasurable contempt'. Only a facile moral perception would condemn these gestures as *mere* self-pity. Reardon really is in a doleful predicament — impoverished by his scruples, deserted by his wife, virtually bereft of sympathetic friends. It is idle to expect, Gissing seems to say, that those in a pitiable situation should never draw attention to it themselves. On the contrary, that is their best means of survival. A similar emotional pattern emerges in the case of the cantankerous Yule. A monster of domestic asperity, Yule never wins our empathy like Reardon, yet he too, in his plodding and painstaking way, is a casualty of the commercial incursion. Yule, who has very few pleasures in life, is a positive epicure in self-commiseration. Eventually his darkest fears materialize and he learns that he is certainly going blind. Even here, though, the author refuses to remit his sharp scrutiny of Yule's crippled spirit. Announcing his fate to Marian, Yule ghoulishly insists on extracting from her the maximum terror and pity; his speech concludes, Gissing grimly records, 'his voice tremulous with self-compassion'.[56] Again, in view of Yule's history and future, a contemptuously smiling response to this passage would scarcely be appropriate. Yule is disgraceful, but he has indeed suffered; not long after this conversation, he goes blind and dies. The man is undoubtedly pathetic — in every sense of the word.

Despite its almost diagrammatic structure, and the closeness of its thesis to Gissing's own emotions, the characterization in *New Grub Street* is both subtle and unsentimental. Even Dora, an unfailingly kindly girl, is shown to be but human in her self-regard. After Harold Biffen's suicide, Dora awaits further information from Whelpdale, thinking 'more of that gentleman's visit than of the event that was to occasion it'. As in all Gissing's fiction, love is egotistic. As usual, too, there is much shrewd perception of the minor psychological quirks of jealousy and despair. When Biffen tells Reardon that, earlier in the day, he passed Amy, with Milvain, in Tottenham Court Road, Reardon demands incredulously, 'In Tottenham Court Road?' 'That was not the detail of the story', says Gissing, 'which chiefly held Reardon's attention, yet he did not purposely make a misleading remark. His mind involuntarily played this trick.' Soon afterwards, Reardon is abandoned by Amy, and again his mind for a moment slips a notch. Returning to the suddenly empty flat, he lights a fire against the cold: 'Whilst it burnt up he sat reading a torn portion of a newspaper, and became quite interested in the report of a commercial meeting in the City, a thing he would never have glanced at under ordinary circumstances.'[57] This trivial incident is more effective than any extravagant outburst. Reardon's emotions recoil in weariness from the fact that his life is now in ashes. His untypical absorption is doubly ironic in that it is precisely the commercial world that has led to his sitting there alone.

We need to say more about the commercial world, for a third major source of the novel's vigour, in addition to its structure and its psychological subtlety, is the way it taps energies already released in Gissing's treatment of this subject. The struggling writers are hedged around by an ominous throng of familiar obsessions. Haggling tradesmen buy books and furniture; gambling card-players drive Reardon to distraction. Whelpdale, his novel refused, has to contemplate life as a commission-agent. Reardon actually takes a job as a clerk: 'His face burned, his tongue was parched'. In a commercial society, imaginative literature is of marginal importance to the mass of the people. When Biffen laments to a dealer in oil that all his books have been burnt in a fire, the other responds sympathetically: 'Your account-books! Dear, dear! — and what might your business be?' To pull through, literature must adapt to the market. Repeatedly, the dodges of advertising are recommended by Jasper Milvain, who can see the point of a catchy title (Reardon, conversely, never thinks of a title until the book has been completed). Jasper can also appreciate the potency of well-placed and well-timed reviews. Curtly rejected in his well-meant offer to turn out a laudatory notice for Reardon, he writes it anyway after Reardon's death — and uses it to seduce his widow.[58]

Periodicals often figure prominently in Gissing, and nearly always with unsavoury connections. In *Demos* Mutimer's hench-man, Keene, is a journalist who serves him by circulating libel. In both *Born in Exile* and *Our Friend the Charlatan* the hero is discredited by the ruinous discovery of a compromising article in a magazine. *New Grub Street* is the richest repository of this deeply imprinted preoccupation. Its pages are packed with periodical titles — fictional for the most part, though two of them, *The West End* and *All Sorts*, were adopted by real magazines. There is *The Study*, rather formal and old-fashioned, deserted by its editor, the malicious Fadge, for the more contemporary pages of *The Current* (eventually edited by Jasper Milvain, now completely in the swim). There is the *Wayside*, which Reardon falls beside when they turn down his article on Pliny, but from which he gets posthumous recompense when commemorated by Jasper. There is the *Will o' the Wisp*, to which Jasper contributes a slanderous Saturday causerie, and the *Balance*, in which, inappropriately, Alfred Yule makes 'a savage assault upon Fadge'. The list of others is almost endless — the *English Girl* and the *Young Lady's Favourite*, the *Evening Budget* and the *Shropshire Weekly Herald*, and *Chat*, which Whelpdale reduces to *Chit-Chat*. This 'multiplication of ephemerides' (Yule's phrase) is a symptom of changes in the literary market. For Gissing, periodicals were substitutes for books. The wealthy philistine John Yule, who has made his money in paper manufacture, reads little else but newspapers. The ill-educated wife of Alfred Yule sits turning the pages of a coloured magazine. Characters are differentiated by their views on periodical literature. Alfred Yule gains credit with his contention that 'journalism is the destruction of prose style'; he loses it by coveting Marian's money for the purpose of starting up a literary monthly, to be used as an outlet for his grudges. Amy, too, condemns herself by her growing attention to the ephemeral press. Capable of forming purely literary judgements, she switches her attention to financial matters — the implications of gossip columns, 'the practical conduct of journals and magazines'. After leaving her husband she turns even more to 'specialism popularised': pieces on philosophy and social science, potted versions of Darwin or Spencer. Amy reads writing about writing, becomes proficient in substitute achievement. The demands of periodicals encourage this, not only for readers but also for writers. *New Grub Street* is full of journalistic incest, the kind of barren, self-predatory activity that Marian despairs of in the British Museum. Jasper, who studies audiences in order to make his goods fit the consumer, converts this research to more immediate account by producing an article on 'Typical readers' — malicious, satirical, highly successful; a masterpiece of ingrown enterprise. Whelpdale, having failed as a novelist, sets up shop as a literary adviser, instructing failed novelists how to publish and write. Another example is the journalist Sykes: a drunkard whose literary career has dried up, he rescues himself by recounting his scrapes ('Through the Wilds of Literary London') in the pages of a regional paper.[59] Literature about literature, failure metamorphosed into success. Oddly, the supreme example of this is the novel *New Grub Street* itself.

The symptoms of commercialization are consistent with those that appear elsewhere; so too is the historical diagnosis. Throughout the novel the squalors of the present are contrasted with the relative decencies of the past. In the literary sphere the past is represented first by the world of Samuel Johnson, whose own Grub Street, though savagely competitive, was not quite so sordidly commercialized. The *new* Grub Street, Gissing felt, lacked the redeeming features of the old. The title of his book is a sardonic signpost pointing towards a historical chasm rather than an unbroken pathway. Gissing explained to his friend Bertz that when Johnson had defined 'Grub Street' in his dictionary, he had added a Greek quotation meaning 'Hail, O Ithaca! Amidst joys and bitter pains, I gladly come to thy earth'. Gissing commented,

'Is not this delicious? Poor old Sam, rejoicing to have got so far in his Dictionary, and greeting the name "Grub Street" as that of his native land'. Johnson's quotation reveals him as feeling, in the literal sense, nostalgic for Grub Street. So was Gissing: but for Johnson's, not his own. His title, he told Bertz, was not 'altogether' meant contemptuously. One reason is that some of the characters — pre-eminently Reardon, but also Yule — still hanker after Johnson's milieu. All that Jasper has picked up from Johnson is his praise of dogged application.[60]

The past is represented secondly by the non-commercial grandeur of the classics. Ithaca, as Reardon's death scene shows, is no longer a metaphor for Grub Street but a yearningly dreamed alternative to it. Reardon discovers that the classics aren't commercial, but this, for him, is part of their attraction. 'Yes, yes', he reflects, reading the *Odyssey*; 'that was not written at so many pages a day.' He and Biffen seek temporary refuge from poverty by discussing Greek metres or Euripides' fragments. He plans to go back to Greece once more, to escape from hardship, frustration and struggle. But as he lies dying he dreams of a ship sailing south to the Ionian islands and is grieved to learn that Ithaca 'had been passed in the hours of darkness'. He awakes to the rented shores of Brighton: 'The glory vanished. He lay once more a sick man in a hired chamber, longing for the dull English dawn.'[61]

The objections to commercialism in *New Grub Street* are also consonant with those in the rest of Gissing's work. He hated commercialism, we recall, partly because it fomented strife and partly because it pandered to the masses. He also regarded it as antipathetic to the healthy purity of nature. This last is admittedly less important in the novel, though Jasper's progress from the leafy lanes of Finden to the metropolitan corridors of power is no doubt symbolically significant: taking the train from the country at the end of Chapter 3, he 'smiled at the last glimpse of the familiar fields, and began to think of something he had decided to write for *The West End*'. Reardon's attack on London anticipates *The Whirlpool*, and his and Biffen's responsiveness to nature contrasts with Amy's preference for the city.[62] The commercially minded are also urban. More important, they are conquerors in a world of strife. It is no accident that Amy reads Darwin and Spencer. In the elemental struggles of the literary jungle, the survivors only prosper if the failures die out. Some of the characters are linked like pendants, one rising to the rhythm of the other's fall. On the day Yule leaves London, blind and broken, a celebration appears of Clement Fadge — at an earlier period his protégé, later his malevolent rival. Both Whelpdale and Biffen begin by writing commercially fruitless realistic fiction, but while Biffen perseveres into penury, Whelpdale shoots off into lucrative fraud. Though both at first are sexually lonely, Whelpdale succeeds in winning Dora: his bouncy announcement of the joyful tidings tips Biffen into suicide. Ironically, the news of Biffen's death is used as a pretext by Amy and Jasper for a meeting that consolidates their mutual attraction. Whelpdale's success prompts Biffen's suicide; Biffen's suicide clinches Jasper's success. The most sustained personal combat is that between Jasper and Reardon; and since Jasper's reward is Reardon's wife, what begins as a contrast of literary outlooks takes on the appearance of a fight for a mate. The superimposition of sexual struggle on a narrative concerned with commercial strife can be seen in the quasi-erotic reproaches that Amy directs at her wilting spouse. 'Don't you feel it's rather unmanly?' she remarks, of his failure to satisfy her material desires; and Reardon agrees that it is. He fears that his 'mental impotence' has cost him not only his livelihood but also Amy's love. As he worries about this in the watches of the night, 'The soft breathing of Amy at his side, the contact of her warm limbs, often filled him with intolerable dread'.[63] Financial collapse causes sexual estrangement; the night before they separate, the couple sleep in different beds. The physical aspects of competitive struggle also embrace the question of health. In the drizzly and fog-choked world of *New Grub Street* it is indeed survival of the fittest. While the statuesque Amy is 'gloriously strong', the crumbling Marian has a 'morbid' complexion and suffers from nervous headaches.[64] Reardon is a mournful anthology of ailments — coughs, colds, sore throats, lumbagoes. The contrasts aren't merely sentimental, for Gissing attributes ill health to hardship, both physical (leaky boots, insufficient food) and mental (anxiety, depression, disappointment). The effect, however, is to suggest that survival, physically as well as morally, is a privilege of the coarser-fibred.

Gissing's third objection to commercialism was that it flattered the masses. The anonymous mass audience weighs heavily in the novel, held in contempt by all the main characters, though some, like Jasper, also wish to exploit it. The most measured and successful attempt to do so is that of Whelpdale with his paper *Chit-Chat*, addressed to the 'quarter-educated' and containing no article longer than two inches.[65] Perhaps the best way of assessing the significance of differing attitudes towards the public is by considering them as a factor in the final reason for the novel's power — its skilful reconciliation of its social and personal themes. In books like *Demos* Gissing had argued that personal conduct could not be detached from public policy. He was clumsy, however, in soldering the links. In *New Grub Street* he effects a smoother continuity between the public and the private — or rather between the public (one's literary career), the social (one's appearance at fashionable occasions) and the personal (one's marital and private life). In the novel's moral architecture, the office is connected with the drawing-room, which in turn communicates with the bedroom. The passages between these three areas are no secret. In a commercial society, a lucrative career depends on a flourishing social life; a flourishing social life in turn depends on a prosperous marriage. Behind these crude economic realities are far-reaching moral and emotional implications. Essentially, the novel suggests, the trading attitude to literature is bound to carry over into personal relations. Those who neglect literary value for the sake of money and social esteem will not only be mercenary in private life, they will also display two other faults: first, capitulation to public opinion; secondly, insincerity and dishonesty.

Public opinion: in Gissing's view there was a deep connection between supplying the wants of the vulgar masses and appeasing the whims of a respectable élite. Though the public in question might not be the same, the underlying mentality was. It involved a surrender of individual judgement, an abject deference to prevailing demands. Those who adopted as their literary starting-point 'What do the masses want to read?' would take as their be-all and end-all in conduct 'What will people think?' Amy Reardon is a case in point. Her mother is of the 'multitudinous kind' who 'lived only in the opinion of other people. What others would say was her ceaseless preoccupation. She had never conceived of life as something proper to the individual'. Amy is intellectually superior to this standpoint but lacks courage to act on her convictions. Arguing with Reardon, she is constantly apprehensive that their poverty will be publicly talked about, and advises him to forestall such detraction by profitably writing for the masses. Jasper, who likewise believes that intellectuals are justified in catering to the mob, is similarly nervous about public opinion, despite his façade of bold frankness. He guards his tongue in his sisters' company, trims his conversation to flatter his hearers, and carefully avoids putting down in writing any statements that might be used against him. He cultivates a 'diplomatic character' and has 'a scent for the prudent course'; ultimately, he convinces himself 'that he cannot afford to despise anything that the world sanctions'.[66] Jasper's final public gesture is to frown down his pretty but prattling new wife when she touches on a perilous story. Characteristically, in both print and talk, he assesses his audience.

Another moral corollary of handing over one's judgement to the public is being too easily influenced. Amy is affected by recent impressions just as much as by market trends. Her husband extends her mind in one way, Jasper's magnetism pulls it another. At home she is even 'subtly influenced' by her mother's insistence that her husband is mad. Jasper, conversely, is deeply disturbed when Amy seems to slight his choice of fiancée. By contrast, characters like Reardon and Marian show remarkable fidelity and consistency, in both literary judgement and personal affection. At the opposite extreme from Amy's mother is Biffen, who cares nothing about reviews or readers and finds drawing-room talk an ordeal. It is not that Biffen is a strident rebel: he is scrupulously well-mannered and tries hard to observe propriety of dress. Intellectually, however, he is fiercely independent. This is what Amy pretends to be, but in truth she is not only socially but mentally acquiescent.[67]

Gissing, then, sees an ignominious affinity between serving up literary fare for the masses and waiting on the words of distinguished diners-out. At times, indeed, these two tyrannous publics seem to be almost the same. Biffen speaks of best-selling novelists who 'are in touch with the reading multitude; they have the sentiments of the respectable'. Jasper and Dora see 'a copy of *Chit-Chat* in the hands of an obese and well-dressed man'.[68] As elsewhere in Gissing, plutocratic vacuity keeps company with impoverished ignorance. The commercial mentality, supplying these publics, is cowardly, servile and quite probably insincere. Jasper and Amy are perfectly aware of the limitations of public opinion; but in practice they defer to what in theory they despise. This insincerity is a final link between the novel's social analysis and its treatment of personal relations. Jasper and Amy, in the Ovidian phrase, see and approve the higher course while following the lower.[69] This is true in both literature and life. Amy's discerning intelligence decamps from literary appraisal to commercial assessment. Perceiving that *The Optimist* was unworthy of Edwin, she still exhorts him to write for the market; similarly, though uneasy in conscience, she still makes off to her mother's. Jasper, too, has considerable potential which is ultimately ruined by insincerity — but in his case this is doubly interesting since his pose is one of brutal candour.

The opening scene of *New Grub Street* sketches the essential lineaments of Jasper (as also of his two sisters). As the clock strikes eight, he cheerfully remarks that a man is being hanged at that moment in London (this opening was significant to Gissing: it was earlier recorded in his scrapbook).[70] His sisters immediately object: Maud does not want to hear about such things; Dora is disturbed by her brother's tone. Characteristically, Jasper justifies his flippancy: what better 'use' could he make of this fact; indignation or misery would not be 'profitable' emotions. He adds that his tone 'needs no justification' because it was 'spontaneous'. We have here Jasper's character in epitome: a brusque acceptance of the fall of others, a competitive attitude to human affairs (another's calamity is a 'consolation' to him).[71] At this stage, though, the potential nastiness of his views is apparently excused by his self-awareness. Admitting that his feelings are not exalted, he enters the defence of frank self-interest. For almost the first two-thirds of the book, his cynicism is mitigated, for the majority of readers, by his cheerful acknowledgement of what he is doing. Gradually, however, our responses change. There is no single turning-point, though the first mention of Miss Rupert, in Chapter 22, is an ominous moral creak. Eventually, Jasper's self-awareness only makes him more contemptible. Able to recognize decency (in the person of Marian Yule), even to be moved by it, he abandons it for profitable dishonesty. This personal behaviour is the direct equivalent of his attitude towards literature, in which, though intelligently alert to merit, he commits himself to money-spinning trash.

Jasper Milvain's is a masterly portrait of subtle deterioration. Fundamentally insincere, he has to find means of reconciling his spontaneous responses with his calculated acts. In the case of literature he accomplishes this through an oxymoronic vocabulary: he praises 'good, coarse, marketable stuff ', 'the genius of vulgarity', 'Honest journey-work ... rubbish ... of fine quality', 'a wholesome commonplace'. More generally, he cultivates a tone of apparently self-critical candour. Continually speaking 'frankly' and 'simply', full of locutions like 'to tell the truth' and 'to put it plainly', he heads off attacks on his stratagems by briskly confessing them first. Jasper's technique might be summarized as 'candour equals self-absolution'. It enables him to justify himself while claiming that he offers no justification. More important, it enables him to lie while gaining credit for the truth.

For of course, while always making a show of putting his cards on the table, he is careful to keep quite a few up his sleeve. Jasper degenerates in the course of the novel as the logic of his specious position is worked out. At first his frankness has a genuine connection with his boyish enthusiasm and vigour. Later he exploits it more consciously, luring Marian with 'the unusual openness of his talk', speaking not candidly but 'in a tone of candour'.[72] Jasper's end is implicit in his beginning. His treatment of Marian is ominously latent in his literary manifesto.

New Grub Street takes for granted that literary values are applicable to life. When books are converted to commodities, people are reduced to investments. Gissing facilitates the association by describing literature in moral terms. Reardon shrinks 'from conscious insincerity of workmanship'. Yule might have been more successful had he 'been content to manufacture a novel or a play with due disregard for literary honour' (like his rival Fadge, perhaps, who specializes in 'malicious flippancy'). Biffen tries to write without the suggestion 'of any point of view save that of honest reporting'. He labours over *Mr Bailey, Grocer* 'patiently, affectionately, scrupulously'. Biffen, of course, is a self-styled realist and Reardon, too, though repelled by Biffen's subject, is 'a psychological realist in the sphere of culture'. In 1895 Gissing published an article on 'The place of realism in fiction'. After making a number of telling distinctions, he concluded by defining realism as 'nothing more than artistic sincerity in the portrayal of contemporary life'.[73] In so far as sincerity is a moral attribute, realism, then, is a literary movement with moral connotations. The relevance to *New Grub Street* is inescapable. Reardon and Biffen are realists not only as novelists but as honest individuals who insist on acknowledging unpleasant facts. The world of Amy and her mother is one of evasion and euphemism.[74] Several of Amy's arguments with Reardon turn on the question of 'realism' — about the admission of their economic plight and the most sensible adjustment to it. Both Amy and Jasper are proud of being 'practical', but their 'practicality' involves untruth. Biffen, hopelessly impractical in their view, is more honestly in touch with the real. Ironically, at the end of the book he allows himself to idealize Amy. The realist dies after fantasy-indulgence: 'He became the slave of his inflamed imagination.'[75]

New Grub Street, an imaginative melting-pot for a number of Gissing's most passionate concerns, is not only an informative sociological document but a skilfully structured psychological study whose social analysis is precisely embodied in its treatment of personal relations. Of course, it has some weaknesses. Written in just under ten weeks — though conceived and planned over a longer period — it occasionally has shoddy patches in the prose and moments of narrative abruptness. Sometimes, too, the tone is disrupted by embarrassingly personal notes: many of these Gissing eliminated when revising the book for a French translation.[76] Overwhelmingly, however, *New Grub Street* survives as a cogent indictment and a moving novel. A tribute to Gissing's will power — 'no book of mine', he later confessed, 'was regarded so hopelessly in the production' — it is deeply pessimistic in argument and structure. Its logic is that of a vicious circle: poverty demoralizes; the best escape from poverty is commercialism; but commercialism also demoralizes. Indeed it describes literal circles of frustration: Reardon's false starts and misleading resumptions — 'endless circling, perpetual beginning'; his fagged-out pacing in the darkness 'round the outer circle of Regent's Park'; and, at the hub of the novel's action, the great circle of the British Museum Reading-Room, with its figure wandering around the upper gallery like 'a black, lost soul'. In the last analysis, the power of *New Grub Street* is that of a pessimistic parable, an almost infernal conception of injustice. Schopenhauer once said that someone should write a 'tragic history of literature', showing how the truly enlightened authors passed their lives in poverty and misery 'while fame, honour, and wealth went to the unworthy'.[77] In *New Grub Street* Gissing wrote it.

4

Poverty, Intellect and Exile

I

A large part of Gissing's fiction takes place inside the minds of outsiders − artistic misfits, rejected lovers, the hopelessly aspiring. In more than the obvious sense it takes place inside his own mind, for he saw himself always as a natural stranger. He lacked, it is true, most of the customary credentials: he was not illegitimate nor homosexual, not Jewish, nor a genius, nor mad. Nevertheless, for much of his life he suffered from both alienation and exile; he felt himself outside all existing communities and doomed to exclusion from an ideal community − both 'unclassed' and 'born in exile'. The causes were complex, but a crucial clue is contained in a letter he wrote to Morley Roberts in 1894. Asserting that his books dealt with many social strata, he added, 'But what I desire to insist upon is this: that the most characteristic, the most important part of my work is that which deals with a class of young men distinctive of our time − well educated, fairly bred, *but without money*'. He went on to list some instances: 'Reardon, Biffen, Milvain, Peak, Earwaker, Elgar, Mallard' − most of them, he said, 'martyred by the fact of possessing uncommon endowments'.[1] This list − which, interestingly, cuts across the lines of explicit authorial approval − might easily be extended to other examples (Waymark, Kingcote and later Will Warburton) as well as to a comparable class of young women (Emily Hood, Rhoda Nunn, the Madden and Milvain sisters). What all these characters have in common, despite their obvious differences, is experience of class displacement. George Orwell once said that Gissing's central theme might be stated in just three words: 'not enough money'.[2] But to these we should append another three: 'too much intellect'. The typical Gissing protagonist is certainly cursed with a shortage of cash, but also with a surplus of brains. Exalted by culture, depressed by poverty, he suffers a double alienation. His exceptional intelligence and aspirations lift him above the majority of people, but his failure to prosper drags him down again — back into a wearing physical proximity to those from whose mental and emotional life he is irreversibly severed. This is the source of his sense of exclusion, the fundamental cause of his discontent. In simplified form we might state it as an equation: poverty plus intellect equals exile.

The equation is excessively simple, of course: it needs to be refined by additional terms. Still, it is a useful formula, and this chapter will argue that poverty and intellect, as well as being central topics in Gissing, are frequently interlocking concepts: properly combined, they provide the key to his permanent obsession with exile. The question of Gissing's own poverty is disputed. His sister, Ellen, anxious for the family image, complained that his hardships had been overstated. Frederic Harrison, keen to emphasize his own generosity, dismissed all talk of hunger and neglect as 'a myth that has grown up'. As it happens, there need be little dispute about Gissing's actual literary earnings, for he kept a detailed 'Account of books'. In 1884 — when, according to Ellen, he had already escaped from the only period 'which he spent in actual poverty and privation' — he earned just over £37. From 1888 to 1895 his earnings slowly but steadily increased, but even in his last years there were times of crisis: 1897, in which he earned less than £102, he dubbed 'the year of terror'.[3] Ledgers, however, cannot rule out further argument, for, as Gissing himself remarked in *Henry Ryecroft*, 'Poverty is of course a relative thing'. Victorian conceptions of poverty were rigorous: thousands of Gissing's submerged contemporaries would certainly have regarded his particular privations as luxury grievances. What matters is that Gissing felt himself to be poor, given his interests and aspirations; and this feeling was never transcended. 'Ceaseless torment about money', he groaned in 1900. 'And so it will be to the end.' In 1901, the year of his maximum earnings (£723), he announced that 'pauperdom stares me in the face' and offered as proof of his 'miserable' poverty the fact that he *never* bought a book.[4] Pauperdom, and in particular the Marylebone Workhouse, were subjects of appalled fascination for years. From 1884 to 1890 Gissing lived opposite that dismal institution, and in 1887 he even got the authorities to take him on a conducted tour. 'The workhouse is before me' became his watchword, chanted repeatedly at home and abroad. Though physically he moved out of Marylebone, in his mind it always hovered close.[5]

Poverty, for Gissing, was a psychological evil as much as a material one. He felt it keenly because of his nerves, but also, in his own view, because of his brains. After stating in *Henry Ryecroft* that poverty is relative, he continues, 'the term has reference, above all, to one's standing as an intellectual being'. A life of high culture demands a high income, but Gissing craved the first without having the second. Like Egremont in *Thyrza*, he discovered that poverty could not annul a 'birthright of brains'; as with Waymark in *The Unclassed*, there was that within him 'which accorded ill with the position made for him by circumstances'. Hosts of his characters are painfully skewered on precisely this discrepancy. Biffen in *New Grub Street* is a classic example: belonging 'to no class', he is 'rejected alike by his fellows in privation and by his equals in intellect'. It was with these, the culturally displaced persons, that Gissing most strongly sympathised. As Roberts said, 'The sort of poverty which crushed the aspiring is the keynote to the best work he did'.[6] If we try to identify the areas of pain that the pressures of poverty were able to produce, the first and most obvious was exclusion from culture from sheer inability to pay. Visiting museums and galleries on the Continent, Gissing found it hard to meet the entrance fees; at home he was barred from West End theatres unless, like Waymark, he would sacrifice a meal. 'Sacrifice — in no drawing-room sense of the word', says Henry Ryecroft by way of explanation of how he managed to obtain his books. An edition of Tibullus could only be purchased by giving up a plate of meat and vegetables. Books, says Ryecroft, were the only commodities on which he would willingly defray expense. Many of Gissing's characters, parched intellectuals, likewise long to have a binge on print. In *Eve's Ransom* Maurice Hilliard yields to extravagance by buying 'a finely illustrated folio, a treatise on the Cathedrals of France', while Eve Madeley only enjoys herself when she takes out a subscription to Mudie's. Without money, and the leisure that money brings, intellectual desires prove punitive. Gilbert Grail in *Thyrza* and Virginia in *The Odd Women* are both the victims of nervous breakdowns from studies undertaken in impossible conditions — in his case, after thirteen hours a day in a factory; in hers, within a life of genteel scrimping.[7]

This leads us to a second pain of poverty intensified by intellect: the outrage of having to immerse oneself in uncongenial work. An idea jotted down in Gissing's scrapbook — 'The degrading effect of mechanical labour. A thoughtful man made a beast by ceaseless work' — is frequently touched on in his fiction, where characters like Waymark, Grail, Hilliard and Warburton, despite their diverse occupations, all share his conviction that repetitive labour is a substitute for a fully human life. Rising each day to face his teaching, Waymark feels like someone being sent to the scaffold. 'Let those smile at this as an exaggeration', says Gissing in a passage later omitted, 'who are so happy as never to have earned their bread by labour they loathed.'[8] The labour Gissing loathed was journalism and the tutoring of private students — not, perhaps, the perfect paradigm of mindless, mechanical and soiling toil, though to Gissing that is evidently how it felt.

A third penalty imposed by poverty was not just uncongenial work but rebarbative human beings. 'You know what it is', says Waymark to Casti, 'to have to do exclusively with fools and brutes, to rave under the vile restraints of Philistine sur-roundings.' The friendship between these two men was based on that between Gissing and Bertz, to whom Gissing wrote many years later: 'we are for ever at the mercy of ignoble creatures, and are forced to live in their hateful proximity.' Life in London lodgings left Gissing with a horror of the snooping, violence and merriment of his neighbours, with whom, like Ryecroft, he 'seldom had any but the slightest intercourse'. A fraught-nerved recoil from their rackety cohabitants is the norm among Gissing's studious lodgers. Golding finds the Pettindund uproar 'intolerable', Kingcote dreads the sight of his landlady's family: 'people of that class', he explains to his sister, 'are a species of dirty object, much to be avoided'. Although such scorn offers temporary relief, Gissing's characters are disturbed by their own responses, quite as much as by the maddening hullabaloo. Kingcote knows that his superior culture 'should have endowed him with tolerant forbearance'; Clara Hewett in *The Nether World* feels herself an outcast even among those 'whose swarming aroused her disgust'.[9] In addition to troublesome feelings of repugnance was the problem of humiliation. Outsiders might well make little distinc-tion between the gifted misfit and his threadbare milieu. 'The one thing I can't stand', says a character in 'A Capitalist', 'is to feel that I am looked down upon.' Gissing would certainly have understood: always hypersensitive to careless condescension, he often suspected that his social superiors (the Frederic Harrisons, for instance) were treating him with disrespect.[10] The phenomenon of shame by association is of paramount importance in *Born in Exile*, where the stubborn tap-root of Peak's discontent is his kinship with vulgarity.

Another source of suffering for the impoverished intellectual was the corollary of enforced proximity to the vulgar — enforced exclusion from the cultured. 'I have the feeling', Gissing wrote in

1891, two months before starting *Born in Exile*, 'of being deserted by all who ought to be my companions: but then these miseries are useful in giving a peculiar originality to my work.' A similar attempt to find solace for his fate can be glimpsed through Gissing's identification with illustrious precedents in exile — especially Johnson, whose early poverty cut him off from his intellectual peers. In *The Nether World* Gissing interrupts the narrative to retail the story of how Edward Cave, publisher of the *Gentleman's Magazine*, once entertained an aristocratic guest who spoke warmly of Johnson's writings; unbeknown to this guest, Johnson himself was having his dinner behind a screen, 'because of his unpresentable costume', and reacted with delight. This passage has more relevance to Gissing's own emotions than to any developments in *The Nether World*. Poverty, hunger and a social exclusion so extreme that the victim is literally screened off — these elements, together with the compensatory power of literary rather than social repute, and the wounded awareness of inappropriate dress, would have leaped to Gissing's attention. In a diary entry for 1890 there is an interesting sidelight on the choice of this story. Returning by ship from Italy, Gissing discovered that his name was known to a clergyman travelling in the first class. 'This is symbolical of my life', he wrote. 'It is the first class people who know me, while I myself am always compelled to associate with the second class'.[11] The parallel with Johnson is manifest: commended as an author by the upper class, but exiled as a social being.

A final pressure point for the cultured near-pauper, wincingly felt throughout all Gissing's work, is the difficulty of marriage. Gissing was convinced that 'educated English girls *will* not face poverty in marriage, and to them anything under £400 a year is serious poverty'.[12] Given this hopeless assumption, however, all the alternatives become unrewarding, as Gissing demonstrated in *New Grub Street* (and went on to prove in his life). A respectable wife reluctant to face poverty is likely to desert her husband (Amy); a work-girl makes him bitter by crippling his career (Mrs Yule); and no wife at all brings only frustration, and possibly suicide (Biffen). Of all the misfortunes of middle-class poverty, exclusion from the comforts of a suitable marriage was, in Gissing's view, the sharpest.

These, then, are the outstanding ways in which poverty imposes alienation or exile on the Gissing protagonist. All, we notice, are relative afflictions — relative to the cultural refinement of their victim. Gissing would not have denied, of course, that poverty also brought absolute miseries. Many are illustrated in *The Nether World*: physical discomfort, inconvenience and hardship; injury to health, including deformity, caused by hard labour and foul conditions; a far higher death rate, especially of infants; a much greater pressure, at times irresistible, to resort to drink or crime.[13] Evils like these were no respecters of character or intellect. Nor were the most oppressive of all — hunger and starvation. Since, in his twenties, Gissing knew both, food soon became a consuming obsession in his work as well as his life. An unmistakably personal note about 'the first terrible pangs of hunger' is plaintively sounded in *Workers in the Dawn* and continued in *The Unclassed*. Unable to afford nutritious food, Gissing had recourse to cheap substitutes — desiccated soup, potatoes in dripping — and, at times, to vegetarianism, which he urged on his brother with a convert's zeal, even posting him a specimen lentil.[14] The reaction, when it came, was sour and explosive. Repulsed by pulses and 'windy insufficiencies', he came to prize a diet, in Roberts's words, of 'gross abundance' — 'of oil and grease and fatness'. In his fiction, hot, nourishing, meaty meals — like Cheeseman's beefsteak pudding in *A Life's Morning* — are served up at moments of expansive escape from the pinchings of poverty. A vegetarian regime is always connected with penury and self-delusion. The eponymous 'Poor Gentleman' resorts to it; so does a clerk in the story 'Simple Simon' who, 'losing flesh and accumulating bile', consults a doctor and is bluntly told, 'Eat and drink like other men, or die!' Virginia in *The Odd Women* is an impoverished vegetarian: plied with choice beef by Rhoda Nunn, she brightens wonderfully.[15] Square meals, in Gissing's view, were the basis of contentment. 'You do not want medicine', he instructed Bertz; 'you want *good food*.' Notoriously, when he lived with Gabrielle, whose mother deprived him of his bacon and eggs, he complained with neurotic futility of his diet, facetiously requesting his friend Dr Hick to send him a slice of roast beef in a letter, and eventually hurrying back to England, to be fattened at a sanatorium.[16]

Hunger was an absolute evil of poverty, but even hunger could have various psychological effects — as Gissing's own history shows. In his fiction, once starvation has been averted, the benefits of eating become relative to the eater. His story 'An Inspiration' shows a salesman's character transformed and fortified by a fine meal. Dining out, says Maurice Hilliard in *Eve's Ransom*, is a potent civilizing influence.[17] But not everyone, of course, can afford to dine out: civilization depends on money.

Gissing believed this, but went even further. In his view, most virtues depended on money: poverty demoralized. For this proposition, as for many others, Gissing found support in Johnson, from whom he quotes twice in *Henry Ryecroft*. Ryecroft argues that the evils of poverty go beyond personal deprivation, for poverty inhibits the exercise of kindness and companionship. 'It would scarce be an exaggeration', he concludes, 'to say that there is no moral good which has not to be paid for in coin of the realm.' Such assertions stretch back a long way in Gissing. 'Put money in thy purse', we are told in *A Life's Morning*; '... for, as the world is ordered, to lack current coin is to lack the privileges of humanity, and indigence is the death of the soul'. In the same novel Mrs Baxendale declares: 'Men and women go to their graves in wretchedness who might have done noble things with an extra pound a week to live upon. It does not sound lofty doctrine, does it? But I have vast faith in the extra pound a week.'[18] That money ennobles and that poverty degrades becomes a central theme in *The Nether World*; by *New Grub Street* it becomes obsessional.

Perhaps we should examine this idea more closely. Expressed for instance in Waymark's aphorism — 'Money means virtue; the lack of it is vice' — it might suggest that in Gissing the poor are vicious and the moneyed virtuous. In fact, no such correlation obtains. Many of Gissing's poorest characters — Biffen in *New Grub Street*, Emma in *Demos*, Sidney in *The Nether World* — are also his most principled. Money brings out the worst in others — Golding, Mutimer, the French sisters of *In the Year of Jubilee*. What's more, the opinion that poverty degrades is often the excuse of the morally shady. Though in *Henry Ryecroft* Gissing himself declares that one of the curses of poverty is that it leaves no right to be generous, in *The Crown of Life* an identical opinion is expressed by the blackmailer Daniel Otway. About poverty, Gissing was bitter but ambivalent. In *New Grub Street* the link between money and virtue is an article of faith for many of the characters — but most of all for Amy and Jasper, who blame poverty to exonerate themselves. What Gissing shows contradicts what he asserts. In the novel's final scene, lucratively married, Jasper announces that a struggle with poverty would have made him detestable: now, he is 'far from the possibility of being vicious'. This scene is placed straight after some cynical manoeuvres and Jasper's callous dismissal of Marian. As Dora says to Jasper shortly before, 'Who ever disputed the value of money? But there are things one mustn't sacrifice to gain it'.[19]

If money is no guarantee of decency, and the shortage of it can be morally resisted, in what sense does poverty demoralize? In so far as it affects the worthier characters, it seems to do so by weakening morale rather than debasing morality. Reardon knows it as 'the chilling of brain and heart ... the dread feeling of helplessness'. 'As a poor devil', he admits, 'I may live nobly; but one happens to be made with faculties of enjoyment, and those have to fall into atrophy.' Poverty is less a detonator of evil than a sapper of confidence and a cause of depression. Hence, when money does confer benefits — as with Rolfe in *The Whirlpool* or Marian in *New Grub Street* — it brings liberty and a balm for bruised self-respect.[20] Poverty, in short, hamstrings positive qualities — friendship, initiative, openness, generosity. It cripples rather than corrupts.

This being so, the damage wrought by poverty is in direct proportion to the qualities it frustrates. Once again material adversity is relative: it bears more heavily on the conscientious, the sensitive, the cultured. According to Roberts, Gissing's 'natural sympathy was only for those whom he could imagine to be his mental fellows'. Such he pitied, although 'in a way all this was nothing but translated self-pity'. Quite probably Gissing would not have denied this: he knew himself reasonably well and he also knew that, for Schopenhauer, all pity was translated self-pity — and that was the basis of morality.[21] Although it is possible to find passages in Gissing expressing sympathy for the poor as a whole, his deepest responses are clearly aroused by those like the heroine of 'An Old Maid's Triumph', who, 'with the instincts and desires of the educated class, had never allowed herself one single indulgence'. Shocked to discover that the working classes did not repine against poverty as he did, Gissing concluded that they did not suffer. A similar discovery and an identical conclusion are frequently enunciated in his work — by Emily in *A Life's Morning*, say, or by Wyvern and Adela in *Demos*. Perhaps his most uncompromising statement of this view occurs in his story 'A Poor Gentleman':

> An educated man forced to live among the lower classes arrives at many interesting conclusions with regard to them; one conclusion long since fixed in Mr. Tymperley's mind was that the "suffering" of those classes is very much exaggerated by outsiders using a criterion quite inapplicable. He saw around him a world of coarse jollity, of contented labour, and of brutal apathy. It seemed to him more than probable that the only person in the street conscious of poverty, and suffering under it, was himself.[22]

Stretched to an extreme, as it sometimes is, this opinion can contort into 'Wyvernism' — the theory of the opinionated parson in *Demos* that 'happiness is evenly distributed among all classes and conditions'. Inconsistently maintained in *Demos* itself, this theory makes nonsense of large chunks of Gissing's fiction. In *The Nether World*, written two years later, Sidney Kirkwood bitterly exclaims: 'Lives may be wasted — worse, far worse than wasted — just because there is no money. At this moment a whole world of men and women is in pain and sorrow — because they have no money. How often have we said that?' Gissing himself had said it often. Nevertheless, it was not usually a 'whole world' of people whom he showed to be suffering the sorrows of poverty, but a much smaller category closer to home. In his fiction, poverty is most sharply injurious to those possessed of intellect and cultural aspirations. It also hurts those with moral sensitivity, which for Gissing was linked — though not synonymous — with mental ability. In his critical study of Dickens, he comments wonderingly on the fact that his author 'very often associates kindness of disposition with lack of brains'. His own view was closer to that of Godwin Peak: 'ignorance and baseness ... speaking generally, go together'. Finally, of course, Gissing tended to identify intellectual ability with educational status. It followed that the miseries of material deprivation were experienced most acutely by the educated classes — perhaps only by them.

This conclusion was not held with absolute rigour. Nor were the connections that underpinned it. It is possible to find characters in Gissing who are morally scrupulous but not educated (for instance, Mary Woodruff in *In the Year of Jubilee*); intelligent but not educated or scrupulous (Joseph Snowdon in *The Nether World*); intelligent and educated but unscrupulous (Jasper in *New Grub Street*). By and large, though, the customary connections are maintained and Gissing is always most sympathetic to characters with his own mix of attributes. The gravest evil of poverty, for him, was that it imposed a cruel sense of exile on people who also possessed other qualities — who were, in his revealing formula, 'well educated, fairly bred, *but without money*'.[23]

I I

'Well educated': the importance in Gissing's work of intellectual cultivation must also be assessed. Few novelists have had a greater respect for the processes and results of learning, especially of literary culture. One could say with scarcely any exaggeration that Gissing's whole life was devoted to books. When he was not writing, he was usually reading. He read voraciously not only in English, but in French, German and Italian literature; though unacquainted with the Russian language, he continually returned to Russian novels (he reread Turgenev's *Fathers and Sons* six times); in the last years of his life he taught himself Spanish, and tackled Cervantes and Galdós.[24] He was also familiar with the Greek and Roman classics. The standard work on this subject is still *George Gissing, Classicist* by Samuel Vogt Gapp. According to Gapp, Gissing's knowledge of Greek 'appears to have been absolutely phenomenal'; his command of classic metres deserves to be called scholarly; he was strong on ancient history and knew some archaeology; but his acquaintance with Greek and Latin literature, though thorough and sensitive, was patchy.[25] As it happens, Gapp underestimates Gissing. His appraisal predated the publication of Gissing's commonplace book, his diary, and several collections of letters. In the case of almost every omission mentioned, it turns out that Gissing's reading of classical authors was more extensive and more sustained than Gapp was able to infer. It is not the case, for instance, that Gissing never refers to Hesiod, or Juvenal, or Suetonius, or Lucretius; that he perhaps never read Martial and scarcely knew Thucydides; that Ovid was only read late in his career, and Plutarch and Tacitus only earlier.[26] Nor is Gapp correct to suggest that Gissing read practically nothing about the present. His diary reveals an astonishing immersion in contemporary literature of all kinds, including popular and ephemeral fiction. And in preparation for some of his books he read widely in current sociology.

His novels, too, are those of an intellectual — in several different ways. His protagonists tend to be bookish and thoughtful, passionate amateurs of scholarship rather than academic specialists. His pages are studded with allusions to authors. Some, like Dante, Homer and Shakespeare, are quoted from repeatedly, but it is not unusual to find a Gissing character referring to Sir Thomas Browne's *Urn Burial* or reflecting fondly on his acquisition of 'the six folios of Muratori'. In Gissing's earlier work especially — when he was still inspired by vast study schemes — characters are ingenuously commended for the zeal and range of their learning. Hilda Meres, a 16-year-old in *Isabel Clarendon*, 'could render you an ode of Horace, could solve a quadratic equation, could explain to you the air-pump and the laws of chemical combination'. Annabel Newthorpe in *Thyrza* is less versatile, but even more determined. First discovered with a copy of Virgil, 'humming over dactylics', she later comes out with the remarkable declaration: 'A London season — and I still have Homer to read!' Like Edwin Reardon, Gissing produced books that 'dealt with no particular class of society (unless one makes a distinct class of people who have brains)', books with 'an intellectual fervour, appetising to a small section of refined readers'.[27] The characters share this intellectual fervour. Gissing's people take self-improvement seriously, and this includes cultural and mental as well as moral and psychological development. Most of his novels feature such development and in three — *Workers in the Dawn, A Life's Morning, The Emancipated* — it constitutes a primary theme.

Again and again Gissing sifts his characters according to their love of books. In *Henry Ryecroft* he cites with approval Johnson's belief that the difference 'between a lettered and an unlettered man' is as great as that 'between the living and the dead'. (In fact Johnson, quoting Aristotle, spoke rather of the learned and the unlearned: Gissing's version exceeds even Johnson's claim for the vitalizing power of literature.) In his fiction the most admired characters are those like Gilbert Grail in *Thyrza*, to whom a printed page is 'the fountain of life'; the most despised are those who themselves despise books, such as Jessie Cartwright in *A Life's Morning*.[28] For those dependent on literature, a library is a life-support system. Gilbert Grail nearly withers away when Egremont's library scheme terminates: for him, loss of Thyrza is fatally bound up with loss of his librarianship. Gissing was impressed in America by the free public library system, and pressed for its introduction in England after his return.[29] In his fiction, libraries of all kinds bulk large. A personal library was, he believed, 'an index to its owner's mind'. 'To know a man's chosen books', he told Gabrielle, 'is, in some degree, to know the man himself.' In *Workers in the Dawn* Mr Tollady's library is a guide to his good qualities, but Will Noble's only serves to classify his mental limitations. In *Thyrza* Gilbert Grail's bookcase — full of history, biography, poetry and fiction — indicates 'a mind of liberal intelligence'; his mother's — packed with products of the Church of the New Jerusalem — is a revelation of the opposite. Mutimer in *Demos* is comprehensively condemned because of his lopsided library: nothing of imaginative literature, only dogmatic and polemical works on social, religious and political topics — a more damaging extension of Will Noble's. In *The Whirlpool* Harvey Rolfe's library shelves are a kind of reverse geological section of his spiritual biography. At the top are the earliest deposits, school books and old volumes from his father; in the middle are 'dozens of French novels', washed up by 'a frothy season, when he boasted a cheap Gallicism'; at the bottom is a bedrock of serious works, acquired in maturity. Given the volume of reading in Gissing, it is scarcely surprising that public libraries are often key meeting-points. In *New Grub Street* Jasper first spots Marian in the British Museum Reading-Room; the friendship between Biffen and Reardon opens in a circulating library in Hastings. In *In the Year of Jubilee* an assignation in Teignmouth library, plus provocative dialogue about a book, leads directly to copulation between Tarrant and Nancy Lord.[30]

As this suggests, books and opinions about them are never purely cerebral matters in Gissing: they are psychologically symptomatic, or crucial to the working out of feeling. For Gissing, intellectual enthusiasm could never be divorced from emotional yearning. This was true of his own passion for the classics. As Samuel Vogt Gapp perceptively observed, Gissing's three main sources of joy — his childhood, his books and Mediterranean travel — were all connected in his mind with the classics. 'By some trick of memory', says Henry Ryecroft, 'I always associate school-boy work on the classics with a sense of warm and sunny days.' An illuminating remark, for Gissing's descriptions of classical scenes in life or literature are often bathed in golden light.[31] Moreover, what drew him so warmly to the classics was not philosophical or speculative writing, and certainly not textual analysis. What he wanted, as Gapp points out, was mellifluous expression of personal emotion: 'His favourite passages are almost without exception those noted for picturesqueness, for the suggestion or depiction of feeling.' He also used classical literature as a refuge, an escape from the harassing squalors of the present, and this was soon translated into a lust to flee to the antique locations themselves. Italy and Greece became Arcadian constructs, idealized lands of serenity and culture; Rome was 'the centre of the Universe'; the light of Greece was 'not of this world'.[32] For Gissing, appreciation of ancient literature had nothing to do with reluctant rote-learning or the practice of a worthy intellectual drill. On the contrary, it thrilled him profoundly.

We should not, of course, exaggerate the singularity of this response. Enveloping the classics in a rosy cloud of feeling was not uncommon in the nineteenth century. From Richard Jenkyns's *The Victorians and Ancient Greece*, we may learn how many features of Gissing's sensibility were shared by his contemporaries. Idealization of the Greek climate and the notion of a 'pilgrimage' to Greece; insistence on the aesthetic coarseness of the north; acknowledgement of the prestige of the classics because of their social and cultural exclusiveness, together with a zeal to introduce them to the masses; worship of Homer and contempt for science; enhanced respect for aristocracy and delight in the pastness of the past — all such attitudes, so typical of Gissing, were endemic to the classically inspired. That Gissing absorbed them is not really surprising: Owens College, after all, was partly set up as a classical bulwark, its ethos intended to leaven the effects of the commercial and the mundane.[33] What is surprising is the depth of Gissing's knowledge and the intensity of his commitment. But in any case his emotional investment in learning was not exhausted by his fervour for the classics. For him the whole idea of intellectual exertion had an almost erotic attraction.

The proof of this is the prevalence in his work of intellectual courtship. Gissing's lovers are stimulated by study; they put their heads together over books; it is certainly not a case with them of 'We read no more that day'.[34] In *Workers in the Dawn* Arthur Golding, as a child, pores over his letters in a rapture of affection for little Lizzie Clinkscales, who duly shows him favour with the present of a spelling-book. In *The Crown of Life* the mature Irene teaches herself Russian for Piers Otway, who responds with an offer of marriage. The lovers often lend one another books, or tempt each other with extracts. In *New Grub Street* Reardon brightens Amy up by reciting Odysseus's praise of Nausicaa, and she enthusiastically asks for more ('Oh, I like that!'). This improbable scene no doubt had its roots in Gissing's holiday rendition of the *Odyssey* to his sister Madge in 1888, as well as readings of Tennyson and Browning to Edith Underwood while writing *New Grub Street*.[35] When he met Gabrielle, the dream revived. 'Oh, darling, you and I will read much poetry together, in many languages!' he sighed to her, adding cautiously, 'As for Latin and Greek, well, life is too short; I shall never ask you to study the old tongues.' Within a couple of months, however, he was carried away with pedagogic ardour: 'Yes, and you shall learn to read Homer, my beloved. That, if anything can, will bring us yet nearer together.'[36]

Oddly, Gissing's most sustained account of a love affair of this kind is contained in a novel which, in this very letter, he contemptuously repudiates. Wilfrid Athel in *A Life's Morning* is

smitten with desire for the family governess on discovering that
she can read German. Greek, too, should therefore be within her
grasp, and one day, perhaps, he might hear her voice caressing
the hexameters. Before long − both of them deeply stirred by
a solo from an oratorio − Wilfrid declares his love for Emily
through a gloss on the literary connotations of her name. 'I could
not sleep,' he tells her, 'so I read of you till dawn in the Knightes
Tale.' His ideal is 'one heart, one brain'; he needs Emily for
completeness of both 'thought and desire'. However, after
defending his choice to his father ('Her intellectual tendencies are
the same as my own'), Wilfrid is forced away from Emily and
much later gets engaged to a girl called Beatrice, a comparatively
superficial *salon* beauty. Beatrice broods darkly on the threat of
Emily ('she was intellectual beyond ordinary women; for Wilfrid
that must have been a rich source of attraction') and tries to
consolidate her own position by offering to spend mornings in his
study. Although Wilfrid cheerily agrees, suggesting she can
'digest a blue-book' for him, this plan is exploded when, in
Bushey Park, he catches sight of a person reading and reflects
that 'a woman never looked more graceful than when walking
with her head bent over a book'. The woman is of course Emily,
and Wilfrid, casting a glance at the book, reopens their former
affair: ' "Are your tastes still the same, I wonder?" "It is Dante,"
she replied.' Wilfrid is stunned by the revelation that Emily now
reads Italian, but she explains 'unaffectedly', 'I have tried to keep
up the habit of study'. Their marriage follows rapidly, and their
honeymoon − naturally in Italy and Greece − puts the final seal
on their blessedness:

> 'Talk to me of Rome'; those were always her words when Wilfrid
> came to her side in the evening. 'Talk to me of Rome, as you alone
> can.' And as Wilfrid recalled their life in the world's holy of holies,
> she closed her eyes for the full rapture of the inner light, and her
> heart sang praise.[37]

Such for Gissing was the platonically perfect affair: love and
learning would joyously unite. But reality was disappointingly
different. Like Reardon with Amy, Gissing promised Gabrielle
that one day they would see Greece together; like the Reardons,
they never did. In *Henry Ryecroft* − written while with Gabrielle −
Gissing speaks sadly of his lifelong dream of shared appreciation
of literature, of 'sympathetic understanding'. 'Such harmony of
intelligences is the rarest thing', he concludes. 'To every man it

is decreed: thou shalt live alone.'³⁸ Anxious to believe that intellectual passion could guarantee rapture with a perfect partner, Gissing discovered the opposite. Since intellect segregated human beings, more often than not the dowry it brought was one of alienation.

The most important reasons for this were connected with poverty and class. The poorest classes, being the least educated, could easily appear the least intelligent. Of twenty-five entries on the lower classes recorded in Gissing's commonplace book, well over half insist on their ignorance and lack of understanding. Intellectuals are naturally élitist in Gissing. Irene's father in *The Crown of Life*, 'like all men of brains, had a good deal of the aristocratic temper'. Such cerebral aristocrats vary little in attitude. Some — like Hubert Eldon in *Demos* — are, when confronted with working people, chokingly antagonistic; others are merely awkward and constrained. Frequently Gissing's own narrative tone proclaims his aloofness from his unlettered characters. His merciless mimicry of their fashionable slang ('it fair mismerizes me', etc.), his sniffily pedantic annotation of their grammar ('the syntax of his periods was often anacoluthic'), are suggestive of a man wincing back from a specimen held up in verbal tweezers.³⁹ In a novel like *The Town Traveller* the rasping illiteracies of the characters are played off against the suavity of the narrator chiefly for comic purposes. Elsewhere the note of contempt is dominant. But always the impression given by Gissing is that learning and perception are forces of estrangement. The brainy are also lonely.

But intellect had an even greater disadvantage: in Gissing's opinion it could only flourish in a climate of financial security. For a long time he resisted this conclusion. He tried to believe that intellect could compensate for poverty, that art could be immune to material circumstance, that the physical world was of secondary importance, that body was subordinate to spirit. At the same time he was all too painfully aware of the crushing power of poverty. Concentration on external events was vulgar, ignoble and self-defeating — as Mutimer's case history was meant to show. Yet external events could cripple and frustrate, could stultify the inner life. This debate in Gissing — relevant to the tension between pessimism and will power — was never altogether resolved. But if anything he moved away from stoicism, from belief in the power of autonomous mind. Ryecroft recalls that while 'literally starving' he spent days reading at the British

Museum 'as disinterestedly as if I had been without a care!' But he adds that, through worry, agitation and fear, he has forgotten most of what he read.[40]

Attaching supreme importance to intellect, Gissing was also alert to the forces that inhibit its fulfilment. Hence his characteristic stress on the plight of intellectually ambitious protagonists entrammelled in the fetters of poverty. It is worth observing that not all such protagonists are strictly intellectual in their aspirations: though they usually are, they need not be of bookish or scholarly bent. What they must possess is imagination, some native urge to reflection or thought. Clara Hewett, of *The Nether World*, is an instance. Despite her 'unfortunate endowment of brains' — unfortunate because at odds with her station — she has no wish to become a student.[41] Nevertheless, her fierce originality, her capacity to formulate her discontent, give her access to the Gissing pantheon.

That intellect is only a relative good is shown by Gissing's treatment of education. An unashamed élitist, he believed that 'education is a thing of which only the few are capable'. Democracy was producing a 'host of the half-educated, characteristic and peril of our time'. Specimens of these, pushy and pretentious, spout and bluster in his later fiction, especially *In the Year of Jubilee*. But Gissing believed that even genuine education could do harm unless rooted in leisure and security, by generating longings that could never be assuaged. The Milvain sisters in *New Grub Street* are examples: the daughters of a country vet, they would have been happier if their education had been 'limited to the strictly needful'. Gissing adds: 'To the relatively poor (who are so much worse off than the poor absolutely) education is in most cases a mocking cruelty'. The sentiment was certainly one of his favourites. 'If only the schoolmaster could be kept away', cries Bernard Kingcote in *Isabel Clarendon*, contemplating the 'worthy clodhoppers' around him: they would then have no 'futile aspirations'. Consulted by his impoverished sister, Kingcote advises her not to grieve that she cannot give her children the education she would wish. Children born to 'day-long toil' will only despair if brought up for leisure. 'Do not heed the folly of those who say that culture is always a blessing; the truth is that, save under circumstances favourable to its enjoyment and extension, it is an unmitigated curse.' Expressed by a man of means and learning, such counsel might well seem ungenerous. But Kingcote sees himself as a casualty of culture — how much better, he tells a friend, if he had been born a clodhopper, too, 'and had never learned the half-knowledge which turns life sour!' In the context of the novel as a whole, such professions ring rather hollow. It is not only that we never see Kingcote — a trained medical student who after years of doing nothing eventually becomes the manager of a bookshop — being crucified by day-long toil. It is also that everywhere else he takes for granted, by the tone and content of his conversation, the superiority of learning. For instance, his ironic reassurance of Mrs Stratton that her robust, bumptious, mindless sons represent his 'ideal of education', makes no sense except on this assumption.[42]

Perhaps, though, the ironies of such a passage could better be interpreted as masochistic. They are rather like Harvey Rolfe's praise of Kipling, which H. G. Wells, among others, took literally.[43] These are the ironies of despair, directed at, as well as from, the speaker's personal ideal; they relieve the feelings of a man convinced that his values are both true and unattainable. The sardonic tone grows out of acknowledgement of a paradox that Gissing could never resolve. Intellectual and cultural self-improvement was of supreme importance for a human being. Yet the fruits of such improvement would always be blighted for those condemned to poverty. The two qualities, poverty and intellect, appeared to be in perpetual conflict: the result was perpetual exile.

I I I

So far the main outlines of the picture are clear. Poverty was in some ways an absolute evil, but more importantly a relative one — relative to the cultural refinement of its victim. Intellect was partly an absolute good, but largely, too, a relative one — relative to the material security of its possessor. Misalignment between poverty and intellect was the primary cause of exile. As Gissing phrases it in *Demos*, 'To rise to the supreme passion of revolt, two conditions are indispensable: to possess the heart of a poet, and to be subdued by poverty to the yoke of ignoble labour'.[44] But this picture is really too clear, for it fails to include some ambiguous shades. One way of bringing these out is to trace the complications that emerge when characters in Gissing try to break through the boundary lines of exile.

Logically, given the predicament defined, only two modes of escape are possible: to relinquish one's cultural aspirations or to better one's economic position: capture money or surrender intellect. For those with no prospects of material comfort, it was preferable, in Gissing's opinion, to forgo all but practical education. But for those already afflicted with learning, already endowed with a craving for thought? Such people could scarcely discard their brains. They could, however, give up the attempt to provide their brains with a suitable environment: they could reconcile themselves to exclusion from contact with the cultured classes. This was the policy of resignation — acceptance rather than release. It seems to have been pursued by Gissing in his first two marriages, especially the second. Wedding Edith and moving to Exeter, he talked morosely of never again meeting with educated people. As we saw in Chapter 2, the concept of sacrifice is prominent in all Gissing's early books. Resignation, too, became a favourite theme (most obviously in *Isabel Clarendon*), while renunciation of normal society is yearningly portrayed in *Henry Ryecroft* and temptingly in *Veranilda*.[45]

The opposite of resignation was revolt. Gissing told Frederic Harrison that a 'passionate tendency of revolt' had been smouldering in him from his earliest years. It was certainly one of his most frequent moods. Even his apparent resignation could be partially fired by defiance and rage: marrying Edith, according to Roberts, was the outcome of 'sudden revolt'. Many of his characters are prone to this impulse, pre-eminently in *The Nether World*: Clara Hewett, her father John, her lover Sidney, her exploiter Scawthorne — all are, in this respect at least, precursors of Godwin Peak.[46] A powerful component in these characters' emotions is resentment of those in the upper world, as it was for Gissing when, in early days, he knew 'revolt against the privilege of wealth' and stood in London 'savage with misery, looking at the prosperous folk who passed'. That these feelings of revolt were ignited by exile — due in turn to a gap between abilities and funds — is suggested by the fact that in 1889 Gissing actually projected a novel called *Revolt*, to be set among 'the poor and wretched educated'.[47]

If revolt against the conditions of exile were ever to be more than a turbulent emotion, it would have to take the form of a practical escape from poverty and its humiliations. Gissing, however, could never make money, and nor can his characters, with the dubious exception of the corrupt accepters of commerce. How, then, to rise into the privileged classes? Godwin Peak's attempt in *Born in Exile* entails a different kind of corruption — hypocritical acquiescence in the standards and beliefs of the class whose refinement he covets. But as soon as Gissing's characters try to break out, the complexity of their prison becomes apparent. One aspect of this has already been suggested. Gissing's typical protagonists, 'well educated' and 'without money', are also 'fairly bred'. To the crucial terms poverty and intellect we must add a third: social class.

Class differences meant a great deal to Gissing: for him, as for Hubert Eldon, they 'argued a difference in the grain'. Like Denzil Quarrier he both felt outside any 'recognized order of society' and believed in 'social subordination'. He was tremblingly sensitive to the tiniest class signals — not only the notorious shibboleths, like pronunciation and table manners (in his study of Dickens, dropping h's and eating with your knife are equated with not knowing that the world is round), but the subtler symptoms of deportment and tone.[48] Even a light novel like *The Town Traveller* is packed with samples of class-based behaviour and upholds the traditional distinctions. Belief in deep-rooted class divisions underpinned Gissing's whole conception of exile. To lament the misalignment of poverty and intellect presupposed, after all, the existence of a system in which, as a rule, brains and breeding went with wealth, and poverty with ignorance. But unfortunately the rule had so many exceptions. Money and class, though closely allied, were not synonymous, as Gissing knew (and showed in his story 'Snapshall's Youngest'). For one thing, a time-lag would operate, so that alteration of financial status would not instantly affect one's class. That is why one might feel *born* in exile: as with Peak, humble origins could determine class identity long after escape from strict poverty. Furthermore, the antique correlations were being shaken and loosened by social mobility. This did not mean that class was less central — as Peak says, 'Classes are getting mixed, confused. Yes, but we are so conscious of the process that we talk of class distinctions more than of anything else'. But it did mean that class was less clear-cut — an impediment for such as Gissing. Many of the poor were intellectually industrious, and at times Gissing wished (like Egremont) to find his companions among them. Many of the leisured were philistines, and hence to rise socially was not always to unite with one's intellectual peers. Gissing discovered this personally when he entered the society of Mrs Gaussen, of Broughton Hall, in the mid-1880s. Though at first he warmed to the atmosphere of easy culture and social refinement, he later found it stifling and stultifying.[49] 'Never yet did true rebel', says *The Nether World*, 'who has burst the barriers of social limitation, find aught but *ennui* in the trim gardens beyond.' Gissing's work is full of onslaughts on 'Society', on the vacuously wealthy and the twittering élite. Even the supposedly educated, he concluded, were often intellectually flaccid. Though intellect flourished best in a climate of comfort, the comfortable classes were not always intellectual. 'Refined — in a sense', says Isabel Clarendon, describing her circle of acquaintance. 'Cultured? — I am not so sure of that.'[50] Intellect could even be a disadvantage within the community in which it should thrive. As Godwin Peak discovers among the Warricombes, it was possible to be socially too retarded, yet mentally too advanced.

The complexities of class were an external factor that qualified Gissing's conception of exile. But equally potent was an internal factor — his mixed feelings about privacy and solitude. To be *born* in exile might be partly the result of inherited temperament. Gissing certainly pined for company, but he also recoiled from unwelcome intrusions. Without doubt much of his life was passed in genuine isolation. 'How few men there must be', he wondered, 'who have spent as much time as I have in absolute loneliness.' His personal writings confirm this assessment: the plaint 'lonely, lonely, lonely' tolls through them incessantly. He was lonely in London, lonely in Wakefield; he sickened for companionship while travelling abroad. 'My solitude', he sighed, 'is a wearisome topic', though he still continued to record it in his fiction, where acute recognition of loneliness often marks a narrative climax.[51]

The fact of Gissing's loneliness is not disputable; the causes of it are. 'It is', he wrote to Gabrielle, 'the life of a hermit; not a happy life; haunted with desires of the impossible, oppressed by great loneliness.' His recurrent descriptions of himself as a 'hermit' provide a clue to which aspect of his solitude afflicted Gissing most. Frustration at the lack of a sexual partner is, as Roberts recognized, an endemic malaise in his work.[52] Frequently his characters work off their energies by pacing compulsively about their rooms — frenzied, fevered, explosively possessed.[53]

The most incontinent distress of exile for Gissing was, it seems, enforced celibacy. Even more curious, then, is the fact that his own exclusion was partly self-imposed. In an often-quoted passage from his diary he laments that after ten years in London there is not one family, not one person, who would certainly receive him with good will. But a week later, after visiting the Gaussens, he writes anxiously, 'What would become of me if I had regular social intercourse?' Two passages in *Henry Ryecroft* about the London fog encapsulate this contradiction. In the first he recalls how it cosily cocooned him; in the second, how it drove him out to tramp the streets, his 'solitude being no longer endurable'. 'I used to suffer from loneliness', he once told his sister Margaret; 'now the difficulty is to get any time at all to myself.'[54] What were the reasons for these split responses? Why did Gissing, to some extent, choose exile?

His most practical reason was the nature of his work. 'Serious literary toil compels solitude', he asserted; his methods of composition meant that he would *never* have society. In the 1890s he was showered with invitations — 'pleasant enough, but ruinous to work'. It was difficult to find a middle course between being stranded and being swamped. In particular it was difficult to accommodate his writing — a cloistered, intensely individual task — with his craving for the company of a wife. This dilemma speared all three of his marriages. Nell, for whom he couldn't find suitable companions, must have asked, like Carrie Mitchell in *Workers in the Dawn*, 'Is it likely as I can live day after day without seeing no one?' Edith, kept away from his family and friends, much resented her social quarantine. To Gabrielle, Gissing explained his problem, confident that she, an intellectual herself, would accept his 'solitary work'. But Gabrielle felt it was taken too far. 'George dislikes my going to see friends', she wrote plaintively in 1901, 'and would like me living in his own solitary way; but that I can't endure.'[55]

A second reason why Gissing chose exile he explained in 1887: 'I cannot get to know the kind of people who would suit me, so I must be content to be alone.' The longer he remained in bookish seclusion, the less he felt able to adjust to society, and therefore the more he shunned it. It was not only that he had no wish to mingle with those he regarded as brutes and louts. He was also repelled by the 'gabble of drawing-rooms', the 'well-millinered and tailored herd', the 'greetings and meaningless phrases'. No doubt his nausea at affluent small talk was the natural symptom of that deadly compound, poverty plus intellect. But as *Henry Ryecroft* makes clear, the alienation this brought on was not unwelcome to his constitution. Describing how he quitted such occasions with relief, he adds: 'Dear to me then was poverty, which for the moment seemed to make me a free man. Dear to me was the labour at my desk, which, by comparison, enabled me to respect myself'.[56] Both poverty and intellect protected him from idle and frivolous activities, the one by preserving him from social obligations, the other by enhancing his esteem. To some extent he was *grateful* for exile, and the causes of this lay deep in his character, as they do with his protagonists. Like Egremont, he 'suffered from the caprices of his temperament'; like Kingcote, he was 'born with the nerves of suffering developed as they are in few men'. Neurotically sensitive to the slightest disturbance, he was sometimes prone to palpitations, like Julian Casti in *The Unclassed*. Fearful of the mildest altercation, he would shrink back immediately into his shell if his tentative conversational feelers encountered any rebuff.[57] He was also self-destructively yielding – singularly so, in his own opinion. 'No man I ever met', he wrote in his diary, '*habitually* sacrifices his own pleasure, habits, intentions, to those of a companion, purely out of fear to annoy.' As this self-excoriating entry implies, he was not only submissive and introverted, but anxiously introspective. As with Waymark, 'it was always needful to him to dissect his own motives'. 'He struck me as morbidly self-conscious', wrote his friend Edward Clodd, recalling their first meeting. Not surprisingly, his happiest moments (as he notes in *By the Ionian Sea*) were when his 'own being became lost to consciousness' – like Hardy in 'The Self-Unseeing'.[58] Painful self-awareness is a primary attribute of Gissing's typical protagonists. Worrying, wincing, self-absorbed, they all share this morbidity.

But perhaps, to Gissing, it was not morbidity; perhaps it was rather a healthy reaction to a woefully distempered world. At times he suggests that in modern society self-analysis and withdrawal are inevitable. In *The Emancipated*, two years before *Born in Exile*, he explicitly connects moral introspection with the disappearance of traditional rules; among the putatively enlightened, each person must become his own casuist. At other times he associates shrinking with superior refinement and delicacy. A good deal of pride and *amour-propre* enters into the brooding of Gissing's excluded. Kept out, they suspect, because they are outstanding, broken down because of their integrity, they relieve themselves by harbouring contempt for those mediocre enough to succeed. Yet, as we might expect in Gissing, scorn of others can easily be twisted inwards, can be curdled into rancid self-disgust. Several of his characters, like Rolfe in *The Whirlpool*, look back with shame on their earlier actions, or despise themselves for their weaknesses now.[59] Keenly resentful, yet masochistic, a peculiar mixture of arrogance and guilt, Gissing was uncertain whether his exile was chosen, imposed or deserved.

These, then, are some of the factors that qualify Gissing's presentation of exile. Class was too rigid and not rigid enough, strongly influenced but not defined by possession of culture and wealth. Gissing's own attitudes were ambivalent and shifting, especially about the causes of his alienation — were his attributes a stigma or a cachet? A few other complications need to be mentioned, and this can be done by looking briefly at three of the symptoms of Gissing's exile — the double life, restlessness and irony.

Pulled apart by poverty and intellect, for much of his life Gissing lived in two worlds. His father — himself an 'alien' in Yorkshire — kept apart from other shopkeepers: 'we hung between two grades of society', wrote Gissing, ' — as I have done ever since in practical life'. In the early 1880s Gissing moved abruptly from poverty and uproar at home with Nell to tranquillity and comfort with his pupils. Marrying Edith, he repeated the pattern: she remained strictly in purdah, while he began to penetrate loftier circles. The place where Gissing lived longest in London, 7K Cornwall Residences, was symbolic of his social position. Backed up against the squalor of the railway and work-house, the building containing Gissing's rooms commanded a prospect from the front of the elegant mansions around Regent's Park; appropriately, perhaps, only the rear view was visible from Gissing's flat. Many of the characters in his fiction are conscious of a 'double existence': Egremont, Scawthorne, Mallard, Peak — above all, Will Warburton.[60] Straddling two worlds sharpened Gissing's interest in other types of doubleness. Some of his protagonists experience alienation in a virtually psychiatric sense. Thyrza is frightened by a vision of people 'who did not seem to be human beings'. Emily Hood has a 'ghastly clairvoyance' when her friends turn into puppets. Kingcote feels 'moonstruck' by perception of absurdity: eventually he becomes so detached from reality as to suffer a nervous breakdown.[61] Less dramatic, but still revealing, are split states of consciousness like those of Peak, when a person steps back from his own activities and regards them with critical wonder.

But doubleness could also take a moral form: the fruit of divided existence in Gissing is sometimes duplicity. Oscillating between opposite social poles is likely to spark off hypocrisy, especially in one who is both very yielding and very contemptuous. The double life connects with the Guilty Secret. Gissing had been briefly locked in prison, and this, he felt, permanently barred him out. According to Roberts, 'The real reason for his almost rigid exclusion from society' was his fear that some 'brute' might expose his past. (Something like this had in fact occurred after Gissing met Frederic Harrison.)[62] Double-crossing is a prominent theme in his novels: at least sixteen of the twenty-two feature betrayal in one guise or other — sometimes a lover's infidelity, more often a friend's treachery. Gissing feared betrayal because he felt anxious, but this feeling was not confined to his crime. He was also uneasy with his dual existence — the evasions, the suppressions, the compromise. His exile was, as Roberts suggests, partly due to anxiety; but anxiety was perversely intensified by the form his exile took.[63]

Another symptom of exile which was also a cause was perennial restlessness. Convinced he was mouldering in 'the wrong world', Gissing continually switched his address in search of his ideal niche. With all his possessions in a single trunk, 'for one reason or another, I was always moving'. By October 1880, after three years in London, he had moved, he claimed, about forty-five times. He would wear out a pair of boots every three weeks. Not surprisingly, he came to hate London lodgings (for Peak, a lodger is a symbolic 'alien'), and the women who kept them, members of a class 'distinguished ... by its uncleanness, its rapacity, its knavery, its ignorance'. In the very first chapter of *Workers in the Dawn* an unscrupulous landlady appears; she reappears, in various revolting shapes, in nearly all his subsequent books. He also pined for a life abroad, frequently planning to leave England for good; living abroad with Gabrielle, he pined for life in England.[64] His restlessness was partly a consequence of his genuinely uncertain position in society. Unclassed and itinerant, he longed for acceptance, for the comforting security of fixed surroundings, for — as he wistfully puts it in *Henry Ryecroft* — 'the unspeakable blessedness of having a home!' The concept of home as a healing oasis springs up repeatedly in his books. It is virtually always a mirage: the norm for his characters is the nomadic life so fiercely denounced in *The Whirlpool*.[65] Yet Gissing's restlessness was also due to his own instability of constitution, his intrinsic discontent. After all, where was his ideal community, the family to which he would wish to belong? It never existed as a tangible group. Perhaps it had once existed in the past: Gissing idealized the milieu of Johnson and, more intensely, the golden world of classical antiquity. He represented his spiritual home as Rome — not the modern city, even less the church, but the legendary centre of the classical world. That this Rome was in more than one sense in ruins was a powerful part of its attraction. Likewise the splendours of ancient Greece: in *Henry Ryecroft* Gissing is anxious to dispel the suspicion that fifth-century Athens could have any application to the present. The classical world was a cherished ideal *because* it was irrecoverable. 'Paradise', as Gabrielle mournfully remarked, 'is always ... where he is not.'[66]

A last, fascinating symptom of exile in Gissing is his use of irony. The connection might not be immediately apparent, for irony can be multi-faceted and can correlate with many moods. Essential to all irony, however, is recognition of incongruity; irony is thus a congenial mode for those with complex, para-doxical or ambivalent responses. Gissing's writings are pervasively ironic both locally and structurally. He had a liking, he said, for ironical titles, and he told his brother that *The Emancipated* contained 'irony of a kind not generally understood — irony of fact and situation'. '*My motives are too subtle*', he added to Gabrielle. 'You know that I constantly use irony ... it is all taken in the most stupid literal sense.' The poorer classes among whom Gissing lived were not notable, he felt, for perception of irony: it was not a weapon, he observed in *The Nether World*, 'much in use among working-people: their wits in general are too slow'. Irony, for Gissing, 'meant intellect': Constance's use of it in *Our Friend the Charlatan* is too fine for the intelligence of her hearers. The liability of irony to be misunderstood was, of course, one of its advantages, especially for a victim of exile. Ross Mallard's father in *The Emancipated*, a talented outsider in a northern town, 'often made ironical remarks, and seemed to have a grim satisfaction when his hearers missed the point'. Gissing responded similarly, and no doubt for similar reasons. Maintaining that 'his greatest gift was perhaps that of irony, which he frequently exercised at the expense of his public', Morley Roberts remembered Gissing's 'joy when something he had written which was ironically intended ... was treated seriously'. Roberts also mentions Gissing's delight in the solemn reception of Samuel Butler's *The Fair Haven*, a parody of Christian apologetics, and this, together with his known love of Gibbon, and Roberts's earlier thought of him using irony against 'some relic of ... the schools', all suggests that Gissing was especially fond of ironies directed against the church — a key point for *Born in Exile*.[67] But it would, of course, be wrong to imply that irony, by its nature or in Gissing's hands, is a purely aggressive strategy. It appealed to him also for its ambiguities, its performance of multiple functions. The manipulation of double meanings was apt for one leading a double life and endowed with divided feelings. Moreover, irony was a perfect device for relieving the tensions of a man in exile, for with it he could, simultaneously, claim allegiance and express disdain. Irony provided a double signal: it repelled the obtuse and, Gissing hoped, attracted the *cognoscenti*.

Irony (the Greek root of the word means 'dissimulation') is integral to *Born in Exile*, but so too are the other ingredients of exile — poverty, intellect, class, deception and the penalties of torn temperament. In this book they achieve their most potent fusion: it is time to see how they do.

I V

Born in Exile, Gissing told Bertz, 'was a book I *had* to write'. Compulsively composed, it makes compelling reading, for its passionate dissection of a hidden pain is performed with considerable artistic skill and psychological penetration. At the novel's centre is our initial equation, poverty plus intellect equals exile, which emerges even in the opening chapter, where Godwin Peak, at a college prize-day, strikes most of the audience as an awkward pariah. Mr Warricombe puts his finger on the young man's predicament. 'Overweighted with brains', he muses, ' ... and by no means so with money, I fear.' Thereafter these twin attributes are frequently stressed. At college Peak's few intimates are chosen from those 'who read hard and dressed poorly'; having, like Gissing, to buy books instead of food, he finds that his hours of 'rigorous study' often leave him with 'ravenous hunger'.[68] The result of his dilemma is isolation. Debarred by poverty from social recreations, he also repels his fellow students by his fierce commitment to work.

The importance of Peak's poverty extends beyond the college scenes, but it is always a relative importance. Although he is born into straitened conditions — his widowed mother has no servant and can scarcely scrape by — these only matter because of the breadth of his cultural aspirations. Half-starved on account of his hunger for books, he lacks money for examination fees. Once, he has to walk home 25 miles, having blown the cash needed for trains and cabs — partly, it is true, on a temporary dissipation, but partly on a visit to the theatre. (The play, prophetically, is *Romeo and Juliet*: lovers doomed by conflicting backgrounds.) Culture costs money, but Peak's hope is that intellect can compensate for poverty: 'If, thus hampered, he could outstrip competitors ... the more glorious his triumph.' The unlikeliness of this is suggested by an episode symbolic of his later fate. Peak studies hard for a scholarship that will grant him free tuition at Whitelaw College, but can't quite make the required grade; he has to fall back on a benefaction that confirms his outsider's status. These events anticipate the novel's main plot, for the essence of Peak's dealings with the Warricombes is that, seeking entry into their world, he tries to transcend his impoverished background by skilful application of his intellect — tries and just fails.[69]

The humiliations rather than the hardships of poverty are what young Peak feels most keenly — as when he must confess to his landlady that he wishes to put off his rent. This point tells against Gillian Tindall's assertion that the hero's college poverty is irrelevant to the story, 'for later we never see Peak as actually destitute'.[70] Hypersensitive to social condescension, the adolescent Peak is thrown into wrath when first Lady Whitelaw and then Mr Moxey express hopes of his finding something 'advantageous'.[71] The word reminds him too painfully that despite his high-flown aspirations, he must indeed remember mundane necessities. Though his later poverty is much less acute, this psychological consequence of it is always kept in view. In his perilous relations with the Warricombes it conditions both his responses and theirs. Though material advantage is not his main aim, it is certainly one of his motives: as he admits to Marcella Moxey, he thinks it likely that Mr Warricombe may be able to help him substantially. Just after his tentative proposal to Sidwell, he is breathless for confirmation of this hope: goaded by 'the curse of poverty', he reminds her he is 'seeking for a livelihood'. Her brother Buckland requires no reminding: the interloper's probable bank balance is one thing that provokes his suspicions. Peak defends himself by using counterfeit candour. Of course, he tells Buckland, some financial incentive — inevitable and surely understandable — lies behind his intention of entering the church. The significance of Peak's comparative poverty is not, then, that it inflicts privation. Rather it determines how he is regarded and how he decides to act.[72] It is true, however, that poverty as such is not a factor in his exile by the end of the book. Left a legacy by his sullen admirer, Marcella, Peak is released from financial care. At this point he formally proposes to Sidwell — but she does not accept. Whatever constrains her, it is clearly not his poverty, but some deeper, more stubborn cause.

Intellectual qualities are also decisive from beginning to end in *Born in Exile*; but as with poverty their power is relative. The book's bookish hero is first perceived at a provincial academic function and last glimpsed at Piale's Library in Rome: despite the implied cosmopolitan advance, he is still unhealthy and lonely. The centrality and futility of intellect are both deftly sketched in the opening scene, the awards ceremony at Whitelaw College, which trains attention on certain key features of intellectual life: competitiveness and rivalry; the grading of intelligence and industry; the disclosure of intellectual bent. The response of the audience reminds us, however, that social performance often counts for more than scholarship or learning. Who wins what is certainly significant. Peak gets first prize in logic and moral philosophy: his chief enterprise later is an 'immoral' scheme pursued, he says, from following his convictions 'to their logical issue'. He also, with Buckland Warricombe, gets equal first in geology — from which, again, layers of irony emerge. Most obvious is his later hypocritical role as an orthodox apologist, protecting religion from attrition by science (geology is presented as fundamental to Victorian secular thought). But Buckland's joint prize is prophetic, too. Buckland, like Peak, is a modern thinker impatient of traditional dogma; years later, Peak's religious professions arouse his incredulity. Surely, he reasons, his old college rival must still, on this subject, be bracketed with him. Hence the irony, in this opening chapter, of what Buckland's father says to Peak about the joint award: 'Let us hope it signifies that you and Buckland will work through life shoulder to shoulder in the field of geology.' In fact it will be Warricombe himself, a piously old-fashioned amateur geologist, with whom Peak pretends to work shoulder to shoulder. Other prizes, too, are ominous or auspicious. Bruno Chilvers is awarded first prize in virtually all the arts subjects, but comes nowhere in philosophy or science. Earwaker, later a journalist, wins prizes for both the poem and the essay. His subjects, 'Alaric' and 'Trades Unionism', said to indicate 'versatility of intellect', also imply flexibility of view — a poetic response to the fall of Rome, a prosaic recognition of the strength of new forces, both germane to his subsequent career.

Though intellectual achievements certainly matter as far as the achievers are concerned, the audience, it transpires, is just as attentive to social attributes. The two main prize-winners, Chilvers and Peak, are contrasted here, as throughout the book. Chilvers, well dressed and glowing with health, exhibits 'perfect self-command'; Peak, ill dressed and pimply looking, betrays an ungainly embarrassment. The fondness of the audience goes forth to Chilvers, who after the ceremony holds court among admirers while Peak stands apart with a few fellow students. Intellect without breeding cuts little ice — and especially with respectable women: 'No lady offered him her hand or shaped compliments for him with gracious lips.' The conservatism of women, a major premise in the novel, is confirmed by their reaction to Professor Walsh, whose work in physics has incurred the 'imputation of religious heresy'. Mrs Warricombe's whispered aside — 'What a very disagreeable face! The only one of the Professors who doesn't seem a gentleman' — is a nice example of class prejudice encroaching on intellectual concerns. The vulnerability of cerebral distinction to the stultifications of social stigma is clear, too, from the chapter's ending. Armoured with academic awards, Peak is unmanned by the sudden appearance of his vulgar Cockney uncle, Andrew, whose plans to open a café near the college will eventually drive Peak from it.[73]

Many issues are foreshadowed in this opening chapter, but especially — in both senses of the term — the vanity of intellect. Peak has an arrogant pride in his brains, but when he tries to use them to win other prizes — for he knows that by birth he is 'of no account' — he fails ignominiously. At first he tries to push forward along the path of conventional academic success, sweating for exams and memorizing facts (the regurgitating gabble of his cousin Joey is offered as a parodic contrast with this), and exhorting his brother Oliver to pursue the same route to salvation. When his kinship with vulgarity expels him from college, these embryonic strivings are roughly aborted. But Peak conceives of a second scheme by which brains might atone for birth. His ambitious imposture as a clergyman-to-be depends at every stage on the exercise of knowledge and intelligence (he even continues to sit exams, but now as a clerical preliminary). Unfortunately, it depends not only on their exercise, but also on their prostitution. This paradox strikes him in the mental turbulence that follows his decisive hypocrisy. Initially he reverts to his earlier assessment — 'Life is a terrific struggle for all who begin it with no endowments save their brains' — in order to excuse his lies. But then, with a thunderclap of self-contempt, the irony bursts upon him: 'he, he who had ever prided himself on his truth-fronting intellect, and had freely uttered his scorn of the credulous mob!'[74] The causes and effects of Peak's self-contortion are what Gissing absorbedly explores.

Peak's exceptional intellect, which has made him dissatisfied with his native sphere, is also, he believes, his only means of escape. But since his intellect is sharply critical, mercilessly probing into moribund dogma, it cannot, in the world he wishes to join, be allowed to operate unsheathed. For this is a world of conservative refinement, attractive to his sexual and aesthetic instincts, promising emotional satisfaction, but demanding some form of conformity, either social or intellectual. Given his known class origins, Peak — unlike Buckland or Bruno Chilvers — cannot gain admittance merely by flashing the accepted social signals. He must conform intellectually, and the most effective type of conformity, as a counterweight to lowliness and a character-testimonial, is to aim at ordination. Thus it is that Peak, the militant freethinker, bends his intellect to orthodoxy.

The ramifications of Peak's false position are explored on a number of levels. In general terms the book mounts a debate between the dignity of mental independence and the necessity of social compliance. Characteristically, the alternatives are crystallized from a rich flow of literary allusion. By instinct Peak is intolerant of consensus or compromise. He laughs approvingly when Earwaker quotes from Sir Thomas Browne's *Pseudodoxia Epidemica* ('*Nos numerus sumus* is the motto of the multitude, and for that reason are they fools'), and in like mood recounts the anecdote from Plutarch of how Phokion, receiving majority applause, asked 'What have I said amiss?' He also delights in the boldness of thought manifested in a book by Justin Walsh, the brother of his old, subversive professor, whose epigraph comes from Voltaire: '*Oui, répondit Pococurante, il est beau d'écrire ce qu'on pense; c'est le privilège de l'homme*'. Immediately following this quotation, however, is a reminder of the article that Peak himself has published in the *Critical Review* — the article in which he has written what he thinks and which will shortly destroy him. The trouble is that by this stage Peak has betrayed what Voltaire terms the privilege of a man, by aiming instead at what he regards as the natural fulfilments of a man. He has indeed embraced social compromise — that expedient, as Steele says, 'to make fools and wise men equal' — but so forcefully as to twist it into fraudulence. Intellectual integrity, he has come to think, is suicidal when opposed to social law. Confronted with Browning's 'Respectability', he rejects its message as an impossible ideal. His own course, as Buckland suggests with shrewd insolence, is closer to that of Bishop Blougram. But his justification is that enforced compliance cannot violate the sanctity of his untouched mind. Hence he adopts the motto of the Renaissance humanists who outwardly conformed to the common faith: '*Foris ut moris, intus ut libet*' (in public, according to custom; within, according to desire).[75]

More specifically, he masquerades as a Christian whose training in modern scientific thought has enabled him to meet the formidable objections of contemporary rationalists. A unifying theme in *Born in Exile*, sustained with impressive precision of detail, is the clash between religion and science. Before commencing work on the book, Gissing had carefully read up on this subject: Asa Gray and Archbishop Temple on possible reconciliations, and, for a conspectus of the range of thought on evolution and geology, works by Charles Lyell, Hugh Miller, George Romanes, and Alfred Russel Wallace, and popularizations by Grant Allen. He also studied that German work, F. H. Reusch's *Bibel und Natur* (1862) which bulks so large in the text. Though initially his reading was 'not for amusement', he evidently became absorbed in the subject, for even after completing the novel he was reading Darwin and Huxley.[76] No doubt his handling of science and religion was also conditioned by earlier reading, especially of Comte, in whose historical scheme theological and metaphysical modes of thought gave way to scientific ones.[77] None of these sources is indispensable, though, for understanding *Born in Exile* — partly through Gissing's tact and skill in explaining the allusions and arguments deployed, mainly because their intrinsic content is always subsidiary to something else: the social significance attached to ideas and the psychology of those who hold them. The attack of science on metaphysical tradition is not 'the real theme of *Born in Exile*', but rather an important subordinate motif.[78] The real theme is the exile of Godwin Peak, its causes, manifestations and effects. Consistently, the treatment of science and religion is designed to illuminate these.

There are two basic premises nailed into the novel, on which the protagonist is eventually impaled. The first is that modern intellectual trends have impugned traditional religion; the second that in respectable circles religious conformity is still required — at least from one without inherited culture, and especially by women. The religious conservatism of women, persistently emphasized throughout the book, is presented by Gissing as the sharpest point of this incompatibility between mental freedom and social acceptability.[79] Certainly Peak discovers that personal opinions must always have a social meaning. His mother, 'a pattern of the conservative female', expresses her desire that her

boy might rise by becoming a clergyman. When he bluntly
replies, 'I don't want to be a parson' — his earliest recorded
expression in the book — she objects to his contemptuous use of
'that word'. Many years later this dialogue is recalled when
Buckland stammers out his astonishment that Peak should wish
to become a — ' "Parson", supplied Peak, drily'. As a child, Peak
hates Christianity, for he associates it with the shallowness of his
female relatives. He even resents time spent in church, though
later (like the youthful Gissing) he reclaims it for intellectual
effort by memorizing academic data. His antagonism is fortified
by science when Mr Gunnery, an irascible local geologist whose
name sufficiently projects what he stands for, bombards the idea
of the Deluge. Encouraged by Gunnery (who bequeaths him his
collections and scientific instruments), Godwin eventually goes to
college, where — maddened by the hymnal melodies vamped on
his landlady's piano — he embarks on a fruitless search for
lectures that will match his own iconoclasm. Geology, however,
is not only presented as attractive for its propagandist value. It is
also a subject that inspires awe. Meditating in a country road on
the 'inconceivable duration' of geologic time, Peak has a kind of
scientific epiphany, 'a sudden triumph of the pure intellect'.[80]

Ten years later, living in London, Peak is working at a chemical
factory; he 'goes in for science — laboratory work, evolutionary
speculations'. By now his social and intellectual impulses are
emerging as inconsistent. Ambitious to achieve a reputation, he
has published articles in an atheist paper, but has since become
ashamed of this connection with street-corner rationalism.
Anxious for admittance to refined society, he has modified his
sentiments regarding women and aspires to marry a lady. Only
gradually does it dawn on him that this might require hypocrisy.
Surrounded by a few congenial friends, he first holds the floor on
a social occasion by sarcastically venting his real convictions,
denouncing those nervously respectable readers who are 'clamorous
for treatises which pretend to reconcile revelation and science'.
Shortly afterwards, he follows up this harangue with an article,
'The new sophistry', which he sends anonymously to the *Critical
Review*. As the phrasing of his earlier denunciation suggests, this
article is not merely a piece of analysis: it is also a vehement,
satirical assault on those who palter with intellectual integrity for
the sake of social acceptance.[81]

It is while he is on holiday in Devon that the incongruities in
Peak's position are ironically consummated. Having gone there
to study geology, he is soon distracted by Sidwell Warricombe,

whom he first sees in Exeter Cathedral. What his life truly needs, he suddenly discovers, is not seashore thoughts and scientific instruments, but 'one touch of a girl's hand, one syllable of musical speech'. Instead of undertaking a geological survey, he makes a social reconnaissance ('Here then. The site was a good one') of the Warricombes' country house. Before long, his subconscious intentions rewarded, he receives an invitation to lunch; and then comes the crisis of his life. Encouraged by a look of approval from Sidwell when he says he has attended the cathedral service, he finds himself expounding the canon's sermon — indeed, embellishing it eloquently, since in truth he scarcely heard it. Peak has held the floor a second time, but now with quite contrary opinions. Mr Warricombe and Sidwell are surprised and impressed; Buckland, astonished and suspicious. A spontaneous surge of intellectual power has given Peak his first foothold in the company he craves. His next step — an announcement that he seeks ordination — takes him into level hypocrisy.[82]

With convincing precision and psychological finesse, the subsequent treatment of science and religion explores and extends the ironies of Peak's dissimulation. The Warricombes, whom he wishes to cultivate, are devoutly, but discreetly, religious. Their values can be glimpsed in the bedroom he is shown to — comforts of a healthy and sensible kind, water-colours of local scenery, volumes of poets, essayists and novelists, and 'Elsewhere, not too prominent, lay a Bible and a Prayer-book'. Peak has to tread very delicately: his pious avowals must never be strident, his arguments against religious doubt never dubiously emphatic. Though Warricombe is something of a scientific fossil, he retains a clear liberal intelligence; he has sensitive antennae for social pretension if not for intellectual pretence. Luckily what he wants is what Peak has researched, though not in a sympathetic spirit: modern science reconciled with religion. Peak's earliest kindness is to translate a tract which reduplicates his own arguments — and then to disparage it mildly. After that he embarks on a laborious translation of a German work of apologetics, F. H. Reusch's *The Bible and Nature*, which he scorns ferociously in private, but commends to Mr Warricombe. As Peak buttresses his perilous position with piles of well-selected pietistic rubble, we never lose sight of the social ambition that underlies his enterprise. Glossing the theologian's account of creation, he is also glossing over his own obscure origins. But eventually the expected landslip occurs. Exposed as the author of 'The new sophistry', Peak has to limp away in shame, just as years earlier he was forced out of college. But whereas that earlier flight was provoked by his rootedness in poverty, this later one is precipitated by the fruits of his intellect. On the day he leaves Exeter he commits to the flames his incomplete translation of Reusch. Later, hearing that someone else has had an English translation published, he sardonically mutters a Hebrew phrase which, in Reusch's arid exegesis, had assumed an obsessive and absurd importance: *thohu wabohu*. The phrase, from the first chapter of Genesis, and meaning 'without form and void', applies not only to Peak's unfinished work, but also to his nebulous and nullified project to create a new world for himself.[83]

The contemporary erosion of religious belief by remorseless waves of scientific discovery is always subservient, in *Born in Exile*, to the ironies of social predicament and personal manipulation. But one element in this theme stands out as decisive on a more fundamental level. The crucial concept of evolution is not only a topic of discussion in the book, but a metaphor that colours its conception. Several characters evaluate evolution; even more exemplify it. Influenced, perhaps, by his preparatory reading, Gissing repeatedly reverts to the notions of variability and heredity, competition and adaptation. The question of 'instinct' emerges as vital, as also does that of 'finding a mate'; characters develop, or fail to adapt; and, perhaps most significant, different classes come to seem like separate species.

Evolution is applied to human ideas and the institutions that embody them. 'Christianity', declares Peak, in his character of enlightened defender of the faith, 'is an organism of such vital energy that it perforce assimilates whatever is good and true in the culture of each successive age'; and certainly, Gissing notes, the reinterpreters of Genesis are 'diligently adapting themselves to the progress of science'. A notable irony in the novel's treatment of religious responses to evolution is that, in being forced to adapt to the theory, individuals unwittingly confirm it. Take, for example, the cunning account of how Mrs Warricombe, faced with her children, has adjusted to a new intellectual climate. First of all, her hereditary structure is suggested: 'She came of a race long established in squirearchic dignity amid heaths and woodlands. Her breeding was pure through many generations of the paternal and maternal lines, representative of a physical type ...'. Then Gissing tells how, after her marriage to a thoughtful but old-fashioned scientist, she was plunged for a time into mental chaos, settling at last for the comfortable opinion that 'though the record of geology might be trustworthy that of the Bible was more so'. But, he continues,

> as her children grew up, Mrs. Warricombe's mind and temper were insensibly modified by influences which operated through her maternal affections, influences no doubt aided by the progressive spirit of the time. The three boys ... were distinctly of a new generation. It needed some ingenuity to discover their points of kindred with paternal and maternal grandparents ... Sidwell, up to at least her fifteenth year, seemed to present far less change of type ... It was a strange brood to cluster around Mrs. Warricombe. For many years the mother was kept in alternation between hopes and fears, pride and disapproval, the old hereditary habits of mind, and a new order of ideas which could only be admitted with the utmost slowness ... Yet in the end her ancestral prejudices so far yielded as to allow of her smiling at sentiments which she once heard with horror.[84]

Evidently Mrs Warricombe's thought has developed by a kind of evolutionary process — which is almost reassuring. But elsewhere not only ideas but actions, the hero's attempts to transcend his exile, are placed in a quasi-biological perspective; and here the results are less hopeful.

Peak is born into a fierce struggle for existence, a desperate 'competition for minimum salaries'; his 'kinsfolk' soon feel it is high time he fought 'for his own share of provender'. No one has leisure to ascertain 'for what employment he is naturally marked'; all they know is that 'He has been born, and he must eat'. He happens, of course, to have been born with brains and these he employs to make headway. But what he most wants is to retreat to a realm fenced off by inherited wealth. 'A spot of exquisite retirement', he reflects, when he fixes his gaze on the Warricombes' house: 'happy who lived here in security from the struggle of life!' The power of biological inheritance is implied very early in the book. 'Do you know', Godwin asks his brother, 'what is meant by inherited tendencies? Scientific men are giving a great deal of attention to such things nowadays.'[85] These tendencies are manifest in Peak himself, whose arrogance, severity and discontent are inherited from his father.[86] Other characters have better genetic luck. Earwaker, though 'his features betrayed connection with a physically coarse stock', is original, vigorous and adaptable — 'naturally marked for survival among the fittest'. Brooding retrospectively on Earwaker's success, Peak perceives that his friend has 'advanced on the way of harmonious development ... Nature had been kind to him; what more could one say?' Chilvers, too, is more successful than Peak, more instinctively adept at hypocrisy: 'He trod in the footsteps of his father, and with inherited aptitude moulded antique traditions into harmony with the taste of the times.' Peak himself has 'aristocratic instincts', but not, it is suggested, the right pedigree. At any rate he tortures himself with the thought that his outbreak of dishonesty is due to 'the ancestral vice in his blood ... The long line of base-born predecessors ... were responsible for this'. Interpreted thus, Peak's destiny would appear to be inescapable: he is born in exile in every sense. 'You have been trying to adapt yourself', Sidwell tells him, 'to a world for which you are by nature unfitted.' His nomadic isolation is hereditary. 'Nature had decreed', we learn near the end, 'that he was to resemble the animals which, once reared, go forth in complete independence of birthplace and the ties of blood.' Sidwell, conversely, is ultimately chained by birthplace and the ties of blood. 'I cannot think and act', she tells her friend Sylvia, explaining her rejection of Peak's proposal, 'simply as a woman, as a human being. I am bound to a certain sphere of life.' But interestingly this statement switches attention back from biology to social class. Class, it suggests, is a more compelling category than either gender or even species.[87] As always in Gissing, in the last resort class is the unbreakable barrier.

Mention of class must make us turn to the specific nature of Peak's exile, and the complicating factors it involves. The most useful way of elucidating these is through the concept of doubleness — of ambivalence, contradiction, dichotomy. Peak's ambitions are doomed from the start because of ambiguities in the social system and uncertainties in his character. The class to which he wants to belong both supplies and cannot supply what he needs. Though containing a high proportion of cultivated people, it is also intellectually orthodox, and for this Peak must often despise it. Likewise, though its women are attractive to Peak — fastidious, refined and feminine — they are also distressingly conservative and disappointingly timid. In his view 'the truly emancipated woman ... is almost always asexual'.[88] Hence his recoil from Marcella Moxey and his idealization of Sidwell.

Riven by poverty and intellect, consumed by both 'militant egoism' and 'an excess of nervous sensibility', Peak is a divided personality with inconsistent aims. Less charitably, he is an impossible person with impossible aspirations. Gissing intended us, of course, to have a mixed reaction to his muddled hero. 'It seems to me', he wrote to Bertz, 'that the tone of the whole book is by no means identical with that of Peak's personality; certainly I did not mean it to be so.'[89] In the early chapters the word 'prejudiced' is used again and again of Peak, and the reiteration of similar terms (arrogance, envy, resentment, scorn) makes it clear that the book is partly a study in psychopathology.[90] Yet Peak continues to interest us; we sympathize even as we wince; we assimilate his own characteristics. His doubleness assumes at least three forms: double attitudes; dual consciousness; and duplicitous behaviour. An ambivalence of response, an instability of judgement, are the hallmarks of his sensibility. At college he nurses a 'bitter envy' of polished and gregarious fellow students, yet is instantly disarmed by a civil word. Seeing one of them at the theatre, ensconced with his family, makes a painful tear in Peak's perforated heart: 'Inasmuch as it was conventionality, he scorned it; but the privileges which it represented had strong control of his imagination.' Similarly, in spite of his restlessness, Peak craves the comforts and security of home. When he leaves his native village, he resents the natural feeling which brings moisture to his eyes. Early on he is astonished by Christian Moxey's 'yearning for domesticity', but later he abhors his own life in lodgings, which he sees as symbolic of his alien status, and in the Warricombes' 'English home' he discovers the qualities he needs. 'I thought longingly of Exeter,' he says poignantly in his final letter to Earwaker, 'of a certain house there — never mind!'[91] This reluctant homesickness relates to the battle, fought out inside his temperament, between conformity and individuality. Proudly independent in his private judgement, Peak nevertheless wishes to belong. Familiar hymns from a church congregation convulse him with involuntary emotion. Mind and heart will not always beat as one. Though mental solitude is endurable, emotionally he still remains desperate for some satisfactory alliance.[92]

Peak — who comes from Twybridge — is trying to bridge two worlds; so pervasive is his sense of alienation that it gradually dominates his mental, and ultimately his moral, life. As a youth, he is awkward in company because his imaginative and speculative faculties, 'absorbed in all manner of new problems', interfere with the suavity of his address. 'Only the cultivation of a double consciousness', we learn, could put him at his ease. Reintroduced ten years later, he has indeed 'learnt to exercise his discernment even whilst attending to the proprieties', but his peculiar facility for splitting his thoughts now emerges as something more idiosyncratic than conventional self-command. Several key moments in the novel occur when Peak is in a heightened state of mental bifurcation. His 'fatal' exegesis of the canon's sermon is poured forth 'under the marvelling regard of his conscious self'; his decisively hypocritical declaration is the outcome of 'somnambulism'. Expounding ideas to Mr Warricombe directly opposed to his real beliefs, Peak is often strangely beset by 'a tormenting metaphysical doubt of his own identity'. He becomes more and more unable to control 'the sense that life is an intolerable mummery', especially after facing danger from Marcella, whose reappearance detonates an explosive mental fission: 'In three seconds, he re-lived the past, made several distinct anticipations of the future, and still discussed with himself how he should behave this moment.'[93]

As these examples indicate, Peak's split consciousness is the mental correlative of his moral hypocrisy. One way he tries to relieve this hypocrisy is through an acute sense of irony. After the shock received from Marcella, 'the ironic temptation' becomes 'terribly strong': 'What a joy to declare himself a hypocrite, and snap mocking fingers in the world's face!' Irony is not only woven into the narrative, but also into Peak's psychology. He has 'ironic habits of mind', and as his 'persiflage' with Chilvers shows, he often employs them as a 'compensation for the part he had to play'.[94] This part is a hypocritical one, but Peak's hypocrisy is not so blatant as to merit outright censure: it can at least, in Sidwell's distinction, be 'excused rather than justified'. For one thing, his duplicity flows almost inexorably from the doubleness of his native condition, over which he has no control. As a young man, he hates the 'elaborate hypocrisy' entailed by trying to be grateful to his aunt, whose values are remote from his own. Likewise, as a pensioner of Lady Whitelaw, having to be thankful for the charity he detests, 'He knew himself for an undesigning hypocrite, and felt that he might as well have been a rascal complete'.[95] Since so large a part of his social manner has had to be learned like an actor's lines, it is scarcely surprising that the script is extended from behaviour to belief.

A second mitigation of Peak's hypocrisy is its paradoxical nature: it is prompted and sustained by creditable qualities as well as discreditable ones. For example, it involves courage as well as cowardice. Early on we learn that 'a coward delicacy' makes him repress his true opinions and that his shame-filled flight from college was 'an indication of moral cowardice', the result of 'a cowardly instinct'. His deceiving of the Warricombes is partly, it seems, a continuation of this cowardice; but it also needs a gambler's courage. Telling Earwaker he has set out on his life's adventure, Peak quotes some valiantly defiant lines by James Graham, Marquis of Montrose (taken, as it happens, from the poem 'Written on the Window of his Jail the Night before his Execution'). And indeed, having launched himself into deception, he finds he has to 'brave it out'. In a sense, like Marcella Moxey at one point, he displays 'the courage of cowardice'.[96] More important, Peak's scheme presupposes and involves a certain kind of honesty. Peak believes — and the book largely bears him out — that for one in his position social acceptance can only be assured by an affectation of religious orthodoxy. But being familiar with modern thought Peak is too honest to be religiously orthodox: as his article 'The new sophistry' demonstrates, he will have no truck with the legerdemain of contemporary apologists. He must therefore be *consciously* hypocritical. In this he differs from thousands of others, who profess belief for fear of social rejection, only in the clarity of his self-understanding (for he never tries to 'play the sophist' with himself). 'But for the prevalence', Sidwell reflects, 'of such a spirit of hypocrisy, Godwin Peak would never have sinned against his honour.' In contrast with Peak is Bruno Chilvers, who requires no deliberate adoption of pretence because of his intellectual dishonesty regarding the conflict between theology and science. If Peak, in his own words, has 'believed the world round, and pretended to believe it flat', Chilvers is willing to talk as if roundness is really the same as flatness.[97] The early chapters are at pains to establish the hero's natural integrity (just as his father would not fiddle his taxes, so the boy would be appalled to cheat in an exam). And in Peak's bitter judgement on himself — 'My good qualities ... have always wrecked me' — there remains (as in himself) much truth.[98]

Born in Exile is built on irony and contrast, not only psychologically and morally but also in narrative structure. It contains a battery of minor characters whose stories are designed to illuminate the hero's — but in fact are overshadowed by it. For the most part these sub-plots operate on a lower level of creative power. Two of Peak's peers succeed where he fails, one deservedly, the other meretriciously. Earwaker, whose 'mirth' at religious intolerance contrasts, in Chapter 1, with Peak's 'rage and scorn', steers a judicious editorial line between compromise and integrity to attain a 'dignified independence'. He makes his name, achieves acceptance, and still keeps in touch with his family — 'All this with no sacrifice of principle'. Less attractively, but more convincingly, Bruno Chilvers, winged with birth and breeding, outstrips Peak from start to finish. At the prize-day he repeatedly comes first to Peak's second, and also wins the ladies' approval; the news of his success in the first stage of his degree coincides with Peak's leaving college. He joins the ranks of Christian apologists about the time Peak is assailing them, and later, now ordained, takes a church in Exeter while Peak is still 'an obscure aspirant'. With his specious tolerance and glib reconcilements — reproduced with a hilariously derisive zest — he effortlessly achieves what Peak must plan; no wonder that by comparison Peak feels himself a bungler. Contemplating Chilvers, he sometimes wonders if his own imposture has been superfluous; but Buckland, who likewise spots the similarities between the two men, is shrewd enough to realize that Peak's humble station is what, in comparison with Chilvers, will always tell against him. In the end it becomes plain to sceptical observers that Chilvers's 'sole object ... is to make a good marriage'. Needless to say, when Sidwell turns down Peak, the announcement of Chilvers's society wedding — appropriately held at St Bragg's Church — immediately follows.[99]

Two other men achieve contentment in marriage, after having for a time roughly paralleled Peak in amorous frustration. Christian Moxey is an amiable drifter where Peak is an unlovable trier, and the term 'sentimental languishment', explicitly dissociated from the hero, is explicitly attached to his friend. However, Christian's futile and protracted devotion to a woman he has vaporously glorified is clearly a parody of Peak's proceedings, as Christian himself implies at the end. Both men quit their lovers in consecutive chapters, but whereas Christian gets another chance (he returns to his homely but affectionate cousin), Godwin is condemned to solitude.[100] A similar pattern, but in broader burlesque, is described by the antics of the extrovert Malkin, whose simplicity, exuberance and blurted directness are all in clanging contrast with Peak's characteristics, but whose marital ideal is largely the same: a woman of education and breeding. Believing he can train a young girl for his purpose — just as Peak believes that after marriage his wife could be taught to 'think as he did' — Malkin concentrates his lofty yearnings on the 14-year-old daughter of a widow who, in fact, means to grab him for herself. Malkin's ingenuous project backfires at the same time as Peak's ingenious scheme, but again the minor character is granted a reprieve: following a sobering sojourn abroad, he fulfils his original wish. One restriction he cannot escape, however. Though loudly intransigent in early days on all matters of personal principle, he has to abandon his confident plan to turn his wife into an atheist: he is forced to marry in church.[101] Criss-cross patterns of apostasy and faith are, of course, a feature of the book's background shading. They even occur with the female characters, who are mostly conservative. Sidwell, for instance, has a friend, Sylvia Moorhouse, who unlike herself is an unbeliever − or at least this is what the reader divines, since Sylvia, in deference to social decorum, carefully conceals her real opinions (and is thus dubbed by Buckland 'a hypocrite'). Even more sharply in contrast with Sidwell is Marcella Moxey, 'a born atheist', who scorns conventional sentiments and prides herself on boldness of thought. In many ways − her intellectuality, her social isolation, her awkwardness − Marcella is a female equivalent of Peak. Like him she hungers, despite her singularity, for the common consolations of human love (hence her over-rich adornment − the counterpart of Peak's over-eager compliance with the requisites of etiquette). And just as Peak embodies his ideals in a single member of the opposite sex, so does Marcella − in Peak. When he rejects her for the orthodox Sidwell, she punishes him by exposing his past. With apt and ironic symmetry, the way she pulls down his deceptive scheme − by gradual stages, undeliberately, but impelled by an urgent, subconscious drive − closely follows the way that Peak originally built it up.[102]

Several of the minor characters − Marcella, Buckland and Sidwell, say − are created with a density of imaginative detail; others − Earwaker, Malkin, Moxey − are much more trans-parently functional. Though the whole novel is conceived and constructed on the principles of contrast and juxtaposition, it seems that the contrasts which are most effective are those *within* particular characters rather than those between them. This would account for the overwhelming dominance of the central character, Godwin Peak. His divided condition, the main subject of the book, is even displayed in his well-chosen names. His fiery father named him after William Godwin − appropriate for his rebelliousness and atheism, inappropriate for his reactionary politics. His pious aunt, on the other hand, imagines him 'named after the historic earl' − appropriate for his aristocratic instincts, but ironic in the light of his birth. His second name, too, is ambiguous, the exalted and aspiring connotations of 'summit' being stricken with morbid suggestions: resentment arising from wounded pride ('pique'), sickly despondence ('peak and pine') and — from a spelling Gissing tried, then rejected — a sense of furtive prying ('peek').[103] The hero of *Born in Exile* is not, of course, the novel's only complex character. Even Buckland Warricombe is multi-layered, and in his case, too, some of these layers are embedded in his Christian name. William Buckland, the geologist after whom he is called, famously attempted to return natural history 'to the explicit service of religious truth'. Since Buckland believes that traditional Christianity has been buried by the flinty findings of science, his name might appear less honorary than ironic. In fact, though, he combines advanced opinions with intense and atavistic class prejudices (fittingly, the MP for whom he works is an aristocratic Radical) and in this sense, rather than the one intended, he does indeed turn out to be a modern thinker who upholds the traditional line.[104] The fact remains, however, that it is Godwin Peak whose predicament dominates *Born in Exile* and whose psychological peculiarities give the book its unique distinction. They do so by arising, vibrating but shaped, from the author's deeply pondered dilemmas. Gissing, according to Morley Roberts, believed that *Born in Exile* was his greatest book. His evaluation is disputable — several of the sub-plots are distinctly weak and a few of Peak's speeches embarrassingly shrill — but also highly understandable. For *Born in Exile* is the base metal of Gissing's life transmuted into art.[105] With its stress on the amalgam of poverty and intellect, it fuses the basic elements of his condition; with its equal emphasis on opposites — irony, antithesis, ambivalence and paradox — it expresses the quintessential attributes of his temperament and technique.

5

Women, Feminism and Marriage

I

Gissing was a woman-worshipping misogynist with an interest in female emancipation. In his personal appreciation of women he was both idealistic and cynical; in his larger understanding of 'their place in the world, their duties, their possibilities', he was more analytical.[1] These shifting appraisals were partly the result of his own unsteady temperament, but partly, too, an accurate register of the movements and upheavals of his age.

Examining the social status of women, Gissing offered thoughts on a number of topics, like marriage, motherhood, education, employment and sexual frankness. His treatment of these topics will be looked at later, but what we need to trace first is the seismic fault running through the feelings on which his theories were built. Like Will Warburton, Gissing was genuinely amazed to be labelled a misogynist. The truth was, he explained to Gabrielle, he had to detest certain women because his ideal of womanhood was 'so very high'. His bitterness broke out from disenchantment — as it does with the husband in 'Mutimer's Choice', whose wife's dishonesty comes upon him like a 'flaw in a fine piece of marble'.[2] The adolescent Gissing was avidly romantic and even gyniolatrous. His attachment to the seedy and pathetic Nell was originally conceived as a '*grande passion*', and the actions that blasted his whole career — thefts from his fellow students at college — were carried out all for love. An insight into his feelings at this time can be glimpsed from the poetry he wrote shortly after coming out of gaol. In autumn 1876 he composed a series of high-flown sonnets dedicated to Shakespeare's heroines. In August, shortly before sailing to America, he penned a tremulous valediction: 'Farewell, my love; though far apart/ Tonight our spirits meet; ... In yon' new world I seek a home/ Far, far from England's shore;/Wait but a while and thou shalt come,/With me to weep no more'.[3] Nell did not come, of course, though they kept in touch by post. The problems of transatlantic fidelity were anxiously raised in his first published story, 'The Sins of the Fathers'.

Blurrily idealized portraits of women crop up in all Gissing's early books, and a few of his later ones. Sometimes they are literally portraits: convinced of the purity of the aesthetic, he makes women into works of art. In one of his Chicago stories, 'Gretchen', the besotted hero moons over a painting of a beautiful woman, 'a divine idealization, whose prototype seemed non-existent'. In fact she does exist and he makes her his wife. Over twenty years later this fairy-tale pattern is repeated on a larger canvas. *The Crown of Life* opens with Piers Otway standing before a picture shop gazing dreamily at engravings of women. Three in particular fascinate him: a lightly-robed maiden from ancient Greece, warm and erotic against cold marble; a lovely and exquisitely arrayed great lady lounging amid luxurious furniture; a glowingly natural peasant girl, 'consummate in grace and strength'.[4] Each one of these icons held a permanent place in Gissing's imagination. While the maiden transparently epitomizes the sensuous appeal of the classics, the other pictures neatly suggest a revealing class-bifurcation: for some years Gissing could not decide between two contrasting ideals of woman — modestly draped refinement or franker earthiness. The graceful peasant, suitably adapted, represents the idealized working girl whose image Gissing fondles in his early books. The image was framed by his hopes for Nell and varnished by his reading of Murger's *Vie de Bohème*; its supreme exemplar is perhaps Ida Starr, the spotless prostitute in *The Unclassed*. Gissing's fantasy of finding a working-class girl who would satisfy his heart's desire, and more, has been analysed by Gillian Tindall. At its centre was the concept of reclamation, of generous compassion for a Magdalen.[5] Though this motive shocked his surviving family, it appeared to be sanctioned by the memory of his father, who had called for the pardon of fallen women in a privately published collection of poems; Gissing gave a copy of this volume to Nell, and found it in her room at her death.[6] Other constituents of the fantasy — hunger for gratitude, sexual excitement, the urge to remould and educate — were to some extent criticized by Gissing even in his early books; but they kept reasserting themselves. Gradually Gissing downgraded this ideal: in his loveless and expedient marriage to Edith he scarcely expected bohemian passion, but only — and equally hopelessly —

docility and domestic comfort. Finally he abandoned it altogether. In his book on Dickens he speaks grimly of young authors, 'misled by motives alien to art, who delight in idealizing girls of the lower, or lowest class'.[7]

The opposite model of femininity − that of 'a refined and virtuous woman' − was moulded just as early but proved more durable. It was based on symbolism and aspiration rather than achievement and knowledge. 'Alas! I have never known a Helen Norman', sighed Gissing, of the heroine of *Workers in the Dawn*, whom the hero describes as 'his idol, the embodiment ... of all that is loftiest'. Looking up to such a paragon in his fiction, preserving belief in its actual existence, became for Gissing a sustaining faith. Up to and including *Born in Exile*, the ambition to marry a well-bred woman is almost ubiquitous in his books; it partially excuses even the behaviour of Dagworthy in *A Life's Morning* and Mutimer in *Demos*. Meeting Gabrielle, Gissing was convinced that at last he had realized his dream. 'Imagine what it means to me', he enthused, 'to be writing to the *ideal woman herself*.'[8] His letters, as we shall see, certainly cast light on what this ideal involved.

In his fiction, woman-worship has three main aspects − aesthetic, moral and intellectual. The first two are somewhat conventional; the third, more idiosyncratic. Aesthetically, Gissing's favoured women combine the stateliness and dignity in fashion at the end of the century with the delicacy and shrinkingness that were prized in earlier decades. A few touches establish his personal signature. Though theoretically he approved of female vigour, several of his heroines are frail and ailing, with the pallid beauty of Annabel in *Thyrza*, of which he writes, 'to the modern mind nothing is complete that has not an element of morbidity'. His women must also have beautiful voices − sweet, mellifluous, yet natural − which 'thrill' on the hearer's nerves. A foreign accent enhances the charm, for it adds an exotic piquancy. Not surprisingly his letters to Gabrielle are full of cadenzas of praise for her voice, which Roberts also appreciated.[9] A final item in the captivating ensemble is − perhaps surprisingly − a grey dress, which seems to connote good taste and decorum, as well as practicality. Lady Revill in *Sleeping Fires* 'was so well dressed that Langley had no consciousness of what she wore, save that it shimmered pearly-grey'. Similarly, with Gabrielle, Gissing remembered 'the grey dress which you wore'. In *The Crown of Life* Irene Derwent is described as 'a grey figure of fluent lines'.[10] The phrase is perhaps apter than Gissing intended, for aesthetically the attractiveness of his women is often rather bland and shadowy. More important, usually, than their physical appearance is their spiritual influence.

Gissing's etherealized accounts of women are shot through with a highly traditional vocabulary of moral commendation. Words like 'purity', 'nobility' and 'soul' are reiterated reverentially; religious and regal imagery abounds — madonnas and haloes, queens and crowns. In many of his early books the virtuous females exalt and purify their menfolk, as Helen does with Arthur, or Emily with Wilfrid; later this motif disappears, though *The Crown of Life* gives it a reprise. Conversely the men pay tribute to their ladies in the ringing accents of courtly love. In *Isabel Clarendon* and *A Life's Morning* great galleons of romantic hyperbole are launched. 'The empire of my passion is all-subduing', foams Wilfrid Athel to Emily. 'Send me to do your bidding; I have no will but yours.' Bernard Kingcote goes even further: 'My pure-browed lady! Your head is like those which come before us in old songs, dark against gold tapestry, or looking from high castle-windows'. Some of these effusions sound uncomfortably close to the fatuous raptures of the gallant Manning ('I am your servitor ... Let me only wear your livery ... You are all the slender goddesses', etc.) in Wells's *Ann Veronica*.[11] Manning is a devotee of Ruskin, whose *Sesame and Lilies* was the classic serenade to Victorian chivalry. Gissing was not consciously a Ruskinite. In *Thyrza*, Egremont is disappointed that Annabel quite likes *Sesame and Lilies*. In *The Odd Women*, too, Gissing shows his acquaintance with feminist arguments (like those in John Stuart Mill) on the shortcomings of chivalry.[12] Nevertheless, his own instincts were incurably chivalrous, and his language often chivalric. Part of his case against the socialists in *Demos* is that they lack respect for women — respect that takes the form of veneration. The English working class, he remarks in this novel, has as little of chivalry 'as any other people in an elementary stage of civilisation'.[13] Any comparable deficiency in the higher orders he tended to attribute to affectation: the character who announces that 'What is called chivalry is simply disguised contempt' is Dyce Lashmar, the charlatan. To Gabrielle, Gissing wrote, 'how vast is your moral superiority ... A man must be content to kneel before you, and grow better by worshipping what he loves'. Though often considered unyieldingly realistic, Gissing's novels are surprisingly full of amorous genuflection. Arthur Golding kneels before Helen's picture and later before Helen herself. Kingcote kneels before Isabel, Wilfrid Athel before

Beatrice. For Emily, Wilfrid sinks even lower: 'He clad her in queenly garments and did homage at her feet'. Mutimer is reproached for not flinging himself at Adela's feet and praying to her.[14] There is also much blushing, and kissing of hands, and hanging on the lover's lips.

Perhaps all this might be waved aside as a reflex reliance on romantic cliché; writing love chapters, Gissing admitted, was always very difficult for him. At a deeper level, though, his emotional responses were more Ruskinite than he thought. Like Ruskin he believed that woman's role was essentially redemptive and sympathetic; and Ruskin's famous celebration of home found a wistful echo in his breast. 'The man in his rough work in the open world must encounter all peril and trial', wrote Ruskin, but the woman must safeguard 'the place of Peace' from the 'hostile society of the outer world'. In *In the Year of Jubilee* Tarrant tells Nancy that 'as a man, it's my duty to join in the rough-and-tumble', but 'You, as a woman, have no such duty; nay, it's your positive duty to keep out of the beastly scrimmage'.[15]

In one area Gissing's appreciation of women was less reflective of contemporary fashion. As we might expect, his attention to their intellects went beyond romantic convention. His protagonists are typically bookish and studious, and the women are no exception. What is noteworthy is that many of the female characters are more expansive intellectually than the men. In *Workers in the Dawn* the heroine's 'Mind-Growth' receives a chapter to itself; the hero's progress seems less secure. In *A Life's Morning* Emily Hood, pursuing an ideal of purity and beauty, dedicates herself to the study of art. Wilfrid's intellectual vitality depends on reuniting with her: otherwise he will moulder in the lower circle of party politics. Adela in *Demos* is another heroine who develops intellectually as well as emotionally; Mutimer's great weakness is that he cannot. Thyrza too improves herself while Egremont regresses. In *The Emancipated*, Miriam's genuine liberation contrasts with her brother's spurious kind; the woman advances, the man does not. This pattern emerges again in *The Odd Women*, in which Monica and Rhoda attain a self-knowledge denied to Everard and Widdowson. Perhaps the explanation of the pattern is that Gissing found it easier to identify with the intellectual predicament of women, since their formal education was more likely than a man's to be incomplete, like his own; an ambitious woman might be more aware of the need for self-improvement. It is remarkable, at any rate, that Monica, Emily, Adela and Miriam are all struggling against the constrictions imposed by traditional training and provincial life. As so often, Gissing writes best about characters who inherit his own aspirations.

Though it is worth recording this motif, we should not over-estimate its significance. For one thing, the woman's educational process is often masterminded by a man. 'I believe I have learnt much from Shakespeare', says Ida to Waymark in *The Unclassed*, 'but there are many things in him I want to ask you to explain.'[16] The sprouting intellect of Ada Warren in *Isabel Clarendon* is pruned and fertilized by Thomas Meres. Miriam's odyssey of self-discovery is influenced and supervized by Mallard. Perhaps, then, women learn more in Gissing because they have more to learn. A second and graver qualification is that the motif goes into reverse. The turning-point is *In the Year of Jubilee*, in which Nancy certainly grows and matures, but in an opposite direction from the filling-out of her mind. Instead she is happily reconciled to her natural role as wife and mother — part-time wife and full-time mother. (Here, too, it is suggested that the hero, Tarrant, callow and arrogant for much of the book, helps Nancy to develop.) After this novel no importance is attached to the value of intellectuality in women until *The Crown of Life* and *Our Friend the Charlatan*, and even here there is greater emphasis on the need for femininity. What transmogrified Gissing's values was the caving-in of his marriage to Edith, whom he wished could be both better educated and more compliantly domestic. *The Odd Women* explores the first aspiration. *In the Year of Jubilee* affirms the second — a patently nostalgic domestic ideal which became increasingly attractive to Gissing throughout the 1890s. We can see it in Mrs Morton in *The Whirlpool*, with her fountain breasts and busy contentment, her devotion to her children and submission to her spouse; or in Mrs Clover in *The Town Traveller*, who, with her gentleness and neatness, her 'little parlour' and 'merry little laugh', emerges as a distinctly Dickensian figurine: partly reminiscent, in fact, of Ruth Pinch, about whom Gissing wrote so yearningly a few months later in his book on Dickens ('thoroughly kind-hearted ... an excellent mother ... cooking ... babies ... never a wry face ... Upon my word — is it a bad ideal?').[17]

Quite plainly, Gissing's glorification of women led him into inconsistencies. His emphatic approval of 'Wife, housewife, mother ... strong and peaceful in her perfect womanhood' (as he puts it in his story 'Out of the Fashion') was partly at odds with his courtly predilections, and very much with his cerebral ones. Like Breakspeare in *Our Friend the Charlatan*, who 'admired intellectual women' but 'heartily approved the domestic virtues', he 'desired to unite irreconcilable things'.[18] But Gissing's inconsistency went further. The pedestal on which he wished to place women was not only fractured in itself, but attached to a vast and immovable rock of hard misogyny. It is not simply that his fiction contains vicious women, but that their vices are frequently indicted as specifically female ones. Vanity, greed and illogicality, jealousy, violence and hypochondria, spitefulness, cynicism and conventionality — the list is so long that any discussion must be greatly abbreviated.

Anxious to reassure Gabrielle, Gissing explained his alleged misogyny in terms of his choice of subject. Most of his books had dealt, he said, with the 'pestilent and loathsome world' of 'uneducated London women', with 'their faults of vulgar egoism and brutal ignorance'; his concentration on this milieu had misrepresented his views. This argument is only partially valid. Certainly many of his onslaughts on women are aimed at the features of the untaught class among which he chose to marry. Nell — no *grisette* but a tippling doxy — is anatomized in *Workers in the Dawn* and then again in *The Unclassed*, where the snivelling malevolence of Harriet Smales, with her fits and foamings, her scrofula and tantrums, provokes her husband to the declaration (which Gissing later edited out): 'What claim had this wretched creature upon him ... ?' Edith — no mutely submissive mate but a raucous asserter of her own desires — is recreated in Ada Peachey, who enlivens *In the Year of Jubilee* by railing 'in the language of the gutter and the brothel', smashing the breakables in her bedroom, and wrestling with her sister on the floor 'like the female spawn of Whitechapel'. What especially shocked Gissing was the readiness of women to resort to physical violence. 'A *gentle*man', he noted in his commonplace book, 'is much more often met with than a *gentle*woman.'[19] Some of the women he conjures up are about as gentle as a broken bottle. In his story 'A Parent's Feelings' two termagant mothers attack a headmaster and leave him with blood streaming down his cheeks. At the end of the mainly comic *Town Traveller* the squalid demise of Lord Polperro is hastened along by the gentler sex: one woman squirts liquid into his ear, another knocks his hat off; a drunken woman strikes the first blow. In *The Nether World* the feral Clem Peckover delights in tormenting a younger girl both physically and psychologically. She also rains blows on her rival, Pennyloaf, whose husband she inspires with her own 'lust of cruelty', inciting him to punch his wife's mouth.[20] Clem is a monstrous, deranged exception even among the lowest classes; but Gissing's coarse women are typically rowdy and sometimes barbarous.

Feminine failings are not, however, confined to the uneducated. Many middle-class women are also obnoxious, but in a contrasting way. Instead of being vehement, anarchic and careless, they are either quietly calculating — mercenary, worldly and self-controlled — or else they are narrowly censorious and obsessed with trivial rules. The first type of woman, the elegant materialist, is ubiquitous in Gissing's later books. Her prototype is Isabel Clarendon, who though excused as 'woman womanly in every fraction of her being', exhibits a number of qualities — respect for society, fear of poverty, a fluency in shifting her affections — which are later perfected in, for example, the deceitful heroine of *Eve's Ransom*, or Amy Reardon in *New Grub Street*, whose coldly uncooperative passivity is also rather reminiscent of Rosamond in *Middlemarch* (the parallels even extend to the detail of both women being absorbed in sewing to resist their husbands' entreaties).[21] The other type of woman is the pious and prudish. Examples are Maud Enderby in *The Unclassed*, Adela and Miriam (at least at first), and Lady Revill in *Sleeping Fires*.

In *Thyrza* Gissing states that the two main dangers for 'English girls of the free born class' are 'frivolous worldliness' and 'Puritanism'. Both dangers are copiously exposed in his fiction and both, despite their differences, are perceived as aspects of a single vice: conventionality. That women were too often conventional, that they lacked the liberality of mind that would save them from either frivolity or piety, was essential to Gissing's indictment. 'Women are the great reactionary force', says Mrs Wade in *Denzil Quarrier*. 'They worship the vulgar, the pretentious, the false.' Certainly middle-class women in Gissing's books tend to cleave closely to current values, whether socially or morally. It was not, however, that Gissing would have wished them to branch out boldly in either sentiment or conduct. On the contrary, he prized the traditional virtues of modesty and submissiveness. He even changed his mind about the role of religion. In *Denzil Quarrier* it is the satirized Vialls who declares that 'Unaided by religion, the female nature is irresponsible', and in *The Odd Women* it is Widdowson who predictably agrees with this. Yet in Gissing's next book, *In the Year of Jubilee*, this notion is proposed quite seriously (though its implications are qualified); and in *Eve's Ransom* the belief is repeated.[22]

The peak period of Gissing's antipathy to women occurred in the 1890s. Wretchedly unhappy in his marriage to Edith, he discharged his bile in a series of works, from *Born in Exile* to his book on Dickens, which offer a crescendo of misogyny. Given such a context, it is scarcely surprising that *The Odd Women* fails of its purpose in parts: the wonder is rather that it ever got written. Its successors — especially *The Whirlpool* and *In the Year of Jubilee* — are bristling with venomous attacks on women, for their coarseness, their credulity, their neglect of children, and above all their reckless extravagance. The war-beat is also kept up in short stories. After planning a story called 'The Woman-Queller', Gissing actually wrote one, in 1894, entitled 'The Tyrant's Apology'. An exasperated monologue spoken by a husband provoked to curtail his wife's spendthrift ways, this story concludes: 'Her rights as an individual? Humbug! She is not an individual; it's the rarest thing to meet a woman who is.' Gissing wrote this just two days after a particularly galling affront from Edith.[23] In 1895 he shortened *The Unclassed*. Some of his changes are informative for the history of his attitudes to women. A ramshackle sub-plot concerning Maud's parents was not only pared down but altered in bias. In the first version Enderby's love for his wife, and responsibility for her behaviour, are stressed as much as her failing of him. In revision, these qualifications are dropped; the wife is entirely to blame. Again, at the end of the first edition Harriet accepts a kindly offer from a lady who will pay her medical expenses. In the second edition she rejects this with insult, falls downstairs and breaks her neck.[24] At times, indeed, in the 1890s, it seems that Gissing was strongly tempted by the thought of using force against women. 'It is astounding to me that they don't get their necks wrung', cries Mr Lord in *In the Year of Jubilee*, at the end of a frenzied diatribe against 'these trashy, flashy girls'. Earwaker in *Born in Exile* has never married because he 'foresaw a terrible possibility — that I might beat my wife'.

The culmination of this mood in Gissing erupted in a book he wrote in 1897, just after fleeing from Edith to the Continent: *Charles Dickens: A Critical Study*. In this, the chapter on Dickens's women struck even some contemporary reviewers as unusually personal.[25] Dickens's verisimilitude, says Gissing, is primarily shown by 'his gallery of foolish, ridiculous, or offensive women'. Most of these are from the lower-middle class and in general lead comfortable lives. 'Yet their characteristic is acidity of temper and boundless licence of querulous and insulting talk ... Invariably they are unintelligent and untaught; very often they are flagrantly imbecile ... In the highways and by-ways of life, by the fireside and in the bed-chamber, their voices shrill upon the terrified ear'. However, since Dickens assembled this gallery, an 'increase of liberty' for women has made things even worse. Were Dickens now writing, Gissing suggests, 'I believe he would have to add ... the well-dressed shrew who proceeds on the slightest provocation from fury of language to violence of act'. But, he continues, what Dickens did observe, he described with perfect accuracy, though also — to Gissing's amazement — with exuberant comedy. Take a woman like Mrs Nickleby — affectionate, well-meaning, apparently harmless; yet 'unhappily the poor woman has been born with the intellectual equipment of a Somerset ewe'. Her bleating talk has killed her husband, but Dickens finds in her matter for mirth. Perhaps this is only for the best. 'She is ubiquitous, and doubtless always will be. She cannot be chained and muzzled, or forbidden to propagate her kind.' Elsewhere, Dickens's treatment of women is more satisfactory to Gissing's sense of appropriate realism. For example, the 'harsh truth' of the punishment meted out to Mrs Joe in *Great Expectations*:

> Mrs. Gargery shall be brought to quietness; but how? By a half-murderous blow on the back of her head, from which she will never recover. Dickens understood by this time that there is no other efficacious way with these ornaments of their sex. A felling and stunning and all but killing blow, followed by paralysis and slow death. A sharp remedy, but no whit sharper than the evil it cures.

Gissing concludes this section of his chapter: 'One does not venture to begin praising work such as this. Eulogy would lose itself in enthusiasm.'[26]

A few months after completing this book, Gissing met Gabrielle Fleury. Now eulogy did lose itself in enthusiasm. 'My own little girlie,' he wrote, 'my pet, my birdie, don't, don't trouble. What a large, *large* heart it is, and how full, full of exquisite love and loyalty! ... Chérie! Bien aimée! Your first kiss when we meet will give me a new life.' For a time she also gave him a new attitude to women — pantingly romantic in *The Crown of Life*, crisply feminist in parts of *Our Friend the Charlatan*. Yet after all, such attitudes were not really new, but simply a revival of earlier responses. And in any case his sourer judgements survived. *The Charlatan* contains a misogynist tirade, largely irrelevant to the thrust of the plot, delivered, we are told, by a 'fine old cynic' in a 'good-natured growl'. In *Will Warburton* there is not only Rosamund Elvan — the elegant materialist again — but also the naggingly

Dickensian Mrs Cross, her face lined 'by long-indulged vices of the feminine will'.[27] The truth is that from first to last Gissing's emotional reaction to women was strangely compounded of romantic desire and disenchanted repulsion. In two linked stories he wrote in Chicago, 'The Death Clock' and 'The Serpent Charm', a man sees a beautiful woman as victim, deserving even the sacrifice of his life, but is later informed she was truly an enchantress, intent upon his destruction. Nearly a quarter of a century later, in the uncompleted *Veranilda*, the winsome heroine with her 'watchet eyes' is contrasted with a shrill-voiced woman called Muscula and a slinky courtesan called Heliodora, whose lustful wiles the hero must elude. Moreover, in the Abbey of Montecassino, Basil suddenly perceives the explanation of the peace and serenity all around him: 'Here entered no woman'. But Basil discovers that he lacks the constitution to commit himself to ascetic life. He leaves the monastery, re-enters the world and is reconciled with Veranilda — the perfect heroine, the feminine ideal.[28]

I I

If the alternation of rapture and disgust exhausted Gissing's responses to women, his fiction would be less problematic and less valuable than it is. The split presentation of the female sex, as either goddess or succubus, was not peculiar to him but a hallowed prejudice of Western art, very prominent in the nineteenth century. Nor is it difficult to account for Gissing's attachment to this dichotomy. A disillusioned but stubborn idealist, who believed that love was 'the crown of life' (the phrase occurs as early as *A Life's Morning* and the concept even earlier), Gissing devoted much of his fiction to sketching the lineaments of his ideal woman, and etching in acid what he had actually found.[29] In other words, he tended to delineate women as potential sexual partners for men (this explains, incidentally, why his books include so few older female characters).[30] But Gissing also had a larger interest in the prospects and problems of contemporary women, a sociological curiosity. This was so especially after 1889, when he roughed out a novel called *The Headmistress*, which dealt with female education. In October he recorded in his diary, 'Worked at Museum, on Woman Literature'. What this work involved can be gleaned from a dossier now in the possession of the Pforzheimer Library, which incorporates a section on 'The Movement' listing books, magazines and societies concerned with female emancipation, as well as containing more specific notes on higher education. By March 1890 Gissing had decided not to persevere with *The Headmistress*, but he noted, 'materials for that will lie over'.[31] The materials were utilized in *The Odd Women*, but Gissing's researches also affected a number of his novels from *The Emancipated* onwards. In these, unlike his earlier books, topics of contemporary feminist interest are dealt with consciously and deliberately. To provide a context for *The Odd Women*, and to give at least a summary indication of Gissing's often ambiguous stance, five of these topics will be briefly discussed: marriage; sex; motherhood; employment; and education.

Criticism of marriage as an institution was a crucial part of the feminist case in the late-nineteenth century. In Britain a continuous campaign for women's rights began only in the 1850s with the organization on behalf of married women's property rights. By the 1890s the case had broadened. In fiction, attacks on marital constrictions became so common that Mrs Oliphant talked darkly of an 'Anti-Marriage League'. Several of the fashionable 'new woman' novels exposed the disadvantages of marriage, some of their authors, like Mona Caird, recommending its abolition. Gissing also took a jaundiced view of marriage, but not usually from a feminist angle. 'Marriage rarely means happiness, either for man or woman', says *The Whirlpool*; 'if it be not too grievous to be borne, one must thank the fates and take courage.'[32] Very few of Gissing's married couples are happy – the Spences in *The Emancipated*, the Liversedges in *Denzil Quarrier*, the Mortons in *The Whirlpool* itself. In his early books, written while living with Nell, Gissing depicts marriage as a maddening cage into which men are manoeuvred by women and goaded by their own desires. In a chapter called 'A Man-Trap' in *The Unclassed*, Harriet coaxes a proposal from Casti by engineering a compromising scene and playing on his sense of compassion. Casti's later expression of regret for his choice – 'Don't use that word "wife", it is profanation ... Curse her to all eternity!' – becomes curiously resonant by the end of the book. Waymark, having got engaged to Maud, declares, 'I have brought a curse upon my life', and Mrs Enderby confides to her husband, 'I am your curse. I have brought you to ruin'.

In the 1890s, possessed by Edith, Gissing had once again to exorcize his feelings on the baneful effects of marriage. Albatross wives are everywhere in his stories and novels of this period.

Though shallow and childish, they are domineering, and though obsessed with their independence, financially irresponsible. Deficient in sympathy and household duties, they nag their servants into rebellion and reduce their husbands to perplexed despair. Their ravages are most starkly seen in *The Whirlpool*, which seems to describe a moral epidemic afflicting the female sex. At its centre is the marriage of Harvey and Alma, which Gissing, according to Clara Collet, imagined he had treated impartially.[33] The marriage is certainly subtly done, but its drift is unmistakable; what conditions our interpretation is that, swirling round this thematic vortex, are dozens of didactic narrative fragments all converging on the same point. The vast majority of the male characters are bled dry or swept towards ruin by women. Poor, bluff Hugh Carnaby is provoked to commit manslaughter because of his malignly imperturbable wife. Feebly good-natured Cecil Morphew goes bankrupt trying to meet the demands of his chilly fiancée's parents; eventually, after years of stalling, she casts him off for having sired an illegitimate child (whose mother, incidentally, swindles Morphew by taking payments after its death). Mrs Abbott's husband, shocked by her disloyalty, dies from an overdose of morphia; the teacher Thistlewood has lost a finger in a quarrel over an 'expensive young woman' who left him for a richer man. Even the most marginal characters are sucked into the novel's thesis. Harvey's cleaner, Mrs Handover, has reduced her husband to a 'vagabond pauper'. His landlord, Buncombe, is deserted by a wife who, obsessed with her independence, becomes a singer in music-halls (when Alma decides to 'come out' as a musician, Harvey starts thinking of Buncombe). Even Harvey's housekeeper, Ruth, can dilate on her brother's afflictions: 'No one can be sorry for his wife's death; she was such a poor, silly, complaining, useless creature ... There's many women of that kind, sir, but I never knew one as bad as her — never.' Evidently Ruth has not read Gissing's novels. In an earlier one, *In the Year of Jubilee*, the hen-pecked — or rather vulture-scarred — Peachey had already expressed Gissing's disenchantment: 'Before his marriage he had thought of women as domestic beings. A wife was the genius of home ... Nowadays he saw the matter in the light of further experience. In his rank of life married happiness was a rare thing, and the fault could generally be traced to wives.'[34]

Gissing had not always felt as bitterly as this. It is true that his fiction contains four case histories — those of Golding, Casti, Peachey and Rolfe — in which the anguish of a husband is

analysed at length. But it also contains three extended examples
of the painfully unmerited plight of a wife. These three have
remarkable similarities, as well as significant differences. One of
them, the marriage of Monica and Widdowson, will be dealt with
in discussion of *The Odd Women*. The others are the marriages of
Adela and Mutimer in *Demos* and Cecily and Elgar in *The
Emancipated*. The Mutimers' marriage is designed primarily as
a warning against class-miscegenation. The novel stresses
Mutimer's savagery and sadism, his desire to pull down and
humiliate his wife, and in this coarse cruelty, often sharpened
by drink, the author perceives an inevitable regression to the
proletarian 'brute-husband'. An emphasis unusual in Gissing is
placed on the sexual element in the wife's disgust. Adela shrinks
instinctively from Mutimer, almost swoons with horror as his face
draws near. She recoils from his rough sexual overtures — 'his
passion was mysterious, revolting' — and after renouncing her
'maiden whiteness' feels 'cast away on shoals of debasement'. For
comfort she turns to another woman, and this relationship,
though oddly inconclusive, is also portrayed with unusual
frankness. Kissed by the 'light-robed' Stella Westlake, Adela
quivers through her whole frame; this time she almost swoons
with ecstasy. Later Stella undresses her and they sleep together in
each other's arms.[35] Yet despite this feminine sympathy, and the
female solidarity throughout the novel — which does indeed
stretch across class divisions, embracing not only Adela and
Stella, but Adela and Mutimer's rejected fiancée — the heroine is
very far from being a defiant lesbian feminist. She is rather a
pure-souled patient Griselda, admired for her loyal submissiveness. 'The high-hearted one!' gushes Gissing. 'To the end she
would speak that word "my husband" ... with the confidence of a
woman who knows no other safeguard against the ills of life.'
Rather different, this, from Monica's reaction, yet in some ways
the masculine oppression is the same. Mutimer's 'primitive ideas
on woman' closely anticipate Widdowson's, and like the older
man he is prone to fits of possessiveness and jealousy. He accuses
his wife of making secret assignations, manhandles her and locks
her in her room.[36] Adela resents this behaviour but endures it;
Monica, similarly provoked, eventually abandons her husband.

The reasons for Adela's marriage are instructive. One is her
mother's unscrupulous pressure in favour of an advantageous
match; another is her own sheltered ignorance, the result of
restricted education. Sketching out a critique of the social forces
that tend to push girls into unhappy marriages, *Demos* looked

forward to more feminist novels like Sarah Grand's *The Heavenly Twins* (1893). Yet, as if to cancel this diagnosis, Gissing, with characteristic pessimism, created another unhappy marriage with causes precisely the opposite. In *The Emancipated* Cecily Doran has been given a liberal education with no undue emphasis on 'purity'; her aunt has encouraged her to be independent, and financially she need not marry. The upshot of her aunt's enlightened training is that Cecily demonstrates her independence by running off with Reuben Elgar. The causes of the marriage are different from those in *Demos*, but the outcome is strikingly similar. At first, like Adela Mutimer, Cecily tries to absorb herself in her husband's confused ambitions; reluctantly, though, she comes to acknowledge the painful truth of his shoddiness. Sensing this, and resenting his wife's superiority, Reuben tries to assert himself by imposing restrictions on her social life. As if to symbolize the demise of their marriage, their sickly child dies in infancy (Adela's baby is stillborn). Eventually — just as Adela finds out about Mutimer's betrayal of Emma Vine — Cecily discovers that her faithless husband has had an affair with an actress. But Reuben remains intransigently self-righteous. Knowing that Cecily has called on Mallard, he upbraids her with 'the violence of jealousy and the brute instinct of male prerogative'. Ultimately — also like Mutimer — he dies in squalid circumstances. In both books, then, the husband's oppression is exerted in a comparable manner. Sustained by crude attitudes to women, but inflamed by a sense of inadequacy, both men resort to jealous bluster and impose patriarchal restrictions. Widdowson thinks and acts the same. There are differences, however, in the reactions of the wives. While all three women refuse to reply to demeaning accusations, Adela staunchly accepts her lot (thus earning the author's fulsome praise), Cecily makes a half-protest against it (only half, for she also blames natural laws for women's unfair predicament), and Monica, alone among the three, is spurred into open revolt.[37]

At one point in *The Emancipated* Reuben reflects, 'How absurd it was for two people, just because they were married, to live perpetually within sight of each other!' He approves of Godwin's 'rational plan' that husband and wife should have separate abodes. In context these sentiments only condemn him (they occur just before his infidelity), but by *Born in Exile* Gissing himself is suggesting that keeping apart a great deal is 'essential to happiness in marriage'; and by *In the Year of Jubilee* this aside has grown into a theory. Lionel Tarrant believes that most marital flare-ups are caused by habitual friction: 'The common practice of man and wife occupying the same room is monstrous, gross; it's astounding that women of any sensitiveness endure it'. When he says this, Tarrant too is a suspect character, but the novel's conclusion endorses his view. Separate dwellings save his and Nancy's marriage: though scarcely delighted, she gives 'rational acquiescence'. Gissing's lugubrious enthusiasm for the value of semi-detached marriage evaporated when he met Gabrielle. 'A profound love between two intelligent persons *demands* a life in common', he insisted. In *The Crown of Life* the intelligent Mrs Borisoff lives apart from her husband for half the year; but theirs, as she admits, is not a profound love; compared with Irene, the book makes clear, she has settled for a lower ideal.[38]

A second alternative to orthodox marriage was to set up a sexual partnership without it — to live in free union. Widely canvassed towards the end of the century, this arrangement achieved notoriety through Grant Allen's nerveless novel *The Woman Who Did* (1895). In *The Odd Women*, published two years before, free union is also prominent; but here, though sympathetically treated, the issue is made subordinate to the intricacies of personal conflict. The campaign for a broader sexual morality, in which Gissing played a modest part, was closely allied with the women's movement in the late nineteenth century. There was, it is true, some discrepancy between the exceedingly correct deportment of the formal activists for women's rights, who needed to remain irreproachable, and the frequently lurid treatment of the subject by poets and novelists. The coupling of female liberation with a revolution in sexual ethics was especially close in the 'new woman' novels.[39] Gissing's own fictional treatment of sex was always liberal, but usually restrained; and his standpoint changed over the years. A man who marries a prostitute is not likely to applaud conventional morals, and in his early books at least Gissing took pains to defy them. *Workers in the Dawn* mounts 'sordid' scenes (like the erotic 'Tableaux Vivants' exhibition); *The Unclassed* overflows with 'frank' conversations. *Mrs Grundy's Enemies* was bowdlerized by Bentley's and eventually rejected altogether. In 1884 Gissing criticized Thackeray for having conciliated Mrs Grundy, and was promptly knocked on the head by *Punch* ('Praised be the gods for thy foulness, Gissing'). In 1886 he complained to Hardy of 'the reticences and superficialities' that so often had to substitute for honest work. Yet Gissing himself was increasingly reticent. Compared with

Hardy's own novels (at least in their non-serial forms), for instance, his later fiction is heavily draped in smoothed-down obliquities of phrase. Of a character in *The Crown of Life*, he writes: 'She had been imprudent, once or twice all but reckless, never what is called guilty'.[40] Compared, too, with some contemporary novels, his work is not sensuously suggestive; the closest he comes to erotic description is perhaps the account of Nancy's seduction in *In the Year of Jubilee*. He never abandoned his angry contempt for the code of the pursed-lipped *bourgeoisie* (see, for instance, his satire of the Mumbray family in *Denzil Quarrier*). But he did become more and more opposed to the blatant discussion of sexual facts.[41]

Once again his alterations to *The Unclassed* provide evidence of changing values. In his preface to the 1895 edition he states that the book was originally written 'a long, long time ago', when most editors were unwilling to have it noticed and people discussed it in whispers; he then reiterates sardonically: 'The date was 1884 — a long time ago'. Gissing implies here that discussion of sex had become more open in the intervening years. This was true in general, but not of himself: the revised edition is in fact toned down. Among the sections Gissing excised are accounts of Woodstock's '*amours de jeunesse*' and Waymark's 'wildest dissipation', as well as Ida's thoughts on her 'vile trade'. According to Roberts, the younger Gissing rejoiced in a statement of Zola's Nana: '*Quand je vois un homme qui me plaît, je couche avec*'. It is hard to imagine such a sentiment on the lips of, say, Irene Derwent, who demonstrates her boldness by refusing to condemn a fictional character whose parents have not married (though when Piers's illegitimacy is spoken about, she has to avert her eyes). By 1900, Gissing told Bertz, he had 'grown to abhor Zola's grossness'.[42]

Motherhood was another controversial topic to which Gissing's responses changed. A number of Victorian feminists were willing to reject the idea that for women maternity was the goal of life. Very few, however, impugned the existence or the value of maternal instinct. Despite this moderation, it was not uncommon for emancipated women to be portrayed as uncomely, mannish, or sterile. Such portrayals were not limited to popular jibes. In his *Principles of Biology* Herbert Spencer explained that overtaxing a woman's brain would probably make her less fertile.[43] In Gissing's case, reverence for motherhood was based on experience of fatherhood. In his early books he pays little attention to any features of parental feeling; children appear only rarely and are usually regarded as intruders. Wilfrid Athel, married to Emily, is glad that 'no child would be born of her to trouble the exclusive-ness of their love'. When Amy and Reardon's son Willie — a shadowy child at the best of times — dies, Reardon remarkably feels 'a deep solace' that Amy can now concentrate on him. Gissing believed that motherhood was in some ways at odds with education — and at first preferred education. The average woman finds maternity absorbing, he writes in *The Emancipated*, because it is 'a relief from the weariness of her unfruitful mind'.[44]

With the arrival of his sons in the 1890s Gissing's understanding of maternity became more respectful — and demanding. It was not that he had great empathy for the feelings of a woman during pregnancy or feeding. 'Edith ill with dyspepsia, or whatever it may be', he wrote impatiently, of what was probably morning sickness. And when their second baby proved troublesome, he recorded, 'of course poisoned by his milk, E. being constantly in sullen rage'. But charting Edith's failings as a mother — her carelessness, incompetence and ill-temper — sharpened Gissing's appreciation of woman's traditional role. In his fiction of the 1890s he writes waspishly about neglect of children and about women who speak of offspring as 'encumbrance'. Ada Peachey (*In the Year of Jubilee*) leaves her baby to cry and overlooks danger: 'A good-tempered cow might with more confidence have been set to watch over the little one's safety.' Nancy, conversely, achieves respect through the perfect love she devotes to her child. Having given birth, she 'knew the exultation of a woman who has justified her being'. 'Nature doesn't intend a married woman', she concludes, 'to be anything *but* a married woman.'[45] Alma Rolfe in *The Whirlpool* disagrees — with instructively chaotic results. Whereas for Harvey fatherhood makes 'a revolution in his thoughts', motherhood has only a distracting effect on Alma's febrile yearnings. Eventually, it is true, she makes some progress, no longer rejoicing in a miscarriage, but accepting 'the common lot of women'; by this time, though, she is already entrammelled in her own web of finespun intrigue. Alma's antics are luridly confirmed by those of other women: Mrs Abbott's child, we learn, has 'died of convulsions during its mother's absence at a garden party'. In these later books it is usually the fathers who display a protective concern for their children and enjoy an affectionate rapport with them (in *The Whirlpool* Walter Gissing's baby utterances are transcribed with precision and tenderness: little Hughie, his fictional counterpart, is the author's most credible child).[46] The mothers, by contrast, intent on their pleasures, default on their natural functions. However, this is true only of the later books. *The Odd Women* — an offspring of feminist research, but the first novel written after Walter's birth — does not rate the merits of maternity higher than the claims of female independence. It does, though, represent them as alternatives.

Like Mill and most other Victorians, Gissing believed that the duties of a mother would not easily combine with a job.[47] Paid employment was therefore for working-class wives, compelled to eke out their husband's wage, or for genteel females without a partner — the numerous 'odd' women, in fact. But though he accepted female employment as an economic necessity, Gissing did not normally think of it as attractive or fulfilling in itself. For this he has sometimes been criticized.[48] The fact is, though, that as a self-employed writer he was not enthralled by paid labour for others on the part of either women or men. When Will Warburton is asked to name his employers, the term rasps on his sensitive temper. But Gissing was also a realistic novelist, and in writing about his characters' jobs he took care to get his details right. He compiled a huge dossier on 'Occupations', which lists no fewer than fifteen books. Some of these — like *The Englishwoman's Year Book* — are exclusively concerned with female work.[49] It must be admitted, nevertheless, that most of his main female characters either do not have a job at all, or have a traditionally 'feminine' job. Helen Norman, Maud Enderby and Emily Hood work in the teaching and governessing line from which Mary Barfoot wants women released. Ida Starr and Carrie Mitchell are prostitutes. Mrs Clover keeps a shop, Emma Vine is a seamstress. Jane Snowdon, Clem Peckover, Thyrza and her sister are all employed in factories; the first two make artificial flowers, the second two trim felt hats. Many of the better-off women are philanthropists — Stella Westlake, Mrs Ormonde, Mrs Tresilian, Miss Lant. A large number of Gissing's minor heroines have vaguely artistic avocations. Clara Hewett is an actress, Beatrice Redwing a singer, Polly Sparkes a theatre-programme seller. Ada Warren and Mrs Wade are writers, Patty Ringrose works in a music shop, Alma Rolfe likes to think of herself as a professional violinist. Olga Hannaford and her friend Miss Bonnicastle design fashion papers and advertising posters. Bertha Cross illustrates children's books, and Maud and Dora Milvain write them. The exceptions to this pattern are few indeed. In *Born in Exile* Janet Moxey is a lady doctor; but paradoxically the strain of her practice is breaking down her health. Despite his carefully researched information, Gissing's conception of female employment was largely conservative. One suspects in fact that the very idea contained in it something rebarbative to him. Asserting that women must have money of their own, Nancy Lord goes in search of 'honest hard work', but quickly becomes discouraged. 'What right had a mother', she asks at last, 'to be searching abroad for tasks and duties? Task enough, duty obvious, in the tending of her child.'[50] In one of the most famous 'new woman' novels, Sarah Grand's *The Heavenly Twins*, a heroine complaining of the social system cries out with characteristic despair: 'I wanted to *do* as well as to *be*'. But in *The Emancipated*, three years earlier, the hero upholds an opposite priority. Reflecting on the plight of Miriam and Cecily, Mallard concludes that 'neither of these women really could *do* anything; it was not their function to do, but to *be*'.[51]

The question of employment for women was closely connected with education; and indeed the educability of women was central to the feminist case. On female education Gissing felt strongly: it was, he told a correspondent, 'the *one* interest of our time, the one thing needful'. According to Jacob Korg and others, Gissing's views on the subject were progressive and enlightened; certainly there can be little doubt that he favoured the extension of learning.[52] Once again, however, complications arise, a few of which are perhaps worth mentioning here. As we have seen, Gissing had reservations about education of any kind, and these applied to women as much as to men. Education could cause loneliness and social estrangement, as it does for the Meres girls in *Isabel Clarendon* and the Milvain sisters in *New Grub Street*. Lacking opportunities for social fulfilment, a girl might regret, like Clara Hewett, that she has ever been taught to read and write. In Gissing, life is simpler for the less instructed. 'The task of an educated wife and mother', he writes in his story 'The Foolish Virgin', is 'infinitely more complex, more trying.'[53] Nor could women remain immune from the virus of pretentious and sham education, satirized (in *The Emancipated*) through the Denyer girls, with their 'fluent inaccuracy' on every subject, and (in *In the Year of Jubilee*) through Beatrice and Fanny French, who have 'done' political economy and 'been through' inorganic chemistry. Such satirical passages have sometimes been taken as proof of Gissing's disbelief that women were capable of education. Since the mockery extends to male examples — Philip Dolamore, Samuel Barmby — the argument is plainly untenable. It is true, though, that Gissing was always uncertain whether formal tuition could achieve very much. This uncertainty shows up in his book on Dickens, where he tells us that, properly educated, Flora Finching might have been 'a charming person', and even Mrs Nickleby 'quite endurable', but then adds, in connection with Mrs Plornish, 'one thinks with misgivings of the day when that increased comfort which is their due, shall open to such women the dreadful possibilities of half-knowledge'.[54]

Gissing had serious doubts, then, about education as such; whether he also believed that women could profit less from it than men is still a question worth asking. Not long after publishing *The Odd Women*, he opined that women should be intellectually trained very much as men are. Apparently this was not always his view. In 1880 he told his sister Ellen: 'A girl's education should be of a very general and liberal character, adapted rather to expand the intelligence as a whole than to impart very thorough knowledge on any subject'; a girl should *not* concentrate on higher mathematics or political economy. Two years later he added that imaginative literature was essential for the character-improvement of women: 'I would rather have a girl well acquainted with Dickens, George Eliot, Shelley and Browning than with all the science in the text books'. These sentiments — shared by Helen Norman's father — are remarkably similar to those of Ruskin in *Sesame and Lilies*.[55] The question of what girls ought to learn was linked with the question of their mental capacity. The common, but no longer universal, view was that women were less intelligent than men, less rigorous and less original. Biological evidence was sometimes deployed in support of this traditional contention. In an article on which Gissing made notes, George Romanes, the friend and follower of Darwin, provided evolutionary explanations of woman's inferiority. Even centuries of education, he argued, conducted in the most favourable circumstances, could not make up for 'the missing five ounces of the female brain'. Romanes also rehearsed at length the argument, which he largely accepted, that 'the physique of young women ... is not sufficiently robust to stand the strain of severe study'.[56] That Gissing made notes on this article does not prove that he seconded its content. The ambiguity of his response emerges from *In the Year of Jubilee*, where the character who echoes Romanes's remarks ('The delicacy of their nervous systems unfits them for such a strain') is the fatuous Samuel Barmby. The twist is that Barmby turns out to be right: Jessica, overburdened by her feverish efforts, has a breakdown following an examination, and babbles out his crushing maxim.[57]

What we can say is that Gissing paid great attention to the implications of evolution and sometimes believed them to be inauspicious for the mental improvement of women. In *Born in Exile* Peak declares: 'The defect of the female mind? It is my belief that this is nothing more nor less than the defect of the uneducated human mind ... A woman has hitherto been an ignorant human being; that explains everything'. But Earwaker replies: 'Not everything; something, perhaps. Remember your evolutionism. The preservation of the race demands in women many kinds of irrationality, of obstinate instinct, which enrage a reasoning man'. Gissing's inner debate is reflected here − but it is notable that with *In the Year of Jubilee* he authorially endorses the Earwaker case. Certainly he was strongly inclined to believe that biology made women less rational.[58]

On the woman question, then, as on most other questions, Gissing's thoughts were ambiguous and shifting; on all the central feminist issues, he offers a characteristic mix of the reactionary and the progressive. The reason, of course, was that his social theories could never be divorced from his personal feelings, and his feelings were deeply divided. Worshipping women, yet despising them, searching desperately for a perfect mate, he adopted positions on women's rights that reflected his pendulum moods. As time went on, he became more conservative; *The Odd Women* constitutes the high-water mark of his sympathy for the female cause. Even here the reforming fervour is qualified: sympathy is not identical with prediction of total success. Part of the problem was that woman's liberation was dependent on her intimate relations with man; and about these Gissing was gloomy. Two factors − typical of his torn emotions, and relevant to *The Odd Women* − controlled his depiction of sexual relations and undermined his official ideal of equality and harmony. The first was his perennial tendency to write about love as a contest of wills and suggest that what women most admire is ultimately masculine strength. The theme of 'woman's instinct of subjection' emerges strongly in *Isabel Clarendon*, in which Gissing says: 'If a man have not strength, love alone will not suffice to bind a woman to him; she will pardon brutality, but weakness inspires her with fear'. The truth of this dictum is demonstrated at all social levels in his subsequent works. It applies not only to the termagants and shrews − Clem Peckover, Ada Peachey, Louise Derrick, Mrs Cross − but to cool materialists like Amy Reardon, feminists like Mrs Wade, and socialites like Sibyl Carnaby. One short story, 'The Honeymoon', is entirely devoted to its proof.[59] His second wife, Edith, appeared to confirm it. In his scrapbook Gissing laconically recorded her expression of delight in an actor called Gurney: 'He always took a villain's part, & *used to thrash women*. I'd have gone anywhere to see him'. Reminiscent of this remark is the incident in *The Town Traveller* when Gammon manhandles Polly: furiously angry at the time, she is yieldingly impressed later. The few successful love affairs in Gissing tend to conclude with female submission and a flourish of 'triumphant manhood'. Gissing's emphasis on sexual inequality was related, of course, to his own anxiety about his inadequate assertiveness. After two years of life with Gabrielle, he saw himself as 'a rather poor creature, living in querulous subjection', and announced:

> I am going to be more worthy of respect in the eyes of my wife.
> After all, the old predominance of the *man* is thoroughly wholesome
> and justifiable, but he must be *manlike* and worthy of ruling. Most
> contemptible is the man who lets himself be dominated even by the
> most beloved woman.[60]

If Gissing's insistence on male supremacy undermined the possibility of equal relations, his preoccupation with jealousy was a threat to harmonious ones. 'Jealousy', as Frank Swinnerton noted long ago, 'is the dominant note in a Gissing lover'; simply to name its most prominent victims would mean listing nearly half his main characters. Take, for example, *The Emancipated*, where Elgar's passion for Cecily Doran is ignited by his jealousy of Mallard, and Mallard's by his jealousy of Elgar; later, Miriam becomes jealous of Cecily because of her passion for Mallard.[61] A connoisseur of jealousy, Gissing normally portrayed it as something destructive, rancorous and mean — for example, Gresham's in *Workers in the Dawn* or Marcian's in *Veranilda* — but at times he was also tempted to view it as a warrant of sincerity: characters wholly exempt from it (for instance, Isabel Clarendon) are often emotionally shallow.[62] If we needed a biographical explanation of Gissing's obsession with jealousy, we could probably detect it in his dealings with Nell. Both Arthur Golding and Osmond Waymark are tortured by suspicion of their prostitute girl-friends, and we know that Gissing was jealous of Black, who temporarily supplanted him in Nell's bed, and that he haunted the streets where she worked, sometimes spying her with other men.[63] More important, though, is that jealousy, within the terms of Gissing's fictive world, is intrinsic to the promptings of love. Gissing's characters are typically insecure. His lovers tend to come from contrasting backgrounds and have to negotiate estranging gulfs of class, occupation, wealth and belief. Socially they are often isolated, with few opportunities of making friends or finding consolation. Psychologically, too, they are handicapped by their pride, self-distrust and high aspirations; add to this their exacerbated introspection and their fatal attraction to opposite types, and it is not hard to see why jealousy should so dominate their lives.

An essentially paradoxical passion — mingling love and hate, resentment and desire — jealousy was the natural accompaniment of Gissing's split vision of women. As usual, his deepest personal emotions — divided, doubtful, pessimistic — both stimulate and qualify his social analysis. This is certainly true of his fictional treatment of the cause of female emancipation. Even *The Odd Women*, his most fervent attempt, is shaded with scepticism.

I I I

Like all Gissing's best novels, *The Odd Women* is a social disquisition in the form of a romance. To a limited extent it constitutes a tract on female employment and education. As its ironic title indicates, it upholds the dignity of singleness. In Victorian England, Rhoda Nunn explains, there are half a million more women than men — 'So many *odd* women — no making a pair with them'. Rhoda's mission is 'to help those women who, by sheer necessity, must live alone — women whom vulgar opinion ridicules'. Conscious, perhaps, of the status of his sisters, Gissing was always decently contemptuous of facile sneers aimed at spinsters (even in his acrid book on Dickens he protests against such ridicule).[64] He knew about the hardships facing single women — like the draggle-tailed Alice and Virginia Madden — with plenty of gentility and little money, or at least no capacity for earning money beyond the traditional and exploited occupations of teaching and governessing. Dingy lodgings, dietary restrictions, postponed enjoyments, futile consolations — so runs the plaintive plight of these sisters who, brought up to rely on male support but having lost a father, are unable to find a husband. Marriage, they believe, would be the golden solution, and their minds turn hopefully to Monica, their younger and prettier sister. But marriage, statistically impossible for many, is no guarantee of fulfilment either, even if achieved on profitable terms — as Monica's destiny proves.

A more realistic escape-route for women is being dug out by Mary Barfoot and her assistant, Rhoda Nunn. Mary wishes to abolish the traditional English lady, helpless, nervous and dependent on men:

> Girls are to be brought up to a calling in life, just as men are ... Women must have just as wide a choice ... I would have no girl, however wealthy her parent, grow up without a profession. There should be no such thing as a class of females vulgarized by the necessity of finding daily amusement.

Miss Barfoot has quietly begun the revolution by training young women for employment in offices; she offers lessons in shorthand, typing, book-keeping and commercial correspondence. Possessed of private means, she also helps women to launch out into more ambitious careers, as chemists, booksellers, publishers. At the same time she tries to steer them away from the drearier shores of education. A number of the girls she trains are drawn 'from the overstocked profession of teaching'; Rhoda, her keenest protégée, has deliberately abandoned it. But Mary hopes to impart something more than technical and vocational skills or the knack of earning money. She wants to instil a fresh philosophy, a new awareness of untapped potential, a feminist consciousness. To this end she circulates improving literature — volumes on the woman question; and every month either she or Rhoda delivers a stirring address. Rhoda's stance is similar but more militant; true to her plainly symbolic surname, she recommends rejection of marriage by women, resistance to the tawdry beguilements of love — even, as one factor in emancipation, 'revolt against sexual instinct'.[65]

Both Mary and Rhoda have been denounced by modern, supposedly feminist critics, the first for being unacceptably moderate, the second for being unattractively extreme. Thus Alice B. Markow stigmatizes Mary as 'somewhat misogynist' and virtually anti-feminist; Jenni Calder says Gissing betrays confusion by making Rhoda 'very unpleasant ... a prig and a puritan'. Historically, such responses are ill-informed. As Kathleen Blake has convincingly shown, Rhoda's insistence on renunciation relates to a persistent and honourable tradition in the history of feminism.[66] As for Mary, more or less all her opinions can be found within the mainstream of the Victorian movement. Admittedly her school, a curious combination of typing college and polemical caucus, might seem unusual in method and purpose — indeed Gissing thought it was unique. Not long after publication of *The Odd Women*, Gissing was befriended by Clara

Collet, a foremost authority on women's employment, and the following year he wrote to his brother:

> Miss Collet ... tells me that she knows of no establishment for the journalistic training of girls, nor yet — save college classes — for commercial occupation. I myself have never heard of such a place. Miss Barfoot's establishment in 'The Odd Women' seemed to me, at the time, an original idea. But probably something of the kind is going on somewhere.[67]

Gissing had no direct model, then, for his feminist training-camp. But Miss Barfoot's views, and even aspects of her work, were by no means unprecedented. A middle-class school for the training of girls as book-keepers and commercial clerks had been opened by the Society for Promoting the Employment of Women (founded in 1859 by Jessie Boucherett and Adelaide Procter) at 19 Langham Place, London (Miss Barfoot's establishment is in nearby Great Portland Street). Gissing was certainly familiar with literature which gave details of the society's work.[68] He also knew the writings of Emily Davies, Victorian pioneer of women's education, and the real-life campaigner who perhaps comes closest to anticipating Mary Barfoot. Her book *The Higher Education of Women* (1866) — listed by Gissing in his manuscript dossier — argued that all too frequently women were purposeless and idle and that the remedy was education and appropriate professional instruction. It contained many touches that Gissing would have liked — as for instance that often a woman's 'perplexity is how to manage the servants'. Elsewhere Emily Davies complains about females who, with 'no vocation for teaching', are 'forced by necessity into a profession for which they are unsuited'. To a modern reader it might seem improbable that Mary Barfoot, a feminist, should say:

> Whether woman is the equal of man I neither know nor care. We are not his equal in size, in weight, in muscle, and, for all I can say, we may have less power of brain. That has nothing to do with it. Enough for us to know that our natural growth has been stunted. The mass of women have always been paltry creatures, and their paltriness has proved a curse to men. So, if you like to put it in this way, we are working for the advantage of men as well as for our own.

But Emily Davies had already written:

> If we look at the great mass, we shall find much to be ashamed of ... This almost complete mental blankness [is] the ordinary condition of women ... I believe I may say ... that any objector is welcome to

assert anything he likes about the inferiority of the female intellect, if only he does not rate it so low as to be incapable of improvement by cultivation. We are not encumbered by theories about equality or inequality of mental power in the sexes. All we claim is that the intelligence of women ... should have full and free development. And we claim it not specially in the interest of women, but as essential to the growth of the human race.[69]

The thought in the two passages runs almost parallel. Clearly, if Mary Barfoot could be called a misogynist, so too could one of the most distinguished contemporary feminists.

As a social disquisition, then, *The Odd Women* is historically authentic; its concerns and arguments faithfully reflect those current in the later nineteenth century. But the novel is more than a disquisition; it is also a romance, though a sceptical one: a study of male-female relations. It is here that we encounter a difficulty. How can Gissing's favourite fictional process — a social problem filtered through a love story — give adequate results when the social problem is precisely that of women who are single? John Goode has rightly noted the peculiarity that the action of a novel about singleness should largely revolve around two pairings; and other critics have complained, either that Miss Barfoot's training-school is not examined as fully as marriage, or that the novel's overt thesis is subverted by its focus on romance.[70] These objections certainly deserve attention, but anticipating slightly, three points might be made. First, the economics and conventions of marriage are clearly relevant to the plight of single women (hence the story of Monica and Widdowson). Secondly, male-female relations in general provided, in Gissing's view, a larger context in which feminist values might be assessed (hence the story of Everard and Rhoda). Thirdly, two facets of the major subject, the economic and the sexual, are differentiated within the novel, social schemes being dealt with quite hopefully, but personal relations much less so.

As at least one contemporary reviewer perceived, Gissing's method in this novel is to offer a representative survey of the courses of action open to women in a society in which they outnumber men.[71] Involuntary spinsterhood is therefore common and many of the reactions to it are destructive or unavailing. Three of these are epitomized in a chapter entitled 'The Burden of Futile Souls'. Miss Eade, 'a not unimportant type of the odd woman', has flared and shrivelled into prostitution; Virginia has become a genteel tippler; and the chapter concludes with Alice at prayer — '*her* refuge from the barrenness and bitterness of life'.

Virginia's addictive resort to gin is traced with pathetic cogency, and Gissing is also acute in suggesting that pets have begun to obsess her.[72] But such reactions to statistical oddness, escapist and plainly inadequate, are not the main objects of Gissing's inquiry. The responses to singleness dealt with most fully are marriage for security (the case of Monica) and principled celibacy and work (the case of Rhoda Nunn).

Monica and Rhoda's ideals are opposites and the greater part of *The Odd Women* is devoted to their differing relations with men. Monica marries the clearly reactionary Widdowson, Rhoda almost marries the apparently progressive Barfoot: the interplay between the two relationships is the novel's main structural device. Their socially representative nature is implied by the way Gissing fits them into a spectrum of possible man-woman relations. For example, varieties of types of marriage are carefully catalogued. One group, dear to Gissing's heart, consists of men cursed with inadequate wives. All of these cases are connected with Everard Barfoot: one of his friends, whose wife lacked humour, has ended up in a lunatic asylum; another, whose helpmeet clacked incessantly of servants, has become a pitiful nomad. Everard's own brother kowtows to a wife who is both a hypochondriac and a vulgar socialite. Uxoriously refusing to assert himself, he eventually dies for his weakness. Reminiscent of much else in Gissing, these gloomy exempla might well be interpreted as disruptively personal. In fact they flow into the novel's main themes. First, they are shown to have prompted in Everard an embattled model of sexual relations ('It's ... uncommonly like women in general who have got a man into their power'), which proves to be warpingly crucial in his later affair with Rhoda. Secondly, Gissing suggests that such cases are not incompatible with feminism. It is Mary Barfoot, after all, who first broaches the subject of blighting wives; and her talk about women as 'paltry creatures' is reminiscent of Everard's dictum, 'Men have kept women at a barbarous stage of development, and then complain that they are barbarous'. The sentiments were indeed Gissing's own, as expressed in a letter to Bertz: 'My demand for female "equality" simply means that I am convinced that there will be no social peace until women are intellectually trained very much as men are. More than half the misery of life is due to the ignorance and childishness of women.'[73] The unsparing logic here, typical of Gissing, is analogous to his treatment of the working class. Whereas earlier he indicted poverty on the ground that it brutalized its victims, here he attacks sexual inequality on the ground that it stultifies them. Women as a whole outnumber men — but educated men, in this society, vastly outnumber educated women. These, for Gissing, were two sides of one evil. Hence his insistence on the miseries arising not only from the general surplus of women, but also from the even greater surplus of trivial and brainless women.

At the rosier end of the novel's spectrum is the marriage between the endearingly pedantic Micklethwaite and his sallowly faithful fiancée Fanny — 'the old fashion in its purest presentment; the consecrated form of domestic happiness'. The pathetic details of this homely portrait are touched in by Gissing almost dutifully, but their sentimental extravagance (the blind sister, the talk of angels, etc.) betrays his fundamental disbelief. Micklethwaite is introduced in a chapter called 'The Simple Faith', and his dated credo of romantic bliss is treated with affectionate irony — and at times with something sharper. When Everard, rejecting his view of women, says to Micklethwaite, 'You belong to the Ruskin school', the charge becomes graver in the light of the testimony supplied by Mary Barfoot: 'I am strenuously opposed to that view of us set forth in such charming language by Mr. Ruskin — for it tells on the side of those men who think and speak of us in a way the reverse of charming.' Even worse for our view of Micklethwaite is an exhortation we encounter later: 'You shall read John Ruskin; every word he says about women is good and precious.'[74] The speaker is Widdowson.

The marriage between Monica and Widdowson stands out as one of the two main blocks in the novel's architecture. In origin and nature it is traditional, but in contrast with that of Micklethwaite, whose wedding occurs in the same chapter, it displays the traditional evils. Monica marries for money and comfort, though she does have urgent incentives. Her past is the numbing routine at the draper's, no sitting down for perhaps sixteen hours a day. For the future she need only glance at her sisters — a frightening prospect of miserable striving and ignominious slump. Monica is caught in the economic trap of respectable unmarried women. The chapter in which she announces her decision is called 'At Nature's Bidding'. The title is not entirely ironic. Monica does not marry for love or children, but self-preservation and security are also natural drives.

Monica's motives are pardonable as Widdowson's treatment of her is not; yet Widdowson is almost as much a victim, of personal misfortune and social convention, as Monica plainly is. Both have lost their fathers in childhood, and even through similar accidents, Monica's father having been thrown from a dogcart, and Widdowson's knocked down by a cab. Neither has received any useful training. Instead they have toiled and absorbed conventions, and both are attached to propriety. Their qualities are largely defined by negatives. Monica has 'no aptitude for being anything but a pretty, cheerful, engaging girl'. Widdowson, though 'not ill-featured', has 'no particular force of character'. Before marrying, they both (in consecutive chapters) receive but ignore well-intentioned warnings. And both, for differing reasons, see marriage as an escape. But the differing reasons are the stumbling-block: the affinities between Widdowson and Monica are noteworthy but superficial; the discrepancies are profound. It is rather like the fact that their birthdays are identical, though their ages are vastly different. A similar appeal to convention cannot save them: their conventional notions are bound to cause conflict, for though conventional, they are incompatible, and because conventional, not easily discussed. Before marriage Widdowson has 'the most primitive male conception of the feminine being'. Women need to be diverted, like children. 'Therefore the blessedness of household toil' and 'the blessedness of child-bearing'.[75] At first Monica gives little indication that she would disagree with this. Unmoved by the arguments of Rhoda Nunn, she speaks with scant sympathy of feminist principles, to her husband's grateful delight. But in fact her aspirations are quite different from his. Socially ambitious in a timid way, she craves for company and variety of scene, as well as independence of movement. But Widdowson, solitary, suspicious and rule-bound, would like to have her programmed to be a neat combination of loving toy and domestic robot. Even early on there are warning signs of just how precise and exacting he can be. During courtship he dogs her movements, avowedly in adoration. It is hardly surprising that after marriage he hires a private detective.

Widdowson's treatment of Monica excellently demonstrates the dangers of his Ruskinite idealizations. He veers between cloyingly chivalrous affection and sourly autocratic rigidity. Generous with money, he makes a butterfly of Monica by buying her costumes that please him. Yet he also wishes to clip her wings, to confine her in the home that Ruskin had hymned — in this case, a stone-faced 'semi' at Herne Hill. Gissing's language skilfully exposes the gap between doctrine and reality:

> His devotion to her proved itself in a thousand ways; week after week he grew, if anything, more kind, more tender; yet in his view

of their relations he was unconsciously the most complete despot, a monument of male autocracy. Never had it occurred to Widdowson that a wife remains an individual, with rights and obligations independent of her wifely condition.

Any display of initiative by Monica gravely troubles Widdowson, who sets out to 'subdue' it 'with all gentleness'. When the wife persists in wilful defiance, the husband's reaction oscillates between rage and regressive doting ('Didn't he behave gruffly last night to his little girl? ... And what can the old bear do to show that he's sorry?') Gradually, their marriage becomes a battle-ground, their quarrels turning, significantly, on words like 'allow' and 'command'.[76]

Rushed towards maturity by her wretchedness, Monica comes to appreciate the principles of Mary and Rhoda. Instinctively opposed to their projects at first, she respects the two women nevertheless, as witness her delight in the 'joke' that Rhoda has consented to come to her wedding. Convincingly for a girl from her background, though, she clings on to some conventionally feminine responses, smoothing the way by a week's studied meekness for an argument against wifely duty, or trying to idealize the tremulous Bevis as the liberating hero of her dreams. Even so, in her earliest clash with her husband, the names of the feminist crusaders come up, and Monica's 'sole bit of real education' endows her with courage and eloquence. Later she looks back almost with despair on the wisdom she had once ignored: 'What unspeakable folly she had committed! And how true was everything she had heard from Rhoda Nunn on the subject of marriage!'[77]

Though sharply anatomizing masculine oppression, Gissing does not bury Widdowson under total condemnation. There was, after all, a good deal in Widdowson that Gissing could well understand: his jealousy, solitude and self-consciousness, his desire for docility in a wife, his amorous idealizations. Pre-eminently, though, Gissing could empathize with qualities which also earned his disapproval: indecisiveness and lack of will. Enraged and dismayed, dictating and pleading, Widdowson emerges as a *feeble* tyrant: that is why he seems to the reader, as to Monica, not only repulsive but pitiful. Misery, and exposure to unwelcome reality, begin to undermine his health. His yearning to rule exceeds his capacity. Ambushed by Monica, he starts to dilate upon ' "the natural law that points out a woman's place, and" — he added with shaken voice — "commands her to follow her husband's guidance" '. The autocrat's voice contradicts his vocabulary. Soon after, he crumbles from despot to suppliant, plucking at Monica with appeals for affection, and bursting into choking sobs. His scheme to whisk her away to Somerset is promulgated with bloodshot bluster — 'I have been absurdly weak, and weakness in the husband means unhappiness in the wife ... I am no tyrant, but I shall rule you for your own good' — but during their climactic confrontation, it is the self-appointed ruler who has to give way. Struggling to bar Monica's exit, Widdowson assumes a determined posture — 'But her will was stronger than his'.[78] Ironically — since Monica dies soon after — this sentence might stand as the epitaph on the couple's relationship.

The marriage of Monica and Widdowson exposes the cracks, the inherent flaws, in traditional attitudes: the affair between Rhoda and Everard shows the snags in more modern ones. The contrast at first seems absolute. The two men could scarcely be more dissimilar. Everard is suave, sexually experienced, libertarian and quite free from jealousy; he is also widely travelled and cosmopolitan. Widdowson is gauche, sexually innocent, authoritarian, furiously jealous and risibly insular. The women, too, appear to be opposites, Monica dainty, nervous, simple, Rhoda vigorous, confident, complex: one feminine, the other feminist. Everard and Rhoda themselves, however, seem at first to be highly compatible. In more than one sense they are similar types. Despite some obvious differences, they are even alike in physical appearance, the initial description of Everard almost echoing that of Rhoda. Rapidly surveying Rhoda's body, Everard spots its resemblance to his own. He also notes the contours of her personality and here too she appears to fit in with him. Both are modern, 'advanced' in outlook, candid, hostile to Grundyism. Both are believers in health and activity: Rhoda can walk 20 miles a day and relishes the prospect of running naked into the sea. Above all, both are independent and stubborn, proud and steely willed. Everard, determined to oppose his father, has persisted in a job for twelve years 'rather than confess his error'. 'An incredible stubbornness', Mary Barfoot reveals, 'has possibly spoilt his whole life.' But Everard rejoices in that quality and declares it 'delightful' in Rhoda too. Eventually, however, it is obstinacy that prises the pair apart.[79]

Everard first finds Rhoda attractive as a 'new woman' whose celibate principles are rather a temptation. Half-jokingly he starts to flirt with her, tentatively feeling for a pulse of sentiment,

curious to observe her reactions. Gradually his intellectual relish
expands into something sexual. Though her spirit and pride
excite his admiration, her willed coolness threatens his ego.
Intent on achieving the satisfaction of inspiring her with passion,
Everard is aroused by Rhoda's strength — so long as his own
strength is greater. This double stimulation is stressed in the
scenes where he forcibly retains her hand. In the gardens of
Chelsea Hospital, 'She was trying to draw her hand away.
Everard felt the strength of her muscles, and the sensation was
somehow so pleasant that he could not at once release her'. A
tense moment — which Everard remembers later with a certain
lingering fondness: 'That forcible holding of her hand had
marked a stage in progressive appreciation; since then he felt a
desire to repeat the experiment. "Or if thy mistress some rich
anger shows,/Imprison her soft hand and let her rave —".' The
quotation from Keats might warn the reader that in the very
temple of Delight there exists the shrine to Melancholy. But
delight alone rules when, some time later, Everard again grips
Rhoda's hand and starts to raise it to his lips — until she wrath-
fully wrenches it away, referring with seeming indignation to his
former coercive clasp. Though Everard has provoked the conflict,
Rhoda rises to the sexual challenge and patently enjoys it ('He
divined in her pleasure akin to his own'). Both are inflamed by
similar feelings, as is shown in the chapter 'Motives Meeting'.
Everard, confident of his power over Rhoda, suspects that
resistance will intensify his ardour. But Rhoda, her vanity
pleased by his passion, is trembling with a 'sense of exultation, of
triumph'.[80] Despite her excitement, she does not love Everard or
intend to become his wife. She wants a proposal of legal marriage,
but only as gratifying evidence of love, after which she will reject
him. Everard's emotions, as they unfold, contort into a similar
ambition. He desires to have Rhoda as his partner, either in
marriage or in free union, providing she accedes to free union
first. Both are determined on a dual satisfaction: proof that the
other's affection is serious; and proof of their own supremacy.

The first climax of their struggle occurs in the Lake District.
Despite the fine weather, the unclouded enjoyment, their idyll
is decked with the language of power. Everard teases Rhoda
deliciously, but his gentle ribbings repeatedly turn on the
question of relative strength. Though Rhoda responds with merry
defiance, there lurks beneath her lover's banter a genuine lust for
dominion. When he pulls her towards him and presses kisses on
her mouth, 'With exquisite delight he saw the deep crimson flush

that transfigured her countenance; saw her look for one instant
into his eyes, and was conscious of the triumphant gleam she met
there'.[81] Even as he looks into Rhoda's eyes, Everard is conscious
of the triumph in his own: the curious syntax beautifully pin-
points the true focus of his attention. But his joy at her surrender
is premature. Rhoda surprisingly betrays a weakness that gives
her the victory. Not content to risk masculine exploitation, she
tacitly but firmly insists on marriage. Everard, overcome by
passion, impulsively yields to her desire.

In the analysis following this temporary truce, the language
of power, no longer just smouldering, explodes all over the
prose: triumphed, slave, conflict, conquer, subdue, domination,
dependence, yielded — a heavy bombardment of such terms,
concentrated on a couple of pages, sharply reveals the belligerent
feelings entrenched in these combative lovers. Reinforcing this is
the language of trial — of proof, testing, explanation — called up
by Rhoda's doubts about Everard after the arrival of Mary's
letter coupling his name with Monica's. Even before this warning
arrives Everard is worrying that his wife-to-be might torment him
with her jealousy. After the letter, the war is official. Rhoda says
Everard must prove his innocence. Everard, still smarting from
his former concession, coldly and aggressively refuses. So it is that
the power struggle culminates twice in a mutual demand for
proof. In the first climax, the constrained proposal, Rhoda
explains that 'It was the only way of making sure that you loved
me', to which Everard replies, 'And what if I needed the other
proof that you loved *me*?' The second climax is their final parting,
and here, though their state of knowledge is different, their state
of mind is the same. 'When you found that I had been wrongly
suspected', he complains, ' ... if you had loved me, you would
have asked forgiveness.' But she retorts: 'I have a reason for
doubting *your* love. If you had loved me you could never have
waited so long without trying to remove the obstacle that was
between us.'[82] Only the point of conflict has shifted: the battle
positions are the same.

Well before the end of the book it becomes unmistakable that
Everard and Rhoda are not simply antitheses to Widdowson and
Monica: their story is not just a heartening contrast, but a
sobering parallel. In each case a cautious love affair snarls up
into a power struggle. With the married couple this is mainly
material, an overt argument about choice and freedom in their
social and private lives. With the lovers it is mainly psychological,
a covert contention for emotional control. In both plots jealousy

bites into the characters. Widdowson is cast throughout the novel as a kind of ignoble Othello. Requiring 'ocular proof' of his wife's movements, he tells her he would rather she died than ceased to love him and broods on a 'tragic close' to his life — 'he would kill himself and Monica should perish with him'; convinced that he has proved her unfaithful, he even pores over her sleeping form, 'muttering savagely under his breath'. 'The Othello business won't do', his former sister-in-law eventually tells him. By this time, though, the symptoms of sexual jealousy have also broken out in Rhoda, and when Everard identifies himself with Othello by resolving that 'He would whistle her down the wind', he unwittingly aligns himself with Widdowson.[83] The similarities of plot extend further, however, than power or jealousy. Both heroines learn from experience, in complementary ways. Monica comes to perceive the necessity of Rhoda's feminist principles; Rhoda admits the force and value of the commonest human emotions. (That the two men fail in corresponding development indicates their lesser potential.) And as well as displaying comparisons and contrasts, the two plots enhance each other's meaning by eventually intersecting. For most of the book Widdowson and Monica are plainly and inexorably moving apart while Everard and Rhoda, on the face of it, are slowly moving together. But the grimmer and more desperate relationship closes in on the hopeful one. When Everard is about to declare his love, his fervours are appropriately quenched by a servant's announcement of 'Mr. and Mrs. Widdowson'. Similarly, the failure of Monica's ambitions paves the way for the thwarting of Rhoda's. Monica gets ready for her meeting with Bevis while Rhoda prepares for her assignation with Everard in the Lake District. Entertaining vague hopes of exotic liberation — Monica yearns to be swept to the Continent, Rhoda dreams of the Orient Express — both women sift through their personal possessions.[84] On account of this, Monica's fiasco with Bevis creates apprehension for Rhoda.

Each of the two main relationships is wound up by two main climaxes. The first climaxes come in consecutive chapters. Chapter 24 concludes with the violent parting of Monica and Widdowson, Chapter 25 with Rhoda's acceptance of Everard's proposal. One of the couples has broken apart, the other has apparently united. But the immediate effect of the separation is to jeopardize the union. Widdowson hastens to Mary Barfoot and complains of his wife's infidelity. The result is the letter dispatched to Rhoda, which severs the already frayed concordat between her and Everard. The death of the marriage poisons the lovers: but only because similar germs of dissension have already undermined their affair.

Between the first climaxes and the second the couples are at deadlock. Their quandaries are almost identical. In each case, one partner is considered unfaithful; and in each, though the evidence for this looks strong, the suspected partner is unrepentant: both Monica and Everard are adamant that the charges must be retracted. It is not simply, then, that both relationships run adrift into jealousy. They founder on the very same suspicion — that Monica has had an affair with Barfoot. In this way their built-in weaknesses are sharply identified.

The second climaxes in each story (also retailed in consecutive chapters) are the death of Monica and the final parting of Rhoda and Everard. The preliminary climaxes, severance and union, were evidently meant as contrasts; the concluding ones, death and separation, are more like parallels. Each story terminates flintily, one partner refusing to relent. Rhoda, recognizing that Everard has never loved her with entire sincerity, declines his insistent offer of marriage. The whole book vindicates this decision. Ultimately, Rhoda is acknowledging what formerly she had only suspected: that Everard's brand of emancipation coexists with a predatory attitude to women, the detailed curiosity of a sexual connoisseur. His admission that he had been 'not quite serious' is confirmed by his behaviour when rejected here: within a fortnight he gets engaged to a charming girl of wealth and culture. Rhoda, it transpires, is right not to relent. The unyieldingness of Widdowson, on the other hand, is not due to perceptiveness or principle. After Monica's baby is born he reads her perfectly truthful confession but is undecided whether to believe it; there is, in any case, no question of pardon. At Alice Madden's woeful request he cynically sends a word of forgiveness. But when his wife dies he does not look upon her face and quits her chamber 'death-pale but tearless'.[85] Both stories, then, come to a close with a stern refusal to relent. For better (in her case) or worse (in his), Rhoda Nunn and Edmund Widdowson remain intransigent.

The Odd Women ends with delicate integrity. Rhoda's final sigh for Monica's baby ('Poor little child!') has a triple significance: pity for Monica, whose dark eyes it has inherited; concern for the baby, both motherless and a female; and, as Rhoda sits alone, 'still nursing', a realization of what she herself has lost. How hopeful, one wonders, is this conclusion? And what prospects does the book hold out for women? The answer, a mixed one, takes us back to the question of the novel's structure. Viewed simply as a survey of single women, the novel is affirmative, even optimistic. It repudiates, for instance, a number of attitudes which elsewhere Gissing was prepared to endorse: that women should be worshipped with protective chivalry; that their natural role is domestic and maternal; that all but a few occupations are improper or unsuitable for them.[86] The dignity of independence is maintained. Despite Rhoda's sigh as she cradles the baby, the conclusion suggests no sense of sterility (Rhoda is 'bright and natural', her feminist projects are flourishing), merely an acknowledgement that, quite literally, a decision is a cutting off. But of course the novel cannot be viewed simply as a study of single women, for its double-plot structure revolves around couples. That *The Odd Women* deals with romance as well as work has been deplored by Patricia Stubbs as carrying the reactionary implication that for women the realm of personal affections must always be of primary importance. This criticism, though, ignores the fact that, within the novel itself, Rhoda scorns the novelistic emphasis on 'love' and Monica eventually rejects it in disgust.[87] It is safer to assume that Gissing's structure was deliberate, that he wished to test the prospects for a feminist outlook through sexual relations as well as social schemes. In this respect the novel is not so hopeful. It suggests, indeed, that a sex-based relationship which is equal, harmonious and free from jealousy is almost impossible to attain. Nor can we console ourselves with the thought that this is due entirely to social convention. It is true that some attitudes to women are indicted and that the case for female employment is vigorously upheld. But although this is relevant to the plight of single women, it offers no assistance in their dealings with men. Typically of Gissing, the 'enlightened' relationship is ultimately just as unsuccessful as the plainly benighted one.

The reasons for this are buried deep in Gissing's pessimistic conception not just of social structures but of human nature. In *The Odd Women* sexual love is presented by Gissing as turbid and febrile. In *The Whirlpool* passion is referred to as a 'calenture' and the connotations of this word — heat, delusion and self-destruction — are apt for its role in his work.[88] Love is like a malarial spasm. Widdowson suffers from 'love-fever' and Monica's 'fervid feelings' for Bevis throws her into 'all but delirium'; Rhoda agonizes in 'mute frenzy', moves around 'in a fever of unrest'.[89] Except for Micklethwaite and his angel-wife, serenity is reserved for the cordoned-off. At any rate all the single women who achieve some cheerfulness and self-reliance are shielded by conventual names: Mildred Vesper, Winifred Haven and of course Rhoda Nunn. Celibacy, it seems, is the safest bet; sexual involvement, by its very nature, is dangerous and delusive.

In so far as calculation enters into love, it does little to dispel the turbulence. At the heart of *The Odd Women* is insecurity — economic insecurity in the first instance, but later, and more insidiously, emotional and psychological insecurity. The crescendo of discord in the novel, the hostilities that crackle through its two-pronged plot, transmit an unmistakable implication that in their most intimate relationships human beings are possessed by a craving for power — for power, influence and domination — but also for reassurance. Failure to achieve power or security sparks off mistrust and possessiveness. Above all, it sparks off jealousy, here as always in Gissing a central passion. Flaring up not only in the two main stories, but also in the lives of Miss Eade and Mary Barfoot, jealousy is more than a symptom of weakness. It is also a signal of intense emotion and its total absence in Everard betrays a deficiency. What's more, it may be employed as a weapon. Monica, embittered by her husband's jealousy, is prompted to 'a perverse pleasure in misleading'. Everard pens a letter to Mary that he knows will come into Rhoda's hands: 'he hoped to sting her with jealousy'.[90] Primitive impulses, perhaps: but that of course is Gissing's point.

The grip of the primitive is, in fact, a notable part of the novel's case against the idea that social enlightenment can generate personal peace. Power breaks into sexual emotions because it climbs up from our deepest instincts. We have seen how Monica's revulsion from Widdowson is caused by his 'unmanliness' as well as his bullying. Her disenchantment with the tremulous Bevis is likewise provoked by his feebleness. Her quailing swain lacks 'virile force ... he trembled and blushed like a young girl'. Women despise, are dismayed by, male weakness. Conversely, they respond to strength. This is true of Rhoda as well as Monica. When Everard divines her delight in conflict, he remarks that 'Love revives the barbarian; it wouldn't mean much if it didn't'. This opinion is confirmed by the curious scene in which Everard, enraged by his sister-in-law, proposes half-jokingly that he ought to thrash her, as he would do if she were a man. Rhoda assents to this argument from equality and her lover's nerves thrill and his pulses throb. Later, Mary senses that Rhoda had felt: 'Face this

monstrous scandal and I am yours'.[91] The feminist is deeply
stirred by power — beaten, in a sense, by her instincts.

As a disquisition on unpartnered females *The Odd Women* is
affirmative and forward-looking. As a treatment of women's
relations with men it is much less optimistic. Social conventions
and economic conditions can, it suggests, be challenged and
improved. But nothing can annul the friction and suffering
intrinsic, in Gissing's view, to personal relations. A crucially
revealing conversation takes place in Chapter 6 between Mary
and Rhoda. Rhoda maintains that the majority of women are
condemned to lead vain and miserable lives largely because they
marry. The older woman disagrees:

> 'Don't you blame the institution of marriage with what is charge-
> able to human fate? A vain and miserable life is the lot of nearly all
> mortals. Most women, whether they marry or not, will suffer and
> commit endless follies.'
>
> 'Most women — as life is at present arranged for them. Things
> are changing, and we try to have our part in hastening a new order.'
>
> 'Ah, we use words in a different sense. I speak of human nature,
> not of the effect of institutions.'

Manifestly, the major split within Gissing, traceable throughout
so much of his work, also extended to his understanding of female
emancipation. It is difficult to doubt that in this conversation
Mary Barfoot's sentiments are essentially his own. And yet, with
characteristic realism, he lets Rhoda answer back: 'Now it is you
who are unpractical. Those views lead only to pessimism and
paralysis of effort.'[92] Only half of Gissing could agree with
Rhoda. With his stubborn belief in the virtue of striving, he could
never approve of 'paralysis of effort'. But that a view led only to
'pessimism' did not for him prove it mistaken.

Conclusion

To round off the argument of the previous chapters, a few words on Gissing's development. What patterns are discernible across his career? How did he come to regard those themes he had dealt with directly in earlier books? And how does his evolution as a writer relate to his inner divisions?

One useful perspective on Gissing's *oeuvre* is provided by Robert L. Selig in his trenchant and concise *George Gissing* (1983). Selig argues that in his earliest novels Gissing remained 'strongly influenced by a sentimental-idealist tradition that, for more than three centuries, had often diluted supposedly "realistic" novels with elements of romance'; only after repudiating this tradition did he hammer out his finest work — ironic, tough-minded, non-didactic. There is obviously much validity in this view. Certainly, in the six novels before *The Nether World*, the head-count of mistily haloed characters — 'moral-aesthetic paragons who love high culture ... sexual partners who excel in courtly graces' — is much higher than later on. It would be difficult, after about 1890, to find anything directly equivalent to the erotic raptures of Arthur Golding, the moist-eyed ministrations of Ida Starr, or the lofty visions of Stella Westlake, 'that high-throned poet-soul'.[1] Gissing's fiction did become less sentimental, less patently a vehicle for passionate ideals. Increasingly, the creaking conventions of romance were smoothed into the social analysis.

Nevertheless, the dichotomy proposed by Selig is probably too sharp. For one thing, it is difficult to assess how far the admittedly greater realism of the later books is due more to a crisper control of style than a deep transformation of values. These books are less overtly idealistic, but less overt in other ways too — less melodramatic, less morally assertive, less prone to harangues and apostrophes. As early as November 1883, Gissing was telling Algernon: 'the secret of art in fiction is the *indirect*. Nothing must be told too plumply'.[2] He did not, at this stage, practise what he preached; he was just completing *The Unclassed*, in which he rather preached what he felt. However, the slimmed-down version of this novel, produced by Gissing in 1895, is by no means roundly representative of the 'sentimental-idealist tradition' — much less so than the other early books. The essential conceptions of character remain — purified prostitute, humanized miser — but stylistic over-ripeness has been skilfully excised. Allowing for an increase in literary tact, the later books are not wholly different from the earlier. A vein of moral idealism throbs steadily through most of them (to read Gissing as a moral relativist, by stressing his Continental affinities, is more often than not to misread him);[3] and at times, as Selig admits, there are even palpitating passages of empurpled romantic fervour. On the other hand, the earlier books are not wholly idealistic. They also contain a strong sceptical current, persistently impugning what they elsewhere proclaim. Golding, Casti, Mutimer, Egremont — all are in differing ways idealists, and in every case their idealism is deflated or undermined. What's more, large parts of these early books are lodged firmly in a sordidly 'realistic' tradition. Contemporary reviewers of *Workers in the Dawn* scarcely mentioned its extravagant idealism. Instead they complained of its darkness and squalor; Frederic Harrison wondered if its moral aim was sufficiently strong to justify 'the deliberate painting of so much brutality'.[4] Tastes change, and the book reads differently now, but such early responses surely call into question Robert Selig's overarching thesis.[5]

Still, it is right to draw attention to the 'blunt self-criticism' in Gissing. For another way of seeing his fictional development is as a series of corrections, or drastic reassessments, of attitudes he had formerly professed. Self-division, as we have seen, is nearly always lodged deeply in Gissing's understanding of his central themes: it also opens cracks across his career. Incurably restless and discontented, he tended to shift from one posture to another; almost masochistically introspective, he would castigate his bygone self. It was not that any of his deepest convictions were capriciously abandoned or dishonestly denied. The rethinkings were rather of two different kinds. Either he would excoriate, in a tone of resentment, the persuasions which had once beguiled his youth. Or, with a suaver sense of irony, he would hasten to repel the pretentious affectation of opinions genuinely his own. The first was a recoil from his past persona; the second, from the unwelcome company of embarrassing contemporary allies. At a deeper level, most of his values survived — only made more immovable, in fact, by the piling up of the years.

A quick survey of the themes of previous chapters will show how this pattern of prickly reassessment, and underlying continuity, can be glimpsed across Gissing's career. As argued earlier, an oscillation between pessimism and will power, negative projections and positive endeavour, was intrinsic to his life and art. Gradually, though, each impulse became less intense. While he never ceased to be a pessimist — 'All goes tolerably ill, as usual', he grumbled typically in 1898 — he did resent being stuck with the label, and made efforts to detach it from his work.[6] He increasingly emphasized the need to resist the paralysis of pessimism (most notably in *The Odd Women*, *The Crown of Life* and *Will Warburton*). He made a few forays into lighter modes (sub-Dickensian bounciness in *The Town Traveller*, polished comedy of manners in *The Paying Guest* and *Our Friend the Charlatan*). And, most remarkable of all, he attempted to de-glamorize depression. Unhappiness, he increasingly insisted, was seldom splendidly ennobling. In *Demos* he had written: 'We are interesting in proportion to our capacity for suffering, and dignity comes of misery nobly borne.' But as early as *Thyrza* he was voicing the view that, 'in spite of idealisms, suffering more often does harm than good', and eventually he told Gabrielle, 'I am convinced that it is through joy, not sorrow, that men become morally better'. It was partly this conviction that lay behind his generous appreciation of Dickens, who became 'a force for good', he suggested, 'by virtue of his ever-hopeful outlook'. Just how far Gissing was willing to go in his sharp reappraisal of prideful dumps can be judged from his scathing tale of 1893, 'The Pessimist of Plato Road'. The eponymous pessimist, Philip Dolamore, a semi-literate South London lodger, vents his conceit by quoting 'Shoppenhaw' and commending himself as a melancholy misfit to his landlady's awestruck daughter. Complaining that 'Intellect has no value in the market', he condemns 'the vulgar aptitude for commerce' and laments his exile from his natural homeland, the world of Greece and Rome.[7] Manifestly an *ersatz* Gissing, Dolamore represents his creator's dread that the grim conclusions of a painful lifetime might be stultified by cheap imitation. Gissing, after all, had not expressed his pessimism through suicide notes to newspapers but rather through a vigorous creative venture — an impressive series of novels and stories autographed by conscientious craftsmanship and unsparing authenticity. Gissing, unlike Dolamore, was wedded to the work ethic, not merely to unremitting woe. Yet here, too, he was anxiously self-corrective, keen to avoid identification with Carlylean strenuousness. Work, he told his puritan sister Margaret, ought to be a means, not an end in itself. The 'monstrous superstition of the saving grace of labour' is mocked by Waymark in *The Unclassed*, as also by Barfoot in *The Odd Women*, who replaces it with something perilously close to unalloyed hedonism.[8] What Gissing came to settle for was a life of quiet industriousness. In aspiration, if not quite in achievement, he retreated from both metaphysical *angst* and hectic activity.

Another area in which he turned against former views, because of a turning-in on himself, was that of social reform. As we saw in Chapter 2, his commitment to reform was rapidly abandoned in his fiction; yet he seems to have felt a permanent urge to punish his youthful credulity. In 1895, nearly ten years after *Demos*, he was still expending satirical scorn on a hollow industrial agitator. Andrew Catterick, the butt of his story 'The Firebrand' (a squib sparked off by a piece in the *Spectator*), is in many ways a caricature version of Gissing. A fatherless boy from a sooty northern town, Catterick goes to London to live by his pen, and breaks out in radical convictions. Having starved and 'worked himself like a machine', he eventually returns, looking very ill, to recuperate at his mother's house, where he stigmatizes his native circle as a 'century or so behind' in civilization, and discomfits his relatives by denouncing the 'grinding tyranny of the present social system'. Only when Catterick starts to stoke up a pit strike do his actions radically diverge from Gissing's — but by this point the satire of 'The Firebrand' has already singed its author.[9] A curiously acrid distaste for reformers remained with Gissing all his life. With the solitary exception of *Sleeping Fires* they are always, in his later books, portrayed with contempt. He particularly regretted his lecturing phase, and from *Demos* onwards those who give lectures are nearly always disgraceful or foolish. Samuel Barmby's oration, in *In the Year of Jubilee*, is followed by 'a tedious debate, a muddy flow of gabble and balderdash'. Perhaps the most odious character in Gissing — Sibyl Carnaby in *The Whirlpool* — is last glimpsed, improbably, planning high-flown lectures for the benefit of working women. The whole notion of well-meaning projects for the poor is mocked throughout *Our Friend the Charlatan*, which is packed with characters who, stricken by the contrast between their own comforts and 'the hopeless level of the swinking multitude', lapse into a 'turbid idealism'. Opening with some abrasive remarks on that 'silly word — altruism' (a central concept in Comtist thought), the novel concludes with the disenchantment of Lord Dymchurch, who decides he must literally cultivate his own garden: 'He had done for ever with schemes of social regeneration, with political theories, all high-sounding words and phrases'. Dymchurch is plainly a surrogate for Gissing, who by 1902 could write, 'I have made it a rule not to take part in any sort of public movement'. The 'public movement' he had in mind was the Dickens Fellowship.[10]

If we needed further proof that Gissing's later social attitudes were largely a recoil from his earlier ones, we might find it in his treatment of religion. As noted earlier, anti-clerical ardour was essential to Gissing's reformist phase; later, like Godwin Peak, he became ashamed of this connection with 'street-corner rationalism'. The result is not simply that his later churchmen (like the Rev. Lashmar in *Our Friend the Charlatan*) are indulgently rather than derisively portrayed (compare Whiffle in *Workers in the Dawn*). It is rather that religion and radicalism, at first perceived as opposites, are increasingly aligned. In 'His Brother's Keeper' (1895) pious Henry Ellerton has a twin brother, Mark, a pugnacious propagandist for secularism. Obsessed by the damage Mark might do, Henry follows him about the country, countering his twin's 'crudely scoffing rhetoric' with excited religious tirades. Even before the story's lurid ending (Henry tries to shoot Mark at a meeting and is taken away to a lunatic asylum), a symbolic equation starkly emerges: freethinking rage and religious fervour are related forms of insanity. Evidently Gissing came to suspect that his own youthful anti-religious crusading had been a species of fanaticism. And yet there was an underlying continuity, for undoubtedly Gissing remained an agnostic. His private opinions scarcely changed; his social judgements about them did. Compare, in this connection, two passages, one from *Workers in the Dawn*, another (twenty years later) from *Henry Ryecroft*. In the first, Gissing contrasts the open-minded agnostic with the more 'prosaic' religious believer, 'who convinces himself that he has ever at his elbow the key to the mystery of the universe'. In the second, he contrasts the agnostic with the 'hidebound materialist', whose certainties rest on 'self-deception'.[11] In each case Gissing's own stance is similar, that of a marvelling sceptic. But the targets he attacks are on opposite flanks: earlier, the smugness of religious belief; later, the arrogance of atheism.

A similar process is discernible in Gissing's retrospective treatment of the commercialization of art. Though his basic perceptions remained unaltered, he shifted his angle of vision. In *New Grub Street* (1891) he made Amy Reardon, his elegant materialist, openly condemn her husband's scruples and exhort him to write for the market. By the turn of the century — when defiance of commercialism had become, in some circles, virtually obligatory — Gissing had switched his line of attack. Even before writing *New Grub Street* he had briefly mocked bogus bohemianism (in the posturing person of Clifford Marsh, the sham artist in *The Emancipated*). But in *Will Warburton*, written in 1902–3, he decided to rework this particular critique by, as it were, updating the marriage of Amy and Edwin Reardon. Like Amy, Rosamund Elvan is a cool, ambitious beauty whose chief passion is for money and respectable success. Unlike Amy, she finds it necessary to conceal her true opinions. A dainty, dilettante water-colourist, who styles herself 'a poor struggler', she takes luxurious lodgings in Chelsea and cants about life in garrets. Having broken her engagement to the painter Franks, on the ground that he has soiled himself as an artist by splashing out sentimental pictures for cash ('A popular success! Oh, the shame of it'), she takes up with Warburton not knowing he is a grocer, but drops him like a rotten vegetable the moment she discovers the truth. Establishing herself rapidly as the wife of Franks — now a plutocratic portraitist — she blandly glosses over their compromised comforts with an image of artistic 'greatness'.[12] This novel also offers an instructive contrast between the two rivals for Rosamund's hand, the tradesman Warburton and the artist Franks. As in *New Grub Street*, success is granted to the man of inferior integrity, but despite this the implications have changed. In *Will Warburton* Gissing's irony is largely directed at the specious assumption of his own beliefs. Hence he prefers the honest squalors of commerce to the venal rewards of art.

Both of the reactions discussed so far — outright rejection of earlier values and determined detachment from their exploitation — appear to be mingled in Gissing's later assessments of poverty, intellect and exile. Though terror of poverty continued to haunt him, it became a less central factor in his fiction, a rather more transient spectre. Conversely, though he always respected intellect, he came to distinguish, in *Henry Ryecroft*, 'between two forms of intelligence, that of the brain and that of the heart', and professed to prefer the second. Certainly the valiant feats of learning once applauded as heroic or at least endearing (one thinks of Hilda Meres with her knowledge of the air-pump) are mercilessly replaced, in the later Gissing, by the memorized claptrap of conceited pedants, like brain-fevered Jessica in *In the Year of Jubilee* ('The doctor heard me one day repeating a long bit of Virgil ... Oh, it was quite an intellectual delirium'), or brainless May in *Our Friend the Charlatan* ('Just now I'm giving half-an-hour before breakfast every day to Huxley's book on the Crayfish'). Partly campaigns against counterfeit currency, such satirical sallies are also directed at the juvenile fervours of an earlier self. May's twitter about 'getting up' various subjects is an echo of Gissing's own letters from college; short stories like 'Christopherson' (a man's marriage imperilled by his mania for books) are wry comments on his literary obsession.[13]

Where Gissing's perspective altered most, however, was in his later views on social exile, the end-product of poverty plus intellect. Perhaps because in his last decade he was less of an outsider, or because *Born in Exile* had exhausted this theme, he largely abandoned his indignant portraits of those racked by the opposing strains of poverty and learning, and even suggested that many such martyrs were self-glorifying malcontents. 'What it is', he writes sneeringly of Dolamore — who 'revolts' against his social 'obscurity' — 'to be intellectual and at the same time poor!' Revolt, a key concept for the younger Gissing, is regarded with suspicion in his later work. The turning-point is perhaps *In the Year of Jubilee*, where Nancy's desire for 'perfect freedom' is meant to embody 'the spirit of her time'. Eventually her callow resentment and defiance are chastened by submission to 'Nature's law' — that a married woman's duty is to slave for her family. 'One might as well revolt', Nancy concludes, 'against being born a woman instead of a man.' *Our Friend the Charlatan* also mounts an onslaught on 'Discontent, the malady of the age'. Dyce Lashmar lays the flattering unction to his soul that not his own weakness but anomalous circumstance accounts for his failure to prosper. While democracy enthrones the second-rate, he complains, 'the true leaders of mankind, as often as not, struggle through their lives in poverty and neglect'. Lashmar absurdly sees the pathos of his plight as similar to that of Gissing's earliest protagonists ('At his age, with his brain and heart, to perish thus for want of a little money!'). Another modern malcontent in the same novel is Constance Bride, who has 'striven for what she deemed her rights — the rights of a woman born with intellect and will and imagination, yet condemned by poverty to rank among subordinates'.[14] Nothing more calculated, one might have thought, to arouse Gissing's sympathetic indignation; yet Constance, though never condemned outright, is portrayed with some acerbity.

The truth was that Gissing became increasingly impatient with anyone claiming to be 'a victim of circumstances': when he used this phrase for the title of a story, it was heavily ironic. He had never, of course, been a thorough determinist: he had always believed in will. Gradually, however, he moved towards an intermediate philosophical position — an unembittered acceptance of fate, coupled with a small but steady faith in the power of individual initiative. 'Heaven forbid', reflects Langley in *Sleeping Fires*, 'that he should have outlived [the] spirit of revolt.' Yet Gissing did outlive it, and in books like *The Whirlpool* he commended, in place of egotistical striving (as displayed by the neurasthenic Alma Rolfe), a modest and tranquil acceptance of duty (as exhibited eventually by Mary Abbott or the teacher Thistlewood). Conversely, he became markedly less tolerant of anything resembling aggressive defiance or whining discontent. In his study of Dickens (1898) there is an interesting passage about Charley Hexam, the board-school boy in *Our Mutual Friend*, for whom he extrapolates, with telling irritation, an entirely extra-textual career: 'Before he was many years older, he became a "secularist" — quite without conviction, — and delivered peculiarly blatant lectures; after that he added "socialism", and pointed to himself as an example of the man of great talents, who had never found a fair chance.'[15] Clearly, Gissing's anger is not aimed solely at a minor character in Dickens's fiction. Gissing himself has enormously changed. Think, for example, of a fictional character roughly analogous to Charley Hexam — another egotistical working-class rebel, moody, petulant, ungrateful, sharp-witted, and avid to rise into respectable acceptance: Clara Hewett in *The Nether World* (1889). Gissing had not sentimentalized Clara, or refrained from exploring her numerous flaws; but when he wrote *The Nether World* he could also understand from the inside such arrogant and agonized ambition. A second comparison makes even clearer the alteration he underwent. It has often been remarked that *Our Friend the Charlatan* is partly a reworking of *Born in Exile*. Both books are the stories of young men without means who attempt to advance themselves by deceit; professing beliefs not really their own, they are finally destroyed by the cruel revelation of a compromising article. The effects of the two novels are, nevertheless, utterly and revealingly distinct. *Born in Exile* is a work of complex empathy — ironic but angry, intelligently intense — while *Our Friend the Charlatan* is an ebullient satire, a skilled exercise in resolute detachment. Gissing's vision has shifted from inner to outer, from critical sympathy to unpitying scorn. Reviewing the theme of social exile, he seems to have wearied of his former engagement — or at least to have grown increasingly concerned to identify spurious variants.

As for his attitudes to female liberation, enough has been said in Chapter 5 to suggest that here, too, we have a similar pattern — a growing acknowledgement of the feminist cause, culminating in *The Odd Women*, followed by a biliously impatient reaction, a suspicion that, as ever, genuine commitment was outweighed by opportunism. 'I hate talk about *women*', says Constance Bride, echoing Gissing to Gabrielle; 'it has become a nuisance — a cant like any other.' Once again the fictional turning-point is *In the Year of Jubilee*, about which Gissing wrote to Clara Collet: 'People are getting very tired of the "woman question" & I don't want this book to be regarded in that light.' He need scarcely have feared that *In the Year of Jubilee* would be welcomed as feminist propaganda: coupled with the more subtly detractive *The Whirlpool*, it offers a crushingly misogynist contrast with the standpoint of *The Odd Women*. The paradox, typical of Gissing's life, was that his anti-feminist fictional upsurge coincided with a phase in his personal affairs when he forged several friendships with emancipated women — for instance, M. M. Dowie, author of *Gallia* (1895), who told him she had purchased *all* his books — and was keeping abreast of 'new woman' novels (he read works by George Egerton and Sarah Grand, as well as by Olive Schreiner). Gissing did not, then, shut himself away from feminist developments in fiction or life. It was rather that he hated conscription to a movement — hated, one suspects, the very idea that any movement was inspiring the masses. 'It must not be supposed', he wrote waspishly, in his stinging little sketch 'A Free Woman' (1896), 'that female emancipation, in the larger sense, is discussed only among educated women; the factory, the work-room, the doss-house, have heard these tidings of great joy.'[16] This sentence is a reminder of how much remained fixed, even as Gissing's outlook changed: class revulsion was a stubborn component.

What were the overall effects on Gissing's fiction of his restless tendency to pick over past themes? A clue to the reorientation of his values is provided in a letter he wrote to Bertz in 1892. 'As yet I have chiefly dealt', he said, 'with types expressing the struggle of natures endowed *above* their stations; now I turn to those who are *below* it.' Though one should not lean too hard on this thematic pivot, it does epitomize the general direction in which Gissing's fiction turns. It turns, by and large, from those deserving better to those who do not deserve so much; from the evils of poverty to the corruptions of comfort; from expansive protest to tautened satire; from obsession with genuine deprivations to the study of sham acquisitions. A large part of this change is explicable, of course, by reference to events in Gissing's life — the failed experiments in marriage, the perspectives gained by travel abroad, the slow rise in social status. At a deeper level, though, the change also relates to reactions seared into his personality by the branding events at college. We have seen that much of Gissing's self-division, especially the fracture between effort and despair, can be traced to the shock he received at eighteen from expulsion and imprisonment. One form which this division took was a double attitude towards his past: a nervous desire to escape from it, a brooding compulsion to return. In his literary career he did just this. In 1887 he told Algernon that every writer should 'throw into a work of art each stage of life's experience ... Let there be something visible, tangible; then move onwards'.[17] But for Gissing moving onwards was often moving backwards. Magnetized by topics connected with his trauma — the necessity and futility of social reform, the vulnerable consolations of art, the baffled predicament of the social exile, the sustaining and injuring quest for love — he returned to them obsessively in his fiction; at the same time — restless, dissatisfied — he continually reappraised them. As we watch Gissing tracking back through the past, keen to hunt down former follies, anxious to open up new trails, we can see once again why he should excel at capturing weakness and doubt in his pages — why his finest trophies are deluded idealists, or tormented deceivers, or frustrated lovers. The figure he was stalking was himself.

Bibliography of Gissing's Works

Dates, and names of publishers, are those of first editions. Details in parentheses are those of editions cited in the text (where different). As in the list of abbreviations and the notes, the place of publication is London, except where otherwise stated. 'Harvester' designates the Harvester Press critical editions of Gissing, published in Brighton, England.

1880   *Workers in the Dawn: A Novel*, 3 vols, Remington (Harvester, 2 vols bound in one).

1884   *The Unclassed: A Novel*, 3 vols, Chapman & Hall (Harvester: text of revised edition, Lawrence & Bullen, 1895).

1886   *Demos: A Story of English Socialism*, 3 vols, Smith, Elder (Harvester).

1886   *Isabel Clarendon*, 2 vols, Chapman & Hall (Harvester, 2 vols).

1887   *Thyrza: A Tale*, 3 vols, Smith, Elder (Harvester: text of revised edition, Smith, Elder, 1892).

1888   *A Life's Morning*, 3 vols, Smith, Elder (Harvester).

1889   *The Nether World: A Novel*, 3 vols, Smith, Elder (Harvester).

1890   *The Emancipated: A Novel*, 3 vols, Bentley (Harvester: text of revised edition, Lawrence & Bullen, 1893).

1891   *New Grub Street: A Novel*, 3 vols, Smith, Elder (Harmondsworth: Penguin, 1968).

1892   *Denzil Quarrier: A Novel*, Lawrence & Bullen (Harvester).

1892   *Born in Exile: A Novel*, 3 vols, A. & C. Black (Harvester).

1893   *The Odd Women*, 3 vols, Lawrence & Bullen (New York: Norton, 1971).

1894   *In the Year of Jubilee*, 3 vols, Lawrence & Bullen (Harvester).

1895   *Eve's Ransom*, Lawrence & Bullen (New York: Dover 1980).

1895   *Sleeping Fires*, Fisher Unwin (Harvester).

1895   *The Paying Guest*, Cassell (Harvester).

1897   *The Whirlpool*, Lawrence & Bullen (Harvester).

1898   *Human Odds and Ends: Stories and Sketches*, Lawrence & Bullen.

1898   *Charles Dickens: A Critical Study*, Blackie (Gresham, 1903).

1898   *The Town Traveller*, Methuen (Harvester).

1899   *The Crown of Life*, Methuen (Harvester).

1901   *Our Friend the Charlatan: A Novel*, Chapman & Hall (Harvester).

1901   *By the Ionian Sea: Notes of a Ramble in Southern Italy*, Chapman & Hall (Richards Press, 1956).

1903   *The Private Papers of Henry Ryecroft*, Constable (Harvester).
1904   *Veranilda: A Romance*, Constable (Oxford: Oxford University Press, 1929).
1905   *Will Warburton: A Romance of Real Life*, Constable (Harvester).
1906   *The House of Cobwebs and Other Stories*, introduction by Thomas Seccombe, Constable.
1924   *The Sins of the Fathers and Other Tales*, introduction by Vincent Starrett, Chicago: Pascal Covici.
1924   *Critical Studies of the Works of Charles Dickens*, New York: Greenberg (reprint, New York: Haskell House, 1965).
1927   *A Victim of Circumstances and Other Stories*, Constable.
1931   *Brownie*, introduction by George Everett Hastings, Vincent Starrett and Thomas Ollive Mabbott, New York: Columbia University Press.
1938   *Stories and Sketches*, Michael Joseph.
1962   *George Gissing's Commonplace Book: A Manuscript in the Berg Collection of the New York Public Library*, ed. Jacob Korg, New York: New York Public Library.
1968   *Notes on Social Democracy*, ed. Jacob Korg, Enitharmon Press.
1970   *George Gissing: Essays and Fiction*, ed. Pierre Coustillas, Baltimore and London: Johns Hopkins Press.
1978   *George Gissing on Fiction*, ed. Jacob and Cynthia Korg, Enitharmon Press.

Abbreviations

In the notes the following abbreviations are used for items cited frequently; short titles of Gissing's works are given except where specified below.

Berg	MSS in the Henry W. and Albert A. Berg Collection of the New York Public Library.
Bertz	*The Letters of George Gissing to Eduard Bertz, 1887–1903*, ed. Arthur C. Young (Constable, 1961).
CB	*George Gissing's Commonplace Book.*
Charlatan	George Gissing, *Our Friend the Charlatan.*
Diary	*London and the Life of Literature in Late Victorian England: The Diary of George Gissing, Novelist*, ed. Pierre Coustillas (Hassocks, Sussex: Harvester, 1978).
Dickens	George Gissing, *Charles Dickens: A Critical Study.*
Fiction	*George Gissing on Fiction.*
Gabrielle	*The Letters of George Gissing to Gabrielle Fleury*, ed. Pierre Coustillas (New York: New York Public Library, 1964).
GG	George Gissing.
GGEF	*George Gissing: Essays and Fiction.*
GN	*Gissing Newsletter.*
Heritage	*Gissing: The Critical Heritage*, ed. Pierre Coustillas and Colin Partridge (London and Boston: Routledge, 1972).
Hick	*Henry Hick's Recollections of George Gissing*, ed. Pierre Coustillas (Enitharmon Press, 1973).
Jubilee	George Gissing, *In the Year of Jubilee.*
Korg	Jacob Korg, *George Gissing: A Critical Biography* (Methuen, 1965).
LMF	*Letters of George Gissing to Members of His Family*, ed. Algernon and Ellen Gissing (Constable, 1927).
Pforzheimer	MSS in the Carl H. Pforzheimer Library, New York, published with the permission of the Carl and Lily Pforzheimer Foundation, Inc.
Roberts	Morley Roberts, *The Private Life of Henry Maitland*, ed. Morchard Bishop (Richards Press, 1958).
Ryecroft	George Gissing, *The Private Papers of Henry Ryecroft.*
Thyrza (i)	George Gissing, *Thyrza*, 1st edn, 3 vols (Smith, Elder, 1892).

Unclassed (i)	George Gissing, *The Unclassed*, 1st edn, 3 vols (Chapman & Hall, 1884).
Wells	*George Gissing and H. G. Wells: Their Friendship and Correspondence*, ed. Royal A. Gettmann (Hart-Davis, 1961).
Workers	George Gissing, *Workers in the Dawn*.
Yale	MSS in the Beinecke Rare Book and Manuscript Library, Yale University.

Notes

(Except where otherwise stated, the place of publication is London and italics in quotations are in the original text.)

Preface

1 *CB*, p. 68.
2 George Orwell, 'George Gissing', in Pierre Coustillas (ed.), *Collected Articles on George Gissing* (Frank Cass, 1968), p. 55.
3 GG to Ellen Gissing, 1 April 1890, *Bulletin of the Boston Public Library*, November 1947, p. 335.
4 On 23 June 1895, GG wrote to Eduard Bertz: 'It is strange how many letters I get from women, asking for sympathy and advice. I really can't understand what it is in my work that attracts the female mind' (*Bertz*, p. 200).

Chapter 1: *Pessimism and Will Power*

1 Ellen Gissing, 'Some personal recollections of George Gissing', *Blackwood's Magazine*, vol. 225 (May 1929), p. 655. (cf. her comment: 'Yet, in spite of all, a note of depression was the most strongly marked of all his characteristics', *LMF*, p. 404.) Roberts, p. 108; Austin Harrison, 'George Gissing', in J. P. Michaux (ed.) *George Gissing: Critical Essays* (Vision Press, and Totowa, N. J.: Barnes & Noble, 1981), p. 23.
2 MS letter, GG to Algernon Gissing, August 1885 (Berg); *Gabrielle*, p. 127; *LMF*, p. 32.
3 *Gabrielle*, pp. 41—2; MS letter, GG to Morley Roberts, 14 August 1898 (Berg); *Wells*, p. 185.
4 *Bertz*, pp. 237, 245, 269; *Gabrielle*, p. 118.
5 MS letters, GG to Morley Roberts, 10 February 1900, 14 March 1901, 1 November 1903 (Berg); Roberts, p. 188.
6 MS letter, GG to Frederic Harrison, 7 November 1895 (Pforzheimer); *Hick*, p. 26; MS letter, GG to Morley Roberts, 27 May 1895 (Berg).
7 *LMF*, pp. 92, 194, 298; *Wells*, p. 138; *Ryecroft*, pp. 243, 249, 256; *Dickens*, p. 98.

8 Unpublished in GG's lifetime; now published in *GGEF*, pp. 75−97.

9 *GGEF*, p. 94. cf. Arthur Schopenhauer, *Parerga and Paralipomena*, trans. E. F. J. Payne, 2 vols (Oxford: Clarendon Press, 1974), Vol. 2, pp. 303−4; and *The World as Will and Idea*, trans. R. B. Haldane and J. Kemp, 3 vols (Routledge, 1957), Vol. 1, pp. 457, 485, 489.

10 *LMF*, p. 193; *Stories and Sketches*, p. 26; *Unclassed*, p. 165; *Thyrza*, p. 118.

11 *Thyrza*, p. 474; *Born in Exile*, p. 195. cf. Schopenhauer, *Will and Idea*, Vol. 3, pp. 115−17, 252−7; and *Parerga*, Vol. 2, p. 268.

12 *Born in Exile*, p. 248. See also *Demos*, p. 79; *Thyrza*, p. 162; *Ryecroft*, p. 105; and *Will Warburton*, p. 227; cf. Schopenhauer, *Parerga*, Vol. 2, pp. 285−6, 291.

13 *Gabrielle*, p. 113.

14 *Nether World*, p. 58 (contrast *Thyrza*, p. 396); 'The Pessimist of Plato Road' is reprinted in *Victim of Circumstances*, pp. 167−83.

15 Pforzheimer, MS 266, 'Ideas'; *Odd Women*, p. 11.

16 See, e.g. 'A Song of Sixpence', in *Human Odds and Ends*, p. 228.

17 Michael Snowdon and Clara Hewett appear in *Nether World*, Walter Egremont appears in *Thyrza*, Dyce Lashmar in *Charlatan*, Richard Mutimer in *Demos*, Arthur Golding in *Workers*, Alma Rolfe in *Whirlpool*, Godwin Peak in *Born in Exile*.

18 *LMF*, p. 65.

19 Thomas Hardy, *Late Lyrics and Earlier* (Macmillan, 1922), p. viii; Roberts, p. 95.

20 Adrian Poole, *Gissing in Context* (Macmillan, 1975), p. 99.

21 Characters in *Unclassed*, *Thyrza*, *Life's Morning*, *Odd Women*, *Eve's Ransom*, *Jubilee* and *Veranilda*, respectively.

22 *Thyrza*, pp. 213, 232; *Sleeping Fires*, pp. 173, 186; *Will Warburton*, pp. 243 ff.

23 *Born in Exile*, p. 178; *Denzil Quarrier*, p. 195; *Crown of Life*, p. 245.

24 See *Unclassed*, p. 226; *Jubilee*, p. 145; and *Whirlpool*, p. 131.

25 George J. Romanes, 'Mental differences between men and women', *Nineteenth Century*, vol. 21 (May 1887), pp. 654−72, at p. 659. Gissing's notes are in Pforzheimer, MS 267, 'Woman'; he gives the title as 'Mental characteristics of women'.

26 Characters in *Isabel Clarendon*, *New Grub Street*, *Born in Exile*, *Jubilee* and *Whirlpool*, respectively.

27 Pierre Coustillas (ed.), *George Gissing at Alderley Edge* (Enitharmon Press, 1969), pp. 16, 23; *LMF*, p. 403; MS letters, GG to Arthur Bowes, Saturday 1873, 7 May 1873 (Yale); *Bertz*, p. 62; Roberts, pp. 158−9.

28 *LMF*, p. 173; cf. pp. 54, 112, 160−1, 172, 403. GG himself knew *some* of Milton's shorter poems by heart (Roberts, p. 226).

29 MS letter, GG to Algernon Gissing, 19 June 1896 (Berg); GG, *Critical Studies of the Works of Charles Dickens*, p. 157 (cf. *LMF*, p. 221); Roberts, p. 158.

30 *Emancipated*, p. 334.
31 *Emancipated*, pp. 14, 9, 107, 113, 170, 175.
32 *Emancipated*, pp. 239, 274, 308, 309.
33 *Emancipated*, pp. 3, 55, 56, 315, 336.
34 *Emancipated*, pp. 435, 438, 439; *Wells*, p. 49.
35 *Emancipated*, pp. 66, 272, 267; F. Scott Fitzgerald, *The Great Gatsby* (Harmondsworth: Penguin, 1968), p. 136.
36 *Emancipated*, p. 420; cf. pp. 63, 110.
37 *Emancipated*, pp. 356, 388, 398, 455, 456. The quotation from Boccaccio is 'Bocca baciata non perde ventura; anzi rinnuova, come fa la luna' ('lips that have been kissed do not lose their chances; they renew themselves like the moon'), *Decamerone*, end of seventh story of second day.
38 *Emancipated*, pp. 118, 401, 42, 288.
39 *Emancipated*, pp. 3, 42, 55, 124, 271, 276, 336.
40 *Emancipated*, pp. 413, 174, 323, 169.
41 *LMF*, p. 53.
42 *Workers*, Vol. 1, p. 275. GG outlined his polemical intentions in a letter to Algernon Gissing (8 June 1880), in which he said that in parts of the novel he was a 'mouthpiece of the advanced Radical party' (*LMF*, p. 73).
43 *Workers*, Vol. 2, p. 378; cf. Vol. 1, p. 109.
44 *Workers*, Vol. 2, pp. 405, 363, 379; *Ryecroft*, p. 289.
45 *Demos*, p. 371.
46 *New Grub Street*, pp. 110, 179; on Reardon's weakness, see pp. 79, 82, 108, 110, 190, 239, 257, 260–2.
47 *Crown of Life*, pp. 31, 103, 163; see also pp. 182, 170.
48 *Crown of Life*, pp. 285, 172.
49 *GGEF*, p. 95. It should be added that, for Schopenhauer, the escape through art, unlike the escape through resignation, is merely transitory 'and is therefore not ... a path out of life, but only an occasional consolation in it' (*Will and Idea*, Vol. 1, p. 346). The possible contradictions in Schopenhauer's views about hard work and aesthetic escape are discussed by Bryan Magee in *The Philosophy of Schopenhauer* (Oxford: Clarendon Press, 1983), pp. 237, 240–3.
50 *LMF*, p. 128 (cf. pp. 126, 138–9); *Unclassed*, p. 117.
51 See Richard Rumbold (ed.), *Letters of Gustave Flaubert*, trans. J. M. Cohen (Weidenfeld, 1950), pp. 28, 37, 104, 108, 113; and Francis Steegmuller (ed.), *The Letters of Gustave Flaubert 1830–1857* (Cambridge, Mass.: Belknap/Harvard, 1980), pp. 30–1, 143. Though Flaubert's sentiments were similar to his own, GG felt that Flaubert's 'laborious effort' compared poorly with Dickens's joyful energy (*Dickens*, p. 226). We know that GG read Flaubert's letters from a diary entry of 7 December 1890 (*Diary*, p. 232).
52 *Jubilee*, p. 214; the characters are from *Thyrza, New Grub Street* and *Crown of Life*, respectively.

53 Characters in *Unclassed, Isabel Clarendon* and *Born in Exile*, respectively.
54 *Ryecroft*, p. 188; see *Crown of Life*, p. 294.
55 *CB*, p. 51; *Gabrielle*, p. 103; *Ryecroft*, p. 20.
56 *Gabrielle*, pp. 109, 123, 119; *Ryecroft*, p. 167.
57 Austin Harrison, 'George Gissing', in Michaux (ed.), *George Gissing: Critical Essays*, p. 28; *Gabrielle*, p. 51.
58 *Unclassed*, pp. 224—5.

Chapter 2: *Workers and Reform*

1 *Nether World*, p. 139; *GGEF*, p. 197.
2 cf. *Workers*, Vol. 2, pp. 360—1; *Isabel Clarendon*, Vol. 2, pp. 314—15, 324—5; *Thyrza*, pp. 258—9, 466, 471; *Unclassed*, pp. 297—8; and George Eliot, *The Mill on the Floss* (Dent, 1908), pp. 445, 451.
3 *Life's Morning*, pp. 237—40, 308—9.
4 *Nether World*, p. 318. For other rejections of self-sacrifice see *Odd Women*, pp. 21—2; *Gabrielle*, p. 40.
5 *LMF*, p. 13 (my italics).
6 *Gabrielle*, p. 63; *CB*, p. 23.
7 For 'A Daughter of the Lodge' (written 1900) see *House of Cobwebs*, pp. 175—91; *Unclassed*, p. 211. cf. *CB*, p. 67: 'Why is it so painful to me to see even a blackguard humiliated?'
8 *LMF*, pp. 44—5; MS letter, GG to Algernon Gissing, 6 February 1879 (Pforzheimer).
9 MS letter, GG to Frederic Harrison, 23 July 1880 (Pforzheimer). (cf. *Bertz*, p. 51: 'I do not feel — have *never* felt — the least vital interest in Christianity itself'.) Roberts, p. 96.
10 MS notebook 'Reminscences [*sic*] of my father' (Yale); MS letter, GG to Algernon Gissing, 9 May 1880 (Yale); *Workers*, Vol. 1, p. 44.
11 MS letters, GG to Algernon Gissing, 9 November 1878 (Berg), 9 May 1880 (Yale); *LMF*, p. 92. On the connections between positivism and socialism see Royden Harrison, *Before the Socialists: Studies in Labour and Politics 1861—1881* (Routledge, and Toronto: University of Toronto Press, 1965), pp. 269—77, 333—42. GG's respect for intellect was encouraged by the writings of Comte himself, who also appears to have influenced him by arguing that 'the speculative class' had much in common with 'the multitude' and that it was the duty of intellectuals to engage in popular education. See Auguste Comte, *The Positive Philosophy*, trans. Harriet Martineau, 2 vols (Kegan Paul, 1893), Vol. 2, pp. 400, 404. Martineau's translation, of which Comte approved, was the one that GG read.
12 *Bertz*, p. 4 (cf. *Gabrielle*, p. 117); *LMF*, p. 90; *Notes on Social Democracy*, pp. 4, 13.
13 MS letter, GG to Algernon Gissing, 4 May 1881 (Berg) (an edited version of this letter is in *LMF*, pp. 97—8). On GG's attitude to

the *Freiheit* see *Notes on Social Democracy*, pp. 8–12 and Martha S. Vogeler, 'Gissing and the positivists: The *Vestnik Evropy* articles', *GN*, vol. 21 (January 1985), p. 9.

14   MS letters, GG to Algernon Gissing, 21 November 1879 (Berg), 19 January 1879 (Pforzheimer); *LMF*, pp. 38–9.

15   *LMF*, p. 52; MS letter, GG to Algernon Gissing, 15 May 1881 (Pforzheimer) (cut version in *LMF*, p. 98).

16   *Demos*, pp. 381–2, 236–7, 249, 252, 284.

17   *Ryecroft*, pp. 113, 194.

18   See Chapter 4.

19   MS letter, GG to Algernon Gissing, 21 December 1880 (Yale).

20   *LMF*, p. 72; MS letter, GG to Frederic Harrison, 23 July 1880 (Pforzheimer).

21   P. J. Keating, *The Working Classes in Victorian Fiction* (Routledge, 1971), pp. 32–40; and Keating (ed.), *Into Unknown England* (Glasgow: Fontana/Collins, 1976), 'Introduction', *passim*.

22   *Workers*, Vol. 1, pp. 3–8, 269–75; Vol. 2, pp. 183–4.

23   Korg, pp. 36–7. (See also Korg's introduction to *Notes on Social Democracy*, p. iv.) *Workers*, Vol. 1, p. 280, Vol. 2, pp. 29, 403, 418.

24   *Workers*, Vol. 2, pp. 54, 16, 19.

25   *Workers*, Vol. 1, pp. 8, 274–5; *Nether World*, p. 102.

26   *Workers*, Vol. 2, p. 6.

27   *Workers*, Vol. 1, pp. 281–2; Vol. 2, pp. 218–19, 306. On the significance of libraries in GG's work see Chapter 4.

28   Jacob Korg, 'Division of purpose in George Gissing', in Pierre Coustillas (ed.), *Collected Articles on George Gissing* (Frank Cass, 1968), pp. 64–79. For further discussion of art and reform, see Chapter 3.

29   *Workers*, Vol. 1, pp. 127–8; cf. Vol. 1, p. 114.

30   On pity as 'fuel to passion' see *Unclassed*, pp. 107, 193, 226–7; and the chapter 'Love or Pity?' in *Workers*, Vol. 2, pp. 49–68. The theme is recurrent in GG's short stories.

31   *Unclassed*, p. 290; Korg, pp. 62, 67.

32   *Unclassed*, pp. 293, 310, 268–75; *Unclassed (i)*, Vol. 3, p. 187.

33   Theodore Stanton (ed.), *The Woman Question in Europe* (Sampson Low, 1884), pp. 122–3 (this book was later listed in GG's scrap-book dossier 'Woman', Pforzheimer, MS 267); *Unclassed*, pp. 272–5.

34   *CB*, p. 53.

35   *Unclassed (i)*, Vol. 1, pp. 48–50; Vol. 2, p. 51; Vol. 3, p. 119; *Demos*, pp. 250, 259–61.

36   *Unclassed*, p. 125; *Unclassed (i)*, Vol. 1, p. 273.

37   *Unclassed*, p. 141; cf. pp. 9, 22, 209.

38   *Unclassed*, p. 243; *Unclassed (i)*, Vol. 2, pp. 280, 315, Vol. 3, pp. 18–20; *LMF*, p. 140; Joseph J. Wolff, 'Gissing's revision of *The Unclassed*', *Nineteenth Century Fiction*, vol. 8 (June 1953), pp. 42–53, at p. 48. The theme of theft and imprisonment, treated

with revealing intensity, occurs also in several of the short stories which Gissing published in Chicago papers in 1877: 'Too Dearly Bought' (reprinted in *Sins of the Fathers*; see esp. pp. 98, 106); 'The Warden's Daughter', 'Twenty Pounds' and 'Joseph Yates's Temptation' (reprinted in *Brownie*); 'A Test of Honor' (reprinted with an introduction by Pierre Coustillas and Robert L. Selig in the *Times Literary Supplement*, 12 December 1980, pp. 1417−18).

39 *Unclassed (i)*, Vol. 2, p. 3; cf. *Hamlet*, Act III, sc. ii, 11. 371−80.

40 cf. *Unclassed*, pp. 117, 212, with *LMF*, pp. 126−39, *passim*. John Halperin, *Gissing: A Life in Books* (Oxford: Oxford University Press, 1982), pp. 52−3. Not all Halperin's details are accurate: at one point (p. 52) he conflates in a single quotation a statement from GG to Algernon Gissing with a statement from Frederic Harrison to GG.

41 *Unclassed*, pp. 116, 229, 154; *Unclassed (i)*, Vol. 3, p. 9.

42 *Unclassed*, pp. 116, 118, 54, 125, 170, 193, 198 ff.

43 *Unclassed (i)*, Vol. 2, p. 277, Vol. 3, pp. 2, 169−170; *Unclassed*, pp. 54, 234−5, 270. On the need for love see *Unclassed*, pp. 291, 296; and *Unclassed (i)*, Vol. 3, pp. 240, 296−7.

44 *Demos*, pp. 66, 411.

45 See *LMF*, pp. 135−6.

46 *Demos*, p. 470; *Ryecroft*, pp. 194−5.

47 *Demos*, pp. 77, 171, 205, 291.

48 *Demos*, p. 167.

49 *Demos*, pp. 49, 66, 118, 311−12.

50 *Demos*, pp. 277, 300−2, 325, 367, 412, 419, 421−2, 466, 477.

51 *Demos*, pp. 118, 137, 141, 207, 219, 238, 244, 287, 386.

52 *Demos*, pp. 264, 238, 9, 149, 235. On GG's confusion, in *Demos*, about the distinction between Radicals and Socialists see John Lucas, 'Conservatism and revolution in the 1880s', in Lucas (ed.), *Literature and Politics in the Nineteenth Century* (Methuen, 1971), p. 191. However, cf. *Born in Exile*, p. 201.

53 A point well made by Adrian Poole, *Gissing in Context* (Macmillan, 1975), pp. 71−2. cf. John Goode, 'Gissing, Morris and English Socialism', *Victorian Studies*, vol. 12 (December 1968), pp. 211−12.

54 *Demos*, pp. 383−6, 393−5.

55 *Demos*, pp. 334, 28, 409, 388, 411, 350.

56 *CB*, p. 26; *Demos*, p. 225. GG also quotes this 'precious sentence' (from Herbert Spencer's *The Man Versus the State* (New York: Appleton, 1884), p. 43) in *Dickens*, p. 238. Spencer's argument in this section of his work − 'that the welfare of a society and the justice of its arrangements are at bottom dependent on the characters of its members' (p. 43) − is fundamental to *Demos*.

57 *Thyrza*, p. 422.

58 *Thyrza*, pp. 140, 426, 381, 240.

59 A feature first observed in the *Whitehall Review*, 12 May 1887: 'The love element of the story is all worked at cross-purposes, and on the

principle of I love thee, thou lovest some one else, he loves her for a time ...' (*Heritage*, pp. 104–5).

60 In the first edition of *Thyrza* there is the further complication of the married Harold Emerson's infatuation with the heroine: see *Thyrza (i)*, Vol. 3, pp. 93–117, 129–46.

61 *Thyrza*, pp. 486–7, 396; see also *Thyrza (i)*, Vol. 2, p. 13.

62 Korg, p. 104.

63 *Thyrza*, p. 173; cf. pp. 15, 143, 421, 167.

64 *Thyrza*, p. 252; on Egremont's restlessness see esp. pp. 8, 10, 174. The sporadic implication that Egremont is weak is furthered by parallels with Mr Newthorpe (*Thyrza*, pp. 4, 156, 477) and, in the first edition, with Harold Emerson (*Thyrza (i)*, Vol. 3, pp. 113–14).

65 Gillian Tindall, *The Born Exile: George Gissing* (Temple Smith, 1974), pp. 89–97.

66 *Nether World*, pp. 1, 2, 32, 190, 263, 264, 391.

67 *Nether World*, pp. 2, 130.

68 Examples from *Nether World*, pp. 292–3.

69 *Nether World*, pp. 249, 345.

70 *Diary*, pp. 24–7, 33, 35; *Nether World*, pp. 54, 104 ff., 247–50.

71 *Nether World*, pp. 24, 52, 93, 102, 218, 252, 296, 368–9.

72 *Nether World*, pp. 378, 252, 86, 104, 217, 218, 252, 138. cf. Samuel Johnson, *Lives of the English Poets*, ed. G. B. Hill, 3 vols (Oxford: Clarendon Press, 1905), Vol. 3, p. 45.

73 *Nether World*, pp. 57, 53, 74.

74 *Nether World*, pp. 109, 218; cf. p. 112.

75 *Nether World*, pp. 276, 220.

76 *Nether World*, pp. 182, 209–10; cf. pp. 181, 187. On 'middle-class Victorian assumptions that all radical behaviour is mixed up with drink', see John Lucas, *The Literature of Change* (Hassocks, Sussex: Harvester, 1977), pp. 67–8. As a revolutionary fanatic John Hewett is anticipated by John Pether in *Workers* (Vol. 1, pp. 355–70, Vol. 2, pp. 9, 82–3, 203–4).

77 *Nether World*, pp. 241, 229, 250–3.

78 *Nether World*, pp. 101, 179, 233, 255, 308, 311.

79 *Diary*, p. 36; MS letter, GG to Thomas Hardy, 25 July 1887 (photocopy at Pforzheimer; MS at UCLA); *LMF*, p. 83.

80 MS letter, GG to Ellen Gissing, 'Day after Shakespeare's birthday' (i.e. 24 April) 1888 (Yale).

81 *Diary*, p. 24; Arnold White, *Problems of a Great City* (Remington, 1886), pp. 23, 47, 130 ff., 138, 141, 216, 220, 223; *Nether World*, pp. 5, 41–3, 104 ff., 247, 274.

82 White, *Problems of a Great City*, pp. 263, 194, 266.

83 *Diary*, pp. 23, 28, 30; *LMF*, pp. 211, 216.

84 Roberts, pp. 107–8, 138; *Diary*, p. 54.

Chapter 3: *Art and Commercialism*

1   *Dickens*, p. 151; *By the Ionian Sea*, pp. 108−9; MS, 'Reminiscences of my father' (Yale), note made in 1896; *LMF*, p. 18. A similar contempt for business is expressed throughout William Gissing's MS diary (Berg).

2   *Odd Women*, p. 43; *Will Warburton*, p. 113; *Life's Morning*, p. 64. On commission agents see, e.g., *Nether World*, p. 198; *Jubilee*, p. 111.

3   Pforzheimer, MS 251; *CB*, p. 44; *Born in Exile*, p. 264; *Crown of Life*, p. 164; *Charlatan*, p. 87.

4   A. L. Morton (ed.), *Political Writings of William Morris* (Lawrence & Wishart, 1984), pp. 109−33, 134−58; *LMF*, p. 127; *Life's Morning*, p. 209; *Demos*, p. 385.

5   *House of Cobwebs*, pp. 106−23; *Will Warburton*, p. 41; *Dickens*, p. 247.

6   *Life's Morning*, pp. 135, 148; *Will Warburton*, pp. 151−3; *Whirlpool*, pp. 45, 208; Charles Dickens, *Great Expectations* (Harmondsworth: Penguin, 1965), p. 233.

7   *Demos*, p. 30; *Nether World*, p. 199; *Jubilee*, p. 380.

8   *Whirlpool*, p. 451; *Nether World*, p. 364; *Jubilee*, p. 219; MS letter, GG to Ellen Gissing, 19 November 1893 (Pforzheimer).

9   Thomas Carlyle, *Past and Present*, ed. A. M. D. Hughes (Oxford: Clarendon Press, 1918), p. 128; *Unclassed (i)*, Vol. 1, pp. 106−7; *Jubilee*, p. 309.

10 E. S. Turner, *The Shocking History of Advertising* (Harmondsworth: Penguin, 1965), p. 132; on *A Beautiful World* see Robert L. Selig, 'A sad heart at the late-Victorian culture market: George Gissing's *In the Year of Jubilee*', *Studies in English Literature*, vol. 9 (autumn 1969), pp. 703−20, at p. 715. *Jubilee*, pp. 164, 194, 245, 74, 64, 388, 424; *Charlatan*, p. 299 (these advertisements are also described in *CB*, p. 45; Gissing saw them in 1893).

11 *Jubilee*, pp. 114, 143; *Isabel Clarendon*, Vol. 2, p. 175; *Will Warburton*, pp. 113−4.

12 *Charlatan*, pp. 48, 405; see Turner, *Shocking History of Advertising*, p. 67; *Stories and Sketches*, p. 140. cf. *GN*, vol. 7 (October 1971), pp. 16−17; *Born in Exile*, pp. 24−8, 77−83.

13 *Nether World*, p. 163; *Town Traveller*, pp. 129−30 (cf. p. 80); *Crown of Life*, pp. 134, 261; *New Grub Street*, p. 330.

14 *Isabel Clarendon*, Vol. 2, p. 280; *Will Warburton*, pp. 159, 160; *Crown of Life*, p. 268; *Life's Morning*, p. 76; *Jubilee*, p. 429; *Born in Exile*, p. 39; *New Grub Street*, pp. 269, 290; *Nether World*, p. 22.

15 *Crown of Life*, p. 164; *Nether World*, p. 207; *Ryecroft*, pp. 91−3; *CB*, p. 61; *Whirlpool*, pp. 13, 28 (cf. *Wells*, pp. 47−8); Korg, p. 238; T. H. Huxley, 'Evolution and Ethics', in Cyril Bibby (ed.), *The Essence of T. H. Huxley* (Macmillan, 1967), p. 178; *Denzil Quarrier*, pp. 32−3 (cf. *Ryecroft*, p. 187).

16 *Life's Morning*, p. 76; *Jubilee*, p. 220; *Will Warburton*, p. 161.

17 *Unclassed*, p. 119; *Jubilee*, p. 251; *Nether World*, p. 164; *Ryecroft*, pp. 10, 85.

18 *Demos*, pp. 416, 444–5, 450–57; *Nether World*, pp. 104–13; *Town Traveller*, pp. 249–56; *Will Warburton*, p. 145.

19 *Demos*, p. 385; *Ryecroft*, p. 113; *Crown of Life*, p. 290; *Eve's Ransom*, p. 99; *Born in Exile*, pp. 264–5, 107, 111, 278.

20 MS letter, GG to Algernon Gissing, 31 January 1885 (Yale); MS letters, GG to Algernon Gissing, 16 June 1879, 21 June 1879 (Berg); *Diary*, pp. 167, 287, 557 (cf. Roberts, p. 135); *Critical Studies of the Works of Charles Dickens*, p. 106.

21 *Crown of Life*, pp. 102, 156.

22 *Ryecroft*, pp. 82–3; *Life's Morning*, p. 73; *Nether World*, pp. 59–60; *Workers*, Vol. 2, pp. 194–6, 302. For 'The Palace of Art' see *The Poems of Tennyson*, ed. C. Ricks (Longman, 1969), pp. 400–18.

23 *Workers*, Vol. 1, p. 169; Arthur Schopenhauer, *Parerga and Paralipomena*, trans. E. F. J. Payne (Oxford: Clarendon Press, 1974), Vol. 2, pp. 428, 50 (the whole section on 'Authorship and style' is relevant to Gissing).

24 W. B. Yeats, 'The Choice', *The Collected Poems of W. B. Yeats* (Macmillan, 1950), p. 278; *Workers*, Vol. 2, p. 269.

25 *LMF*, pp. 126, 134, 128; *Unclassed (i)*, Vol. 3, p. 11 (cf. *Emancipated*, pp. 95–6), 6–7; *Charlatan*, p. 299.

26 *Workers*, Vol. 1, pp. 102–3; *Unclassed*, p. 150; *Emancipated*, pp. 437–8, 313, 352; John Spiers and Pierre Coustillas, *The Rediscovery of George Gissing* (National Book League, 1971), p. 18.

27 *Gabrielle*, pp. 26, 113, 119; *Diary*, p. 52; *By the Ionian Sea*, pp. 118–19; *LMF*, p. 155; *Thyrza*, p. 423; *Born in Exile*, p. 270.

28 *Diary*, p. 41; *Bertz*, p. 33; Pforzheimer, MS 250, 'The World of Art. Stage etc.'; *Workers*, Vol. 2, p. 79; *Jubilee*, pp. 6, 34, 62, 89, 91, 173, 382. On the significance of popular songs in *Jubilee* see Selig, 'A sad heart at the late-Victorian culture market', pp. 709–14.

29 *Bertz*, p. 119; *Fiction*, pp. 69–71; *CB*, p. 34.

30 *Charlatan*, p. 77; *Ryecroft*, pp. 64–9; *Thyrza*, p. 63; *CB*, p. 68. There is of course a large modern literature (associated especially with the names of Q. D. and F. R. Leavis) on the cultural questions raised by GG in *Ryecroft*. Scholarly support to GG's contention that the contemporary expansion of the reading public, and the multiplication of printed matter, led to a debasement of literary standards is offered by Louis Dudek, *Literature and the Press: A History of Printing, Printed Media, and Their Relation to Literature* (Toronto: Contact Press, 1960); see esp. pp. 10–11, 149, 151, 163.

31 *Bertz*, pp. 140–1; *LMF*, p. 183; *New Grub Street*, p. 493; *Ryecroft*, p. 55.

32 *New Grub Street*, p. 493; Turner, *The Shocking History of Advertising*, p. 54 (cf. Samuel Squire Sprigge, *The Methods of Publishing* (Incorporated Society of Authors, 1890), p. 83); Thomas Babington

Macaulay, *Critical and Historical Essays*, ed. A. J. Grieve, 2 vols (Dent, 1907), Vol. 2, p. 646; *CB*, p. 69.

33 GG, 'An author at grass', *Fortnightly Review*, vol. 71 (1902), p. 918. For other comments on reviewing see esp. *CB*, pp. 34, 55—6; *LMF*, p. 62; *Bertz*, pp. 125, 128; *Hick*, pp. 64—5; *Diary*, p. 288; and *Fiction*, p. 68.

34 *CB*, p. 39; *Bertz*, p. 140; *Fiction*, p. 68; *Gabrielle*, p. 124.

35 *Emancipated*, p. 316; *Whirlpool*, p. 372; *Diary*, pp. 233, 243, 309, 558; *Bertz*, p. 203; *Fiction*, p. 67; *CB*, p. 37; *Wells*, p. 138; *Ryecroft*, p. 210.

36 MS letter, GG to Algernon Gissing, 11 January 1891 (Berg); Schopenhauer, *Parerga*, Vol. 2, p. 502; Roberts, p. 100; *Charlatan*, p. 399.

37 See Schopenhauer, *Parerga*, Vol. 2, pp. 447—8; *Crown of Life*, p. 158; *Bertz*, p. 213; and *Ryecroft*, p. 95.

38 *Thyrza*, pp. 93, 420 (in *Thyrza (i)*, Vol. 2, pp. 12—13, Egremont gives a lecture denouncing newspapers); *Jubilee*, pp. 57, 58.

39 GG, 'An author at grass', p. 918; *Diary*, p. 228; MS postcard, GG to Morley Roberts, 16 November 1903 (Berg); MS letters, GG to Algernon Gissing, 16 March 1883 (Berg), 28 March 1883 (Yale), 30 January 1881 (Yale); *Whirlpool*, p. 50.

40 *Jubilee*, p. 5; MS notebook (Yale); Catherine Morland is the heroine of Jane Austen's *Northanger Abbey* (1818); *Unclassed*, pp. 102, 106; (cf. pp. 21—2); *Demos*, pp. 110, 190 (cf. pp. 254, 277); *Town Traveller*, p. 286. The effect of cheap romances is also shown in *Life's Morning*, p. 182; *Odd Women*, p. 295; and *Charlatan*, p. 317.

41 MS letter, GG to Algernon Gissing, 24 April 1887 (Yale); *Emancipated*, p. 288; *Charlatan*, pp. 164, 133, 309, 405; *Human Odds and Ends*, pp. 277—83; *Victim of Circumstances*, pp. 167—83, 257—70.

42 *Whirlpool*, p. 381; Roberts, p. 141; *Diary*, p. 316; *Bertz*, pp. 177, 202 (cf. pp. 199, 211); MS letters, GG to W. M. Colles, 12 August 1895, 14 December 1895, 6 October 1896 (Pforzheimer); MS letter, GG to A. H. Bullen, 20 June 1898 (Berg).

43 *Workers*, Vol. 1, p. 223; *Isabel Clarendon*, Vol. 2, pp. 168—9, 190; *Fiction*, pp. 35—6; *Thyrza*, p. 478; *Sins of the Fathers*, p. 33; *Ryecroft*, p. 211. George Moore followed up his article in the *Pall Mall Gazette* of 10 December 1884 with *Literature at Nurse, or Circulating Morals* (Vizetelly, 1885).

44 *Life's Morning*, pp. 70, 112, 239, 303.

45 MS letter, GG to Algernon Gissing, 11 April 1893 (Berg) ('I, too, shall have to make concessions of some kind to popular taste, or fall into penury again'); *Fiction*, p. 50.

46 Frank Swinnerton, *George Gissing: A Critical Study* (Martin Secker, 1912), p. 167; P. J. Keating, *George Gissing: 'New Grub Street'* (Edward Arnold, 1968), p. 9.

47 *Bertz*, p. 121.

48 *New Grub Street*, pp. 81, 196, 368—9, 550—1.

49 *New Grub Street*, pp. 97, 256, 163, 545; for Dora's condemnations

see pp. 500, 520, 546.
50 *New Grub Street*, pp. 96, 136; on reclusiveness see pp. 90, 210; on 'hunger' see pp. 95, 219, 227, 364.
51 *New Grub Street*, pp. 383, 388, 230, 531−8.
52 Mabel Collins Donnelly, *George Gissing: Grave Comedian* (Cambridge, Mass.: Harvard University Press, 1954), p. 161.
53 *New Grub Street*, pp. 80, 451, 256. Rosamond Vincy appears in George Eliot's *Middlemarch* (1872); Henrik Ibsen's *Hedda Gabler* was written in 1890.
54 *New Grub Street*, pp. 219, 327, 507, 366.
55 *Bertz*, p. 134; *New Grub Street*, pp. 190, 239.
56 *New Grub Street*, pp. 373, 377, 460.
57 *New Grub Street*, pp. 531, 244, 267.
58 *New Grub Street*, pp. 259, 470, 106−7, 192, 502−4.
59 *New Grub Street*, pp. 126, 67, 199, 99, 397, 104, 414−5; *Born in Exile*, pp. 341−2, 371−405; *Charlatan*, pp. 244−5, 322−7.
60 *Bertz*, p. 122; *New Grub Street*, pp. 39, 123, 337. For a fuller account of Johnson's influence on GG see my article 'The annual return to Old Grub Street: what Samuel Johnson meant to Gissing', *GN*, vol. 20 (January 1984), pp. 1−27.
61 *New Grub Street*, pp. 155, 485; on the antithesis between commerce and the classics see pp. 89, 108, 155, 158, 172, 403−4, 407.
62 *New Grub Street*, p. 75; on contrasting attitudes to nature and the city see pp. 379, 405−6, 417, 474, 479, 529.
63 *New Grub Street*, pp. 80, 223, 227, 152.
64 *New Grub Street*, pp. 95, 46.
65 *New Grub Street*, pp. 496−7.
66 *New Grub Street*, pp. 274, 43, 62, 109, 514.
67 *New Grub Street*, pp. 384, 397.
68 *New Grub Street*, pp. 412, 516.
69 Ovid, *Metamorphoses*, Bk VII, l. 20.
70 Pforzheimer, MS 266, 'Ideas'.
71 *New Grub Street*, p. 35; cf. p. 535.
72 *New Grub Street*, pp. 43, 214, 424, 359, 534.
73 *New Grub Street*, pp. 83, 126, 127, 174, 463, *Fiction*, p. 85 (cf. Roberts, p. 79).
74 See *New Grub Street*, pp. 275, 280, 297−8, 387, 418.
75 *New Grub Street*, p. 525.
76 Michael Collie, *The Alien Art: A Critical Study of George Gissing's Novels* (Folkestone, Kent: William Dawson, 1979), pp. 120−25, specifies the passages in *New Grub Street* which Gissing eliminated for Gabrielle Fleury's translation.
77 *Bertz*, p. 121; *New Grub Street*, pp. 153, 86, 138; Schopenhauer, *Parerga*, Vol. 2, p. 564.

Chapter 4: *Poverty, Intellect and Exile*

1 *Heritage*, p. 244.

2 George Orwell, 'Not enough money', *GN*, vol. 5 (July 1969), pp. 1–4, at p. 2.

3 Ellen Gissing, 'Some personal recollections of George Gissing', *Blackwood's Magazine'*, vol. 225 (May 1929), p. 653; *Wells*, pp. 231–3. GG's 'Account of books' is at Yale: it is reproduced in George Matthew Adams, 'How and why I collect George Gissing', *Colophon*, pt 18 (1934). I am grateful to Pierre Coustillas for supplying me with a copy of this ledger. For other information on GG's earnings see *Diary*, pp. 366, 389, 550, 561; and Korg, pp. 157–8.

4 *Ryecroft*, p. 14; *Bertz*, p. 298; MS letter, GG to Morley Roberts, 15 December 1901 (Berg).

5 MS letter, GG to Algernon Gissing, 22 January 1890 (Berg). GG's visit to the Marylebone Workhouse in September 1887 is described in Pforzheimer, MS 269, 'Local government'. cf. *Workers*, Vol. 2, p. 217; *New Grub Street*, pp. 151, 416; Roberts, p. 92; and Pierre Coustillas (ed.), *The Letters of George Gissing to Edward Clodd* (Enitharmon Press, 1973), p. 57.

6 *Ryecroft*, p. 14; *Thyrza*, p. 177; *Unclassed (i)*, Vol. 1, p. 166; *New Grub Street*, p. 526; Roberts, pp. 239–40.

7 *Diary*, p. 143; *Unclassed*, p. 61; *Ryecroft*, pp. 36–8; *Eve's Ransom*, pp. 41, 76; *Thyrza*, p. 68; *Odd Women*, p. 13 (cf. *Ryecroft*, p. 51).

8 Pforzheimer, MS 266, 'Ideas'; see *Unclassed*, p. 62; *Thyrza*, pp. 67, 108; *Eve's Ransom*, pp. 11–12; and *Will Warburton*, p. 162; *Unclassed (i)*, Vol. 1, p. 170. cf. *CB*, p. 65.

9 *Unclassed*, p. 44; *Bertz*, p. 121; *Ryecroft*, p. 30. cf. *Born in Exile*, p. 129. *Workers*, Vol. 2, p. 77; *Isabel Clarendon*, Vol. 2, pp. 111, 116; *Nether World*, p. 274.

10 *House of Cobwebs*, p. 37; MS letter, GG to Algernon Gissing, 28 December 1886 (Berg).

11 *LMF*, p. 313; *Nether World*, p. 51; *Diary*, pp. 209–10. For a fuller discussion of the significance of this passage in *Nether World* see David Grylls, 'The annual return to Old Grub Street: what Samuel Johnson meant to Gissing', *GN*, vol. 20 (January 1984), pp. 1–27, at pp. 7–9.

12 *Bertz*, p. 112.

13 See *Nether World*, pp. 15, 24, 36, 56, 62, 109, 130, 141, 217, 296, 374. cf. Warburton's realization that life itself is dependent on money (*Will Warburton*, pp. 164–5).

14 *Workers*, Vol. 2, p. 209; *Unclassed*, p. 61; *CB*, p. 25 (cf. *Wells*, p. 268; and Biffen's diet in *New Grub Street*, p. 245); MS letter, GG to

Algernon Gissing, 23 March 1879 (Berg) (the specimen was of an Egyptian split lentil).

15   *Ryecroft*, p. 246; Roberts, pp. 47, 89; *Life's Morning*, p. 138; *House of Cobwebs*, pp. 113–14; GG, 'Simple Simon', *The Idler*, vol. 9 (May 1896), pp. 509, 511; *Odd Women*, p. 23 (cf. p. 122). Despite his attacks on vegetarianism, GG, persuaded by his sister Margaret, gave up meat again in 1899 (*Diary*, p. 512).

16   *Bertz*, p. 209. (cf. MS letter, GG to Ellen Gissing, 25 October 1892 (Pforzheimer): 'Do you, I wonder, *eat* quite enough? I am convinced that the food department is of great importance'.) *Hick*, p. 58. On the question of GG's starvation in France see Roberts, pp. 196–200; and John Halperin, *Gissing: A Life in Books* (Oxford: Oxford University Press, 1982), pp. 319–24.

17   *Human Odds and Ends*, p. 60; *Eve's Ransom*, p. 45.

18   *Ryecroft*, pp. 15–16; cf. James Boswell, *Life of Johnson*, ed. R. W. Chapman (Oxford: Oxford University Press, 1953), pp. 1189–90; *Life's Morning*, pp. 84, 212.

19   *Unclassed*, p. 53; *Ryecroft*, p. 231; *Crown of Life*, p. 249; *New Grub Street*, pp. 550, 545.

20   *New Grub Street*, pp. 97, 232. On money bringing liberty see *Whirlpool*, p. 332; *New Grub Street*, p. 348; and *Charlatan*, p. 382.

21   Roberts, p. 107; *GGEF*, p. 94.

22   *Human Odds and Ends*, p. 200; *Life's Morning*, p. 75; *Demos*, pp. 383, 282; *House of Cobwebs*, pp. 120–21. On sympathy for the poor as a whole see *Life's Morning*, pp. 209–10; *Nether World*, p. 374; and *CB*, p. 54.

23   *Demos*, p. 383; *Nether World*, p. 377; *Dickens*, p. 117; *Born in Exile*, p. 269; see 1 above.

24   Roberts, pp. 94, 224–30; *Diary*, p. 211; *Bertz*, pp. 310, 315, 318.

25   Samuel Vogt Gapp, *George Gissing, Classicist* (Philadelphia: University of Pennsylvania Press, 1936), p. 84; cf. pp. 51, 55, 177.

26   Gapp, *George Gissing, Classicist*, pp. 100–114, *passim*. The main sources for GG's reading of these authors are *Diary*, *Bertz* and *CB*.

27   *Isabel Clarendon*, Vol. 1, p. 121, Vol. 2, p. 134; *Whirlpool*, p. 128; *Thyrza*, pp. 18, 365; *New Grub Street*, p. 93. cf. P. F. Kropholler, 'Gissing's characters and their books', *GN*, vol. 5 (April 1969), pp. 12–16. For GG's study schemes see *LMF*, pp. 41, 69; *CB*, p. 26; and *Ryecroft*, pp. 262–3.

28   *Ryecroft*, p. 128; Boswell, *Life of Johnson*, p. 1074; *Thyrza*, p. 67; *Life's Morning*, p. 111.

29   *LMF*, pp. 16, 33, 43; MS letter, GG to Algernon Gissing, 9 November 1878 (Berg).

30   *Workers*, Vol. 2, pp. 218–19, Vol. 1, p. 114; *Gabrielle*, p. 56; *Thyrza*, p. 59; *Demos*, pp. 42–3; *Whirlpool*, pp. 21–2; *New Grub Street*, pp. 50, 172–3; *Jubilee*, pp. 119 ff. GG's respect for bookishness shows up comically in his story 'Joseph' (*Lloyd's Weekly Newspaper*, 17 May 1896, p. 8), in which a young lad who is a model servant is revealed

to have 'a select library' of 200 volumes — poets, essayists and superior novelists. The menu cards he prepares for a suburban dinner-table include French names, accurately written.

31 Gapp, *George Gissing, Classicist*, p. 184; *Ryecroft*, p. 101. For golden light in classical scenes see *CB*, p. 69; *LMF*, p. 181; *Bertz*, p. 84; and *New Grub Street*, pp. 406—7.

32 Gapp, *George Gissing Classicist*, p. 180; *LMF*, p. 172; *Bertz*, p. 81. cf. *By the Ionian Sea*, pp. 20—21.

33 Richard Jenkyns, *The Victorians and Ancient Greece* (Oxford: Basil Blackwell, 1980), pp. 7, 58, 65, 168, 192 ff., 210—11, 276, 331—2; see Michael Sanderson, *The Universities in the Nineteenth Century* (London and Boston: Routledge, 1975), p. 92.

34 Dante, *Inferno*, Canto V, 1. 138. In *Emancipated* (p. 144) Miriam marks a line in Canto V.

35 *Workers*, Vol. 1, p. 97; *Crown of Life*, p. 315; *New Grub Street*, pp. 155, 158; *Diary*, pp. 40, 229; MS letter, GG to Algernon Gissing, 21 August 1888 (Yale).

36 *Gabrielle*, pp. 49, 74.

37 *Life's Morning*, pp. 14, 16—17, 43, 49, 51, 56, 280, 288—92, 302—5, 343—4. The ending of this novel was, admittedly, rewritten for Smith, Elder at the insistence of James Payn (Roberts, pp. 78—9; and Coustillas, 'Introduction', Harvester edn, pp. xvi—xvii).

38 *New Grub Street*, p. 411; *Gabrielle*, pp. 46, 74; *Ryecroft*, p. 63. cf. H. G. Wells's views in *Experiment in Autobiography*, 2 vols (Cape, 1934), Vol. 1, pp. 377—8: 'In the long run, if we live long enough, we find ourselves standing alone ...'.

39 *CB*, pp. 52—4; *Crown of Life*, p. 317; *Demos*, pp. 375—6, 237; *Ryecroft*, pp. 47, 127; *Town Traveller*, p. 3.

40 *Ryecroft*, pp. 52—3; cf. pp. 184—91 (on stoicism). On intellect as a compensation for poverty see *Diary*, p. 188; and *CB*, p. 21.

41 *Nether World*, p. 79.

42 *New Grub Street*, p. 70; *Isabel Clarendon*, Vol. 1, pp. 178—9, 185, 239.

43 *Whirlpool*, pp. 449—50; *Wells*, pp. 46—50, 242—59; *Heritage*, pp. 336—7.

44 *Demos*, p. 166.

45 MS letter, GG to Mrs Frederic Harrison, 21 April 1891 (Pforzheimer); *Isabel Clarendon*, Vol. 2, p. 315; *Ryecroft*, p. 91; *Veranilda*, p. 300.

46 MS letter, GG to Frederic Harrison, 24 June 1884 (Pforzheimer); Roberts, p. 121; *Nether World*, pp. 26, 276—7, 295, 79, 119, 58, 270. For other passages on 'revolt' see *Born in Exile*, p. 128; *Life's Morning*, pp. 252—3; *Demos*, p. 370; *Thyrza*, p. 371; and *Charlatan*, p. 113.

47 *Ryecroft*, p. 194; *LMF*, p. 291 (cf. *Diary*, p. 223). This novel probably became *Born in Exile*.

48 *Demos*, p. 334 (cf. p. 202); *Denzil Quarrier*, pp. 23, 35; *Dickens*, p. 254; see *Odd Women*, p. 17.

49 *Stories and Sketches*, pp. 71—88; *Born in Exile*, p. 362; *Bertz*, p. 242 (cf. *Thyrza*, p. 213); MS letters, GG to Algernon Gissing, 25 August 1884, August 1885 (Berg).

50 *Nether World*, p. 277; *Isabel Clarendon*, Vol. 1, p. 125. On the short-comings of the educated see *Bertz*, p. 64; and *CB*, p. 46.

51 *Diary*, pp. 288, 35, 137, 168; *Bertz*, p. 85. For recognition of loneliness at a narrative climax see, e.g., *New Grub Street*, p. 289; and *Denzil Quarrier*, p. 307.

52 *Gabrielle*, p. 28; *LMF*, pp. 154, 167, 191; Roberts, p. 109.

53 See *Workers*, Vol. 2, p. 43; *Isabel Clarendon*, Vol. 2, p. 176; *Emancipated*, p. 142; *Odd Women*, p. 287; *Eve's Ransom*, pp. 40, 115; *Crown of Life*, p. 26; and *Will Warburton*, p. 186. cf. *Diary*, p. 35; *Wells*, p. 164; and *Gabrielle*, p. 91.

54 *Diary*, pp. 32—4; *Ryecroft*, pp. 31, 232; *LMF*, pp. 149—50.

55 *Bertz*, pp. 186, 200 (cf. Roberts, p. 115); MS letter, GG to Algernon Gissing, 11 March 1880 (Yale); *Workers*, Vol. 2, p. 190 (cf. *Unclassed*, p. 163); *Hick*, p. 13; *Diary*, p. 277; *Gabrielle*, p. 69; *Wells*, p. 184.

56 *LMF*, p. 192; *CB*, p. 66; *Ryecroft*, p. 114.

57 *Thyrza*, p. 230; *Isabel Clarendon*, Vol. 2, p. 212; *Unclassed*, p. 164 (cf. *LMF*, p. 95); *Ryecroft*, p. xii; *Crown of Life*, p. 183.

58 *Diary*, p. 51 (cf. *Hick*, p. 10); *Unclassed*, p. 170; Edward Clodd, *Memories* (Chapman & Hall, 1916), p. 165; *By the Ionian Sea*, p. 22 (cf. *Ryecroft*, p. 26; *Will Warburton*, p. 227). *The Collected Poems of Thomas Hardy* (Macmillan, 1930), p. 152.

59 *Emancipated*, pp. 423—4; *Human Odds and Ends*, p. 140; *Gabrielle*, p. 94; *Whirlpool*, pp. 331—3.

60 Roberts, pp. 24, 45; *CB*, pp. 23—4; *Nether World*, p. 269 (cf. *Thyrza*, p. 83); *Emancipated*, p. 82; *Born in Exile*, *passim*; and *Will Warburton*, *passim*.

61 *Thyrza*, p. 468; *Life's Morning*, p. 165; *Isabel Clarendon*, Vol. 1, pp. 176—7, Vol. 2, p. 255.

62 Roberts, p. 121; Korg, p. 6. On the Guilty Secret see Gillian Tindall, *The Born Exile: George Gissing* (Temple Smith, 1974), pp. 122—57.

63 See esp. *Will Warburton*, pp. 187, 316.

64 *Bertz*, p. 108; *LMF*, pp. 82, 93, 381; *Ryecroft*, pp. 29—30, 82; *Born in Exile*, p. 298; Coustillas (ed.), *The Letters of George Gissing to Edward Clodd*, p. 100; *Dickens*, p. 107 (cf. p. 175).

65 On 'home' see *Ryecroft*, pp. 112, 8—9, 260; *Emancipated*, p. 78; *New Grub Street*, p. 473; *Born in Exile*, pp. 103, 505; *Denzil Quarrier*, p. 306; *Jubilee*, p. 297; and *Whirlpool*, pp. 327—8. cf. Ellen Gissing's comments in J. P. Michaux (ed.), *George Gissing: Critical Essays* (Vision Press, and Totowa, N. J.: Barnes & Noble, 1981), p. 16.

66 *Ryecroft*, pp. 197—8; *Wells*, p. 176 (cf. p. 169).

67 *Bertz*, p. 199; MS letter, GG to Algernon Gissing, 4 November 1889 (Berg); *Gabrielle*, p. 119; *Nether World*, p. 32; *Emancipated*, pp. 93, 78—9; *Charlatan*, p. 338; Roberts, pp. 48, 229.

68 *Bertz*, p. 153; *Born in Exile*, pp. 22, 46, 48—9.
69 *Born in Exile*, p. 49; cf. pp. 42, 44, 57—9, 72, 94—5, 97.
70 Tindall, *The Born Exile*, p. 137.
71 *Born in Exile*, pp. 94, 101.
72 *Born in Exile*, p. 365; cf. pp. 313, 177.
73 *Born in Exile*, pp. 439, 21, 18, 16, 20, 19, 24—8.
74 *Born in Exile*, pp. 61, 66, 80, 217, 244, 179.
75 *Born in Exile*, pp. 133, 266, 346, 287, 141, 176, 194.
76 *Diary*, pp. 233—54, *passim*. GG was particularly reliant on his sources for the pastiche of contemporary apologetics in Peak's conversations with Martin Warricombe. e.g., *Born in Exile*, pp. 251—2, is a cunning interweaving of passages from Frederick Temple, *The Relations between Religion and Science* (Macmillan, 1884), p. 114 (and cf. pp. 61—2, 232) and Asa Gray, *Natural Science and Religion* (New York: Scribner, 1880), pp. 105—7.
77 See *GGEF*, pp. 12—16; T. R. Wright, 'George Gissing: positivist in the dawn', *GN*, vol. 20 (April 1984), pp. 1—20 (though p. 15, on *Born in Exile*, contains inaccuracies); and Martha S. Vogeler, *Frederic Harrison: The Vocations of a Positivist* (Oxford: Clarendon Press, 1984), *passim*.
78 Jacob Korg, 'The spiritual theme of *Born in Exile*', in Pierre Coustillas (ed.), *Collected Articles on George Gissing* (Frank Cass, 1968), p. 139.
79 *Born in Exile*, pp. 19, 32, 170, 503.
80 *Born in Exile*, pp. 34, 175, 61 (cf. p. 450); Pierre Coustillas (ed.), *George Gissing at Alderley Edge* (Enitharmon Press, 1969), p. 22.
81 *Born in Exile*, pp. 123, 118; cf. p. 212.
82 *Born in Exile*, pp. 148, 146, 156—8, 175.
83 *Born in Exile*, pp. 167, 223, 253, 435, 449. In *Born in Exile*, p. 253, GG used passages from F. H. Reusch, *Bibel und Natur* (Freiburg im Breisgau: Herder'sche Verlagshandlung, 1862), pp. 85—97, 124—48, 347—59. In the English translation by Kathleen Lyttelton, *Nature and the Bible*, 2 vols (Edinburgh: T. Clark, 1886), the relevant passages are at Vol. 1, pp. 111—22, 165—88, Vol. 2, p. 250. GG may not have consulted this version: where he quotes from Reusch in *Born in Exile* (p. 253), his translation differs markedly from Lyttelton's.
84 *Born in Exile*, pp. 251, 253, 224, 225, 226.
85 *Born in Exile*, pp. 39, 146, 65. One such man with whose work GG was acquainted was Théodule Ribot, on whose *L'Hérédité psychologique* (1873) he had made extensive notes in 1889 (*CB*, pp. 59—62).
86 *Born in Exile*, pp. 30, 32, 437. Peak's father's fate anticipates his own: 'his strong impulses towards culture were powerless to obliterate the traces of his rude origin' (p. 30).
87 *Born in Exile*, pp. 108, 109, 443, 260, 130, 179 (cf. p. 380), 402, 436—7, 490.
88 *Born in Exile*, p. 247; cf. pp. 119—20, 130.

89 *Born in Exile*, p. 54; *Bertz*, p. 153.
90 *Born in Exile*, pp. 34, 37, 41, 51, 88, 92, 129.
91 *Born in Exile*, pp. 51, 58, 103, 86, 126, 135, 298, 170, 505.
92 *Born in Exile*, pp. 300, 169.
93 *Born in Exile*, pp. 71, 154, 157, 178, 252, 307, 303.
94 *Born in Exile*, pp. 307, 254, 352.
95 *Born in Exile*, pp. 454, 53, 95.
96 *Born in Exile*, pp. 54, 83, 180, 220, 250, 296, 516 n.; Graham, 'I'll never love thee more', in Helen Gardner (ed.) *The New Oxford Book of English Verse 1250−1950* (Oxford: Clarendon Press, 1972), p. 308.
97 *Born in Exile*, pp. 215, 392, 405.
98 *Born in Exile*, p. 482; cf. pp. 30−31, 35.
99 *Born in Exile*, pp. 24, 284, 498, 443, 15−16, 20, 102, 114, 257, 260, 353, 375, 456, 481.
100 *Born in Exile*, pp. 245, 287, 473, 405, 420.
101 *Born in Exile*, pp. 141, 187, 189, 191, 281−2, 219, 502−3.
102 *Born in Exile*, pp. 322−3; 113, 243, 286−97, 329−42, 447.
103 *Born in Exile*, pp. 31, 33; *Diary*, p. 267. GG first called the book *Godwin Peak* (after thinking of calling it *Raymond Peak*), *Diary*, p. 241. He temporarily altered the hero's name from 'Peak' to 'Peek' while revising the book in manuscript. The significance of this change was first discussed by Jacob Korg in 'The spiritual theme of *Born in Exile*', in Coustillas (ed.), *Collected Articles on George Gissing*, p. 140.
104 Charles Coulston Gillispie, *Genesis and Geology* (New York: Harper, 1951), p. 98; *Born in Exile*, pp. 144, 151, 225, 339, 371, 380. Buckland is indeed his father's son: 'Buckland *Martin* Warricombe' (p. 15; my italics).
105 Roberts, p. 236; *Bertz*, p. 153.

Chapter 5: *Women, Feminism and Marriage*

1 *Charlatan*, p. 219.
2 *Will Warburton*, p. 16; *Gabrielle*, p. 84 (cf. p. 42); *GGEF*, p. 248.
3 GG's allusions to *'grandes passions'* are recorded in his Chicago notebook; the sonnets and the poem 'A Farewell' are in a notebook entitled 'Verses 1869−[1882]' (both Yale).
4 *Sins of the Fathers*, pp. 40−41; *Crown of Life*, pp. 1−2.
5 Gillian Tindall, *The Born Exile: George Gissing* (Temple Smith, 1974), pp. 71−100.
6 Mabel Collins Donnelly, *George Gissing: Grave Comedian*, (Cambridge, Mass.: Harvard University Press, 1954), p. 25. See *Margaret and Other Poems*, by an East Anglian (Simpkin Marshall, 1855), pp. 1−23, esp. p. 19; *Diary*, p. 23; Robert L. Selig, 'Gissing: Father and Son', *GN*, vol. 16 (January 1980), pp. 9−10; and Selig, *George Gissing* (Boston: Twayne, 1983), pp. 5−6. The authorship of GG's

father was revealed by Arthur C. Young, in 'Poems by Thomas Gissing', *Rutgers University Library Journal*, vol. 30 (December 1966), pp. 23–6.

7 *Dickens*, p. 87; see also *Critical Studies of the Works of Charles Dickens*, p. 22. For GG's rejection of his tendency to idealize working-class girls see *Bertz*, p. 134; and *Gabrielle*, p. 122. A clear rejection of the working-class woman in favour of the middle-class ideal occurs in *Sleeping Fires*, p. 39.

8 *Unclassed*, p. 82 (cf. *Unclassed (i)*, Vol. 1, p. 234); MS letter, GG to Frederic Harrison, 23 July 1880 (Pforzheimer); *Workers*, Vol. 2, p. 4; *Gabrielle*, p. 42.

9 *Thyrza*, p. 362. On beautiful voices see *Workers*, Vol. 1, p. 252; *Isabel Clarendon*, Vol. 1, p. 153, Vol. 2, p. 72; *Life's Morning*, pp. 11, 327; *Nether World*, p. 283; *Born in Exile*, p. 52; *Crown of Life*, pp. 27, 63; *Veranilda*, pp. 21–2, 65, 349; *Gabrielle*, pp. 27, 31, 57, 61, 75; and Roberts, pp. 178–9.

10 *Sleeping Fires*, p. 109; *Gabrielle*, p. 67; *Crown of Life*, p. 73. See also *Unclassed*, p. 48; *Life's Morning*, p. 42; *Nether World*, p. 127; *Charlatan*, p. 7; and *Will Warburton*, pp. 211, 227.

11 *Life's Morning*, pp. 89, 93; *Isabel Clarendon*, Vol. 2, p. 72 (cf. Vol. 1, pp. 286–7); H. G. Wells, *Ann Veronica* (Virago, 1980), p. 231. A turning-point in GG's conception of the ennobling effects of women on men was *Emancipated*: see the cancelled passage reproduced by Pierre Coustillas in the Harvester edition, p. xxiv.

12 *Thyrza*, p. 5; *Odd Women*, p. 135; J. S. Mill, *The Subjection Of Women* (Cambridge, Mass.: MIT Press, 1970), pp. 85–6.

13 *Demos*, p. 149; cf. pp. 85, 246, 256, 272, 289; and *Nether World*, p. 215.

14 *Charlatan*, p. 66; *Gabrielle*, p. 67 (cf. p. 92); *Workers*, Vol. 2, pp. 4, 359; *Life's Morning*, pp. 285, 344 (cf. p. 151); *Demos*, p. 273.

15 *Diary*, p. 268; John Ruskin, *Sesame and Lilies* (Smith, Elder, 1871), pp. 91–2; *Jubilee*, p. 429.

16 *Unclassed (i)*, Vol. 2, p. 174.

17 *Whirlpool*, pp. 324, 337; *Town Traveller*, pp. 312–13; *Dickens*, pp. 191–2.

18 *Human Odds and Ends*, p. 308; *Charlatan*, p. 135. For GG's hope that intellectuality in women might be united with domestic efficiency see Donnelly, *George Gissing: Grave Comedian*, p. 55; *LMF*, p. 105; and *Dickens*, p. 192.

19 *Gabrielle*, pp. 83–4; *Unclassed (i)*, Vol. 2, p. 298; *Jubilee*, pp. 248, 253; *CB*, p. 67.

20 *Human Odds and Ends*, p. 255; *Town Traveller*, pp. 252, 254; *Nether World*, pp. 5 ff., 262, 333.

21 *Isabel Clarendon*, Vol. 1, pp. 34, 45–6, 284; *Eve's Ransom*, p. 46; *New Grub Street*, p. 183; George Eliot, *Middlemarch* (Harmondsworth: Penguin, 1965), p. 814; cf. also *Middlemarch*, pp. 698, 816, with *New Grub Street*, pp. 225, 261–2.

22 *Thyrza*, p. 158; *Denzil Quarrier*, pp. 180, 325; *Odd Women*, p. 154; *Jubilee*, pp. 243–4; *Eve's Ransom*, p. 109.

23 *Diary*, pp. 337, 351, 350; *Victim of Circumstances*, pp. 241, 254.

24 *Unclassed*, p. 312; *Unclassed (i)*, Vol. 2, pp. 112, 137, Vol. 3, p. 303.

25 *Jubilee*, p. 44; *Born in Exile*, p. 138; John Halperin, *Gissing: A Life in Books* (Oxford: Oxford University Press, 1982), p. 270 (cf. Roberts, p. 112).

26 *Dickens*, pp. 156–8, 167–9, 171, 173.

27 *Gabrielle*, p. 79; *Charlatan*, pp. 138–40; *Will Warburton*, p. 326.

28 *Sins of the Fathers*, p. 92; *Veranilda*, pp. 57, 66, 182, 188, 246, 300, 341.

29 *Life's Morning*, p. 174; *Isabel Clarendon*, Vol. 2, p. 81 (cf. *Victim of Circumstances*, p. 103).

30 As May Yates was the first to notice, 'There are surprisingly few middle-aged or elderly women in Gissing's world': *George Gissing: An Appreciation* (Manchester: The University Press, 1922), p. 70.

31 *Diary*, pp. 169, 211; Pforzheimer, MS 267, 'Woman'.

32 Constance Rover, *Love, Morals and the Feminists* (Routledge, 1970), pp. 12, 24, 25, 45; Gail Cunningham, *The New Woman and the Victorian Novel* (Macmillan, 1978), pp. 2, 48, 69–73; M. O. W. Oliphant, 'The Anti-Marriage League', *Blackwood's Magazine*, vol. 159 (January 1896), pp. 135–49; *Whirlpool*, p. 382. Mona Caird's most famous book was *The Daughters of Danaus* (1894).

33 *Unclassed*, pp. 206, 297, 302; MS letter, Clara Collet to Morley Roberts, 23 November 1904 (Berg).

34 *Whirlpool*, pp. 24, 25, 49, 207, 291, 351, 376–7, 398–401; *Jubilee*, p. 243.

35 *Demos*, pp. 284, 317, 299, 372, 286; cf. pp. 156–7, 185, 285, 292, 300, 302, 350, 374.

36 *Demos*, pp. 346, 272 (cf. *Odd Women*, pp. 152, 236), 366–8.

37 *Emancipated*, p. 418. On male accusations cf. *Demos*, p. 371; *Emancipated*, p. 420; and *Odd Women*, p. 251.

38 *Emancipated*, p. 308; *Born in Exile*, p. 225; *Jubilee*, pp. 178, 413; *Gabrielle*, p. 69; *Crown of Life*, pp. 195–7.

39 Rover, *Love, Morals and the Feminists*, pp. 47 ff., 55, 132; Patricia Stubbs, *Women and Fiction: Feminism and the Novel, 1880–1920* (Brighton: Harvester, 1979), p. 57; Cunningham, *The New Woman and the Victorian Novel, passim*.

40 *Workers*, Vol. 2, pp. 381–2; Royal A. Gettmann, *A Victorian Publisher* (Cambridge: Cambridge University Press, 1960), pp. 196–7, 215–22; *Heritage*, pp. 72–3; MS letter, GG to Thomas Hardy, 30 June 1886 (photocopy at Pforzheimer; MS at UCLA); *Crown of Life*, p. 207.

41 *Jubilee*, pp. 113, 115, 122–3, 130; *Denzil Quarrier*, pp. 120–22; *Ryecroft*, pp. 280–82.

42 *Unclassed (i)*, Vol. 1, pp. 46, 143, Vol. 2, pp. 11–13; Roberts, p. 74; *Crown of Life*, pp. 116, 207; *Bertz*, p. 285.

43 Herbert Spencer, *Principles of Biology*, 2 vols (Williams and Norgate, 1898), Vol. 2, pp. 512−13.
44 *Life's Morning*, p. 344; *New Grub Street*, p. 486; *Emancipated*, p. 270.
45 *Diary*, pp. 247, 263, 403; *Stories and Sketches*, p. 273; *Jubilee*, pp. 241, 276, 404.
46 *Whirlpool*, pp. 135, 162, 361, 28, 384−5. cf. GG's comment in *Gabrielle*, p. 59: 'I have the highest opinion of a mother's rights and duties; I am very sure that social progress is only possible in that direction ... I tried to make this clear in "the Whirlpool".'
47 Mill, *The Subjection of Women*, p. 48.
48 e.g., by Stubbs, *Women and Fiction*, pp. 124−5.
49 *Will Warburton*, pp. 125−6; Pforzheimer, MS 270, 'Occupations'.
50 *Born in Exile*, pp. 414−15, 474; *Jubilee*, pp. 280−81, 296−7. For further comments on GG's treatment of female employment see Alice B. Markow, 'George Gissing: advocate or provocateur of the women's movement?', *English Literature in Transition*, vol. 23 (1982), pp. 64−7.
51 Angelica in *The Heavenly Twins*, quoted in Cunningham, *The New Woman and the Victorian Novel*, p. 55; *Emancipated*, p. 398 (cf. *Jubilee*, p. 429).
52 GG to William Blackwood, 6 December 1892, quoted in Halperin, *Gissing: A Life in Books*, p. 184; Korg, pp. 184−7.
53 *Isabel Clarendon*, Vol. 2, p. 132; *New Grub Street*, p. 70; *Nether World*, p. 82; *Victim of Circumstances*, p. 204.
54 *Emancipated*, pp. 37−8; *Jubilee*, p. 7; Markow, 'George Gissing: Advocate or provocateur?' pp. 60−62; *Dickens*, pp. 170, 172, 178.
55 *Bertz*, p. 171; *LMF*, pp. 72−3, 107−8; *Workers*, Vol. 1, pp. 127−8; Ruskin, *Sesame and Lilies*, pp. 96−8.
56 George J. Romanes, 'Mental differences between men and women', *The Nineteenth Century*, vol. 21 (May 1887), p. 666. For a modern critique of Romanes's article see Susan Sleeth Mosedale, 'Science corrupted: Victorian biologists consider "the woman question" ', *Journal of the History of Biology*, vol. 11 (Spring 1978), pp. 1−55, esp. pp. 16−24; for a contemporary feminist objection see Emily Pfeiffer, *Women and Work* (Trübner, 1888), pp. 159−86.
57 *Jubilee*, pp. 223, 225−6. cf. GG's advice to Gabrielle: 'Remember your health, sweet, and never overtax yourself with study' (*Gabrielle*, p. 53; see also p. 89).
58 *Born in Exile*, p. 138; *Jubilee*, p. 368. See also *Dickens*, pp. 161−2.
59 *Isabel Clarendon*, Vol. 2, pp. 48, 217; *Nether World*, pp. 35−6; *Jubilee*, pp. 246, 249, 379, 385; *Paying Guest*, p. 56; *Will Warburton*, p. 326; *New Grub Street*, pp. 261−2; *Denzil Quarrier*, p. 166; *Whirlpool*, p. 277 (cf. p. 253); *Victim of Circumstances*, pp. 147−64.
60 Pforzheimer, MS 266, 'Ideas'; *Town Traveller*, pp. 97, 104, 133, 186; *Crown of Life*, p. 327 (cf. *Demos*, p. 477; *Emancipated*, pp. 173, 341, 449; and *Sleeping Fires*, p. 221); *Gabrielle*, p. 138.
61 Frank Swinnerton, *George Gissing: A Critical Study* (Martin Secker,

1912), p. 80; *Emancipated*, pp. 84, 135, 170, 194, 218, 345, 367, 411. The same novel includes Miriam's jealousy of Mrs Welland, and Mrs Travis's envy of Cecily (pp. 202, 386).

62   *Workers*, Vol. 1, pp. 313–33, 348–9, Vol. 2, p. 38; *Veranilda*, pp. 141, 145, 198, 221, 236, 268; *Isabel Clarendon*, Vol. 2, p. 224.

63   *Workers*, Vol. 2, pp. 99–106; *Unclassed*, pp. 111, 118; Pierre Coustillas, 'George Gissing à Manchester', *Études Anglaises*, no. 3 (July–September 1963), pp. 255–7; Roberts, p. 30.

64   *Odd Women*, pp. 37, 182; *Dickens*, pp. 163–4.

65   *Odd Women*, pp. 98–9, 54, 61.

66   Markow, 'George Gissing: advocate or provocateur?', p. 65; Jenni Calder, *Women and Marriage in Victorian Fiction* (Thames and Hudson, 1976), p. 201; Kathleen Blake, *Love and the Woman Question in Victorian Literature* (Brighton: Harvester, 1983), esp. pp. 95–8, 101–45.

67   MS letter, GG to Algernon Gissing, 1 March 1894 (Pforzheimer). For GG's meeting with Clara Collet see *Diary*, p. 310; for their friendship see Ruth M. Adams, 'George Gissing and Clara Collet', *Nineteenth Century Fiction*, vol. 11 (June 1956), pp. 72–7.

68   e.g., in his scrapbook (Pforzheimer) GG mentions Theodore Stanton (ed.), *The Woman Question in Europe* (Sampson Low, 1884), which contains a chapter on the society by Jessie Boucherett herself (see esp. pp. 98–106). Later, in a letter to Algernon Gissing of 1 March 1894 (Pforzheimer), GG recommended Mrs H. Coleman Davidson's *What Our Daughters Can Do for Themselves* (Smith, Elder, 1894) as 'probably the best manual of female employment'; this, too, contains information on the society. Mrs Davidson makes clear (p. 261) that the society, like Mary Barfoot, would sometimes advance premiums to enable girls to take a good position in business. See also Duncan Crow, *The Victorian Woman* (Allen & Unwin, 1971), pp. 158–61.

69   Emily Davies, *The Higher Education of Women* (London and New York: Alexander Straton, 1866), p. 101. (For GG's views on women's inability to manage servants see *CB*, p. 50; *Jubilee*, p. 53; and *Whirlpool*, p. 366.) Davies, *Thoughts on Some Questions Relating to Women* (Cambridge: 1910; New York, Kraus Reprint, 1971), pp. 3–4, 67, 71, 72–3 (the paper from which the quoted extract comes was written in 1864); *Odd Women*, pp. 136–7.

70   John Goode, *George Gissing: Ideology and Fiction* (Vision, 1978), pp. 145, 150; Cunningham, *The New Woman and the Victorian Novel*, pp. 134–5; Stubbs, *Women and Fiction*, p. 125; Nina Auerbach, *Communities of Women: An Idea in Fiction* (Cambridge, Mass.: Harvard University Press, 1978), pp. 144, 151.

71   *Pall Mall Gazette*, 20 May 1893, quoted in *Heritage*, p. 219.

72   *Odd Women*, pp. 299, 305; on pets see pp. 157, 240.

73   *Odd Women*, pp. 175, 102; *Bertz*, p. 171. cf. Everard's dictum with Ruskin, *Sesame and Lilies* (p. 104): 'You bring up your girls as if they

were meant for sideboard ornaments, and then complain of their frivolity.'

74 *Odd Women*, pp. 176, 93, 135, 153.
75 *Odd Women*, pp. 11, 39, 236.
76 *Odd Women*, pp. 152, 156, 167, 164.
77 *Odd Women*, pp. 121, 162–3, 168, 201.
78 *Odd Women*, pp. 164, 224, 252.
79 *Odd Women*, pp. 86, 144; for the descriptions of Everard and Rhoda see pp. 20–21, 77; on 'obstinacy' see pp. 85, 137, 144, 265, 267, 273, 278.
80 *Odd Women*, pp. 128, 142, 182, 148.
81 *Odd Women*, p. 262.
82 *Odd Women*, pp. 268–9, 267, 325.
83 *Odd Women*, pp. 150, 167, 196, 244, 330, 273; *Othello*, Act III, sc. iii, 11. 266, 366. cf. also Widdowson's, 'What? You go time after time to the private chambers of an unmarried man ... and it means no harm?' (p. 250); with Iago's, 'What,/To kiss in private? ... Or to be naked with her friend abed,/An hour, or more, not meaning any harm?' (*Othello*, Act IV, sc. i, 11. 2–4).
84 *Odd Women*, p. 145; cf. pp. 220–21, 226.
85 *Odd Women*, pp. 326, 334.
86 *Odd Women*, p. 336; for repudiation of the attitudes mentioned see pp. 2, 136, 152, 167.
87 Stubbs, *Women and Fiction*, pp. 125, 152; *Odd Women*, pp. 58, 295. For a similar criticism of Stubbs, see Blake, *Love and the Woman Question*, p. 108.
88 *Whirlpool*, p. 39 (cf. pp. 102, 114). 'Calenture' is also used in *Victim of Circumstances* (p. 135) and *Charlatan* (p. 399). *The Shorter Oxford Dictionary* defines 'calenture' as 'A disease incident to sailors within the tropics, characterized by delirium in which, it is said, they fancy the sea to be green fields and desire to leap into it'.
89 *Odd Women*, pp. 153, 246, 283, 287.
90 *Odd Women*, pp. 202, 287.
91 *Odd Women*, pp. 228–9, 182, 189.
92 *Odd Women*, p. 59.

Conclusion

1 Robert L. Selig, *George Gissing* (Boston: Twayne, 1983), preface, p. 22; *Demos*, p. 470. cf., e.g., *Workers*, Vol. 2, p. 315; and *Unclassed (i)*, Vol. 3, p. 263.
2 *Fiction*, p. 27; cf. p. 29; and *LMF*, p. 166.
3 As Michael Collie does in *The Alien Art: A Critical Study of George Gissing's Novels* (Folkestone, Kent: William Dawson, 1979): see esp. pp. 86, 116, 148, 149, 157. On Collie see David Grylls, 'A second view of *The Alien Art*', *GN*, vol. 16 (July 1980), pp. 32–8.

4   *Heritage*, p. 54; cf. pp. 11, 50, 57–64.
5   This thesis is pinned, in any case, to a local misapprehension. In his preface Selig quotes from GG's diary entry for 13 June 1888, on the 'wearisome' rewriting of 'Chap. XII' of *Nether World*: 'it is poor stuff, all this idealism; I'll never go in for it again'. Selig's general account of GG is made to pivot on this remark, which he interprets as 'blunt self-criticism of a persistent tendency' in the early work. However, Selig thinks that the chapter in question is 'Io Saturnalia!' (*George Gissing*, pp. 40, 148 n. 21). In fact, as other diary entries show, it is Chapter 12 of the second volume (Chapter 25 of one-volume editions), 'A Double Consecration'. Since this chapter diagnoses the early complications of Michael Snowdon's morbid idealism, it is unlikely that the sentence in the diary refers to a tendency in GG himself. cf. what GG wrote to Bertz about the novel: 'The note re philanthropy is good; I shall perhaps never again deal directly with that subject' (*Bertz*, p. 56). He had dealt with it, of course, very critically.
6   *Hick*, p. 52.
7   *Demos*, p. 395; *Thyrza*, p. 331; *Gabrielle*, p. 40; *Critical Studies of the Works of Charles Dickens*, p. 56; *Victim of Circumstances*, pp. 170, 173, 174–5.
8   *LMF*, p. 116; *Unclassed (i)*, Vol. 1, p. 227; *Odd Women*, pp. 82–3 (cf. *Ryecroft*, p. 267).
9   *Human Odds and Ends*, pp. 41, 43, 46. 'The Firebrand' (written 1895, published 1896) was inspired by a cutting from the *Spectator*, 2 August 1890 (Pforzheimer, MS 266, 'Ideas').
10 *Jubilee*, p. 306 (cf. p. 66); *Whirlpool*, p. 452; *Charlatan*, pp. 109, 213, 6, 401 (cf. *Sleeping Fires*, pp. 29, 159, 161–2, 167, 210–11); MS letter, GG to F. G. Kitton, 20 October 1902 (Pforzheimer). The exception to GG's hostile treatment of lectures is *Odd Women* (1893).
11 *Born in Exile*, p. 123; *Stories and Sketches*, pp. 91–111; *Workers*, Vol. 1, p. 282; *Ryecroft*, pp. 177–8. An early embodiment of the alignment described is Bunce in *Thyrza (i)* (1887): 'He was the kind of man whom a little judiciously directed persecution would have driven to the point of sacrificing his life for his unbelief' (Vol. 3, pp. 46–7).
12 *Will Warburton*, pp. 212, 132, 273.
13 *Ryecroft*, p. 48; *Isabel Clarendon*, Vol. 2, p. 134 (see Chapter 4, above); *Jubilee*, p. 267; *Charlatan*, pp. 158, 221; Pierre Coustillas (ed.), *George Gissing at Alderley Edge* (Enitharmon Press, 1969), p. 17; 'Christopherson' (reprinted in *House of Cobwebs*, pp. 47–67) was written and published in 1902.
14 *Victim of Circumstances*, pp. 170, 175, 180; *Jubilee*, pp. 96, 404; *Charlatan*, pp. 213, 397, 387, 236.
15 'A Victim of Circumstances' (reprinted in *Victim of Circumstances*, pp. 3–36) was written in 1891 and published in 1893 (cf. GG's use of the phrase in *Town Traveller*, p. 265). *Sleeping Fires*, p. 169; *Whirlpool*, pp. 376, 388, 418–19, 422; *Dickens*, pp. 257–8.

16 *Charlatan*, p. 141 (cf. *Gabrielle*, p. 89); John Spiers and Pierre
    Coustillas, *The Rediscovery of George Gissing* (National Book League,
    1971), p. 99; *Diary*, pp. 147, 360, 364; *Human Odds and Ends*, p. 292.
    On M. M. Dowie see Gail Cunningham, *The New Woman and the
    Victorian Novel* (Macmillan, 1978), pp. 73–6.

17 *Bertz*, p. 144; MS letter, GG to Algernon Gissing, 9 December 1887
    (Berg).

Index

(All books except those of Gissing cited in the text are cross-referenced to the author's name. Citations in the notes to this book of Gissing's books are not included in the index.)

Wyvern (*Demos*) 42—3, 58, 67, 106, 107

Yates, May
  George Gissing: An Appreciation 212n.
Yeats, W. B. 71, 202n.
Young, Arthur C. 211n.
  The Letters of George Gissing to Eduard

Bertz, 1887—1903 192, 194—217, *passim.*, in notes
Yule, Alfred (*New Grub Street*) 5, 88—92
Yule, Marian (*New Grub Street*) 5, 20, 63, 83—7, 89, 93, 97, 106, 110

Zola, Emile 8, 157